Fu*ked up in Dubai!

EMILY BROOK

© Copyright Emily Brook 2022

All rights reserved.

This book is sold subject to the condition that it shall not, by way of trade or otherwise, be hired out, lent or resold, or otherwise circulated without the author's/publisher's prior consent in any form of binding or cover other than that in which it is published and without a similar condition including this condition being imposed on the subsequent publisher.

The moral rights of the author have been asserted.

Disclaimer

All names and identifying details have been changed to protect the privacy of individuals.

Firstly, and foremostly I thank my family for their unconditional love and support. You know who you are. I love you now as I will love you forever.

Secondly, to the Girls of Bur Dubai, past and present, God bless and I pray you will go home soon.

To the British Embassy and Prisoners Abroad - thank you for all that you do.

To George, Sheila and Klaudia - thank you for your friendship, advice and laughter. It means more to me than you will ever know.

Acknowledgements

Angela Orora – thank you for your blessings and guidance in recommending Michelle Emerson to help this new author edit and to share this story. May you both continue to share your gifts and do what you do brilliantly.

Natalia Pokorniecka - for creating the front cover image. You imagined and developed so creatively the visual description that was necessitated and I thank you.

Part 1

'Oh fuck, fuck, fuck!' I was knelt on a cold, dark concrete floor holding myself, rocking back and forth whilst gripping my arms tightly. My fingers and nails indented my upper arms. I had never experienced real police handcuffs before, only the toy ones I had bought for purely entertainment purposes. My consciousness went into overdrive with repetition from the moment they arrived, to my journey, to where I am now, with every single aspect of what had happened in the timeline repeating itself trying to map out what I had done wrong.

What had I done? What the fuck had I done? What the fuck had he done? Shit! Shit! Shit! And no one, no one at all, knew where I was. I lowered my head and the tears rolled and rolled until there was a constant stream. My body and breathing shuddered uncontrollably and I gasped to try and control it. This was a cry like no other. In all my years on this planet I had never experienced anything like this; a cry for loss of all I was and knew. And oh my God, my baby, my little girl. What the fuck was going to happen to her? I did not understand anything. What were they saying to me and showing me? What did they want me to sign? Why couldn't they get me a translator or someone who spoke English? I was not a bad person and had not broken the law, as far as I knew. I mean, I only arrived here two days ago on the bloody 29th of July, 2010. What the fuck had I done? And more importantly, how the fuck was I going to get out of this fucking mess and shithole of a cell? Never ever, even in my worst nightmares, had I ever had one where I was locked up in a bloody cell and not a bloody foreign one. I mean, come on, it was a proper cell with thick metal cold bars, a concrete floor, and no window. This was crazy, and I was sitting in the middle of this craziness. I bowed my head and knew I was fucked, truly fucked. What the fuck had I done?

Small in length and width, I looked at the grey metal bars in front of me and smelled the aroma of the heat-infested toilet behind me. The room, or more apt named 'cell from hell,' had poor lighting that flickered, but I could not distinguish whether the tears of my eyes had affected my sight. I could hear the wailing shrieks and cries of others, the men, I believe? I could only imagine that they were the wails of pain, loss, the uncertainty of the life they now found themselves in and pure desperation for help and freedom. Just like me, and how I fucking felt! I believed the mix of noises I heard came from the men in the cells I had passed in the corridor to the unknown of where I am now.

I wiped my sobbing tears and droplets from my nose onto my hands and arms, as there was no tissue or toilet paper. I did not want to stain my dress with this green wet web of snot. So, my arms and hands it was. As my snot dried, it looked as though a drunk slug had wandered onto my arms, and the remnants of its slime had dried to reveal a light flaky layer of skin. I had nothing on except for the G-string knickers covering my waxed privates and my flowery, black, off-the-shoulder maxi dress with no bra. I was hanging out, literally. I could feel my heart breaking as the electric bolts of lightning stung within me and penetrated me deep to my core. I was so scared and all alone. I had no one. No one at all. My body tried to deal as best as it could with the shock. I knew I needed to relax my breathing and body jolts, as I did not want to go into actual shock; shock that needed medical assistance. So, I lay on the cold, rough concrete floor and got into the foetal position. I closed my eyes and concentrated on controlling my breathing with big and slow inhales. My body slowly relaxed, but my brain was still active as my eyes moved quickly from side to side, processing images and re-enactments of what had occurred since getting here. I clenched my right hand and held it to my lips, which were moist and salty from the tears that continued to fall uncontrollably. The heat from my breath and the saltiness of my taste buds made the air around me stale as the resonating air from the air conditioner surrounded me.

I was scared, more than scared, petrified; petrified that this was the start of things. I was alone here in a foreign country far away from the UK. But, in many ways, what made this country so far away from my home was that it was an Arabic/Muslim country. Whilst I did not know or understand its legal system, I knew it was foreign to the one I had grown up with, respected and knew. Whilst I knew it had stopped the practices of beheadings, lashings, and stoning, I still knew that their sentences had caused outcry internationally, due to their harshness. This I knew. I am and was truly fucked! I knew this was just the beginning, and I had no idea when it would end. I could be here for years. Bloody fucking years! 'Oh God!' I pleaded, whispering, 'Help me! Please, please help me. God, please… I beg you?' I wailed with cries of anguish, shaking uncontrollably, and gasped for breath.

Decision made – I've had enough, I'm fucking off!

A new life beginning and exciting times lay ahead of me after three years of absolute heartbreak and pure bloody depression. My relationship had ended very badly with things said and done that I could not forgive or accept for myself, let alone for my beautiful innocent baby girl. I made the most difficult decision to end the relationship after daily and hourly light bulb moments for such a long time, that I could not even tell when it all started to go wrong. I realised and knew deep down that the life and love that I had with my parents as a family unit, would not be that for my beautiful little girl, Sahara, my little blond monkey, with her biological father.

I had no guilt for ending our physical relationship as I tried for so long, and things just did not get any better. They got worse, and as they did, so did the words of hurt, accusations and pure bullshit. Did I have regrets? Of course, I did. It broke my heart that he did not want me, and because of this, he didn't want us. All I wanted was to be happy and healthy with my family, with all of us together. But the continual work of trying to make the relationship work with her biological father, or more apt 'the Sperm Donor', had to come to an end. We were making each other miserable with pure frustration and resentment. Everyone around us could see it too, but life should not have been the way it was with us. The innocence of love and laughter had gone, and the relationship came to an end, of all places, outside the local wine bar one bitterly wintery cold Saturday night. We stood outside, each smoking a cigarette, when he told me in a confident and arrogant manner that, 'It's me or your family.' That was the statement from a man who I had supported financially, whilst travelling the world working full time, whilst he was in the pub, and who I had loved for all his opposite traits to me, which whilst being bizarre to me, also pulled me like a bee to a honey pot. Being with him was like an adventure I had never experienced before as I was not in control. He was an enthusiast of pubs, horse racing, sports, gambling, and he was ok in the sack. Well, it, Sperm Donor's willy, was working as he impregnated me successfully with it. We had broken up many times throughout the five-year relationship, but when we both found out that I was pregnant, he promised, 'I will change now, I promise, and the little one will want for nothing.'

The saying 'leopards do not change their spots' has foundation because as my pregnancy progressed his behaviour did not change. If anything, it got worse. I would not see him for days as he always had plans. He made me feel alone in our relationship, and he did not respect me. My parents became guarantors on a terraced cottage that we bought. If they hadn't, we would not have been able to get a mortgage because of his gambling and monetary situation. The mortgage company wanted bank statements and when I initially saw his for the past three months, I had no idea that his gambling was so out of hand. I am not talking small bets of £5 or £10; we are discussing bets of £50, £100, and more. Yes, he did win some money back, but the money credited never met his bets. Initially, at the start of our relationship, I got the adrenaline from watching a horse race, watching the horse that you have the bet on running and jumping with support and hope. But, like anything new, it soon wore off. I mean, it was not my bet, but I did share in his winnings. He treated me to a new pair of trainers and sandals in the five years we were together. We had fun trips away that were always financially split equally. It was a good laugh eating good food, drinking excessively, sleeping, and having hot sweaty sex whenever we bloody felt like it. We even travelled further afield to Australia, New Zealand, and Thailand. We had lots of adventures and laughs, but with time and experience, we did not grow together, and what once had tickled me with enjoyment now alienated us from each other. I grew out of wanting to go out to the pub to spend time with him and not seeing him due to football, cricket, rugby, or a funeral. Ye, funerals were popular with him even if it was not someone close that he knew. If there was a boy in the club whose parent died, then he would end up going on an all-day bender. Any bloody excuse, it was! I could not compete with any social life, and if I am honest, I should not have had to. His need for his own life did not fit in with us, and whilst he didn't see my need for him to be there for me and us, it was real and I felt the abandonment every morning when I rose, and every evening before I lay down to sleep by myself. We just did not fit. But one thing is for sure, and that is that there was a time when we were happy and in love, I hope, but I can only remember a few moments that stand out. I cannot explain it, but my memories with him seem to have clouded over into a huge grey cloud where only a few openings reveal the location of the happy events we once shared together. Sadly, I cannot find many.

One of the funniest and best moments in our relationship that I can remember was when I took a short four-month lecturing contract in Amsterdam. 80% of the time, he lived with me and flew back and forth from Swansea Airport, as he had walked out of his job after winning a couple of thousand in a lottery syndicate. I had only been living there a couple of days when there was a knock at the front door. I was in the kitchen, and he answered it as he was nearer to it in the living room. I remember the event so well because it was the first time I met my Dutch neighbour, and I remember it well because it was so bloody strange and weird. He had opened the door and had called me. So, in front of us was a red-haired woman in her twenties holding a pot plant. Now, I know you are wondering what the hell is strange about that? Well, what is strange is her opening conversation after my initial 'Hello.' Her response in a mild Americanised Dutch accent was, 'Hi. My name is Kitty, and I am a bi-sexual witch.'

I frowned, looked at him and then returned my gaze at her as to question: did I hear her right? So, politely I questioned, 'Excuse me?'

She repeated, "Hi. My name is Kitty, and I am a bi-sexual witch.' She smiled and then continued, 'It is nice to meet you,' whilst holding out the pot plant. I looked at him and smiled before returning my gaze and realised that yes, I did hear her right. We shook hands with Kitty and his smile was so big. What is it with men and bi-sexual or lesbian women? She came in and handed me the pot plant and we had a quick chat whilst sitting down. She said she could not be long and just wanted to welcome us to the street as she had to work. We found out that she worked in a coffee shop and in at a herbal shop. She wrote down the names of the shop and cafe and told us to go and see her there and that she would sort us out. Well, sort us out, she did. One night she gave us a concoction of different weeds to smoke and then an assortment of herbal pills to take at certain times throughout the evening. That night I laughed so much with hourly fits of giggling and hiding in the bathroom from the man that shared my bed, because every time I looked at him, he made me laugh; an uncontrollable laugh that was deep-rooted at the bottom of my tummy. I do not know how many times I peed myself that night, but I know I ended up taking my knickers off and sat on the toilet for hours. His features were alien to me, distorted and all over the place and I could not believe I could be with such a man. So, I ran around the apartment trying to get away from him and to stop laughing, as he made me wet myself continuously through the loss of control down there from laughing. I, in turn, was making him laugh uncontrollably by running around and telling him to stay away from me and trying to push doors closed to separate us. I screamed whilst running and laughing, 'Stop it! Get away! You're making me pee!' It went on for hours, and I was weak with laughter with the severe loss of control.

Yes, we had some fun moments and some caring ones too. When we were in a huge shopping centre in Thailand, I really needed new Levi's, well, copies anyway. We were served by many female Thai shop assistants and when they wanted to know my size and I told them I was a size 14 to 16, they laughed. 'You big girl!' And they were giggling and passing these big arsed jeans to me. He could see that my patience and offended scale was rising to new heights, so he butted in, 'You calling my Mrs Fat?' They all laughed except me. That same night we were out drinking, and two major things happened. Firstly, whilst standing at the doorway of a bar, a worker came over to us and asked, 'You want me tonight? We go back to your hotel to have a party?'. I saw him flustered and shocked for the first time, well, initially anyway. 'Ay, Ay. No, no, no. No, we do not want that. Jesus! My Mrs isn't into things like that.'

I just laughed and turned to my left, so I was not facing either of them. When she departed, I turned around to face him, and he had droplets of sweat coming down his forehead. 'Well, that was crazy, wasn't it?'

'Yes, I get labelled fat by you all this morning and now one is asking to have sex with me ... and you? What a bloody day?'

But it was funny, odd, and strange events that made us work for a while. I remembered earlier in our relationship that we had awoken on a Sunday morning with big hangovers and I was peckish and needed some meat and salt. No, not the meat you are thinking of. I am speaking of a cooked chicken from the local supermarket, and so that is what I did. I went for a quick shop and purchased my ingredients: chicken and a loaf of sliced bread. I returned to Sperm, who was still in bed, and proceeded to make a chicken sandwich with a light dusting of salt. However, to my dismay on pulling the chicken out of its plastic bag and placing it on a plate to slice, well, there was hardly any meat on the breasts, if they were breasts at all. I had to literally pull the meat from the chicken to make a measly two-sliced sandwich. So, when I returned to bed, he was still sort of sleepy but awake. He turned to say, 'You took your time.'

I was upset a little and said, 'I am not going to buy a chicken there again. It did not have much meat on it. What a bloody rip off. I would like to know where the hell they are getting their chickens from. I could only make this measly sandwich out of the bloody breasts, and I had to really pick at it, as it was stringy. I have never had a bloody chicken like it. There should be more bloody meat on a chicken breast.'

He looked at the sandwich and up at me, perplexed somewhat, with a frown. I stated he could share my sandwich even though deep down I wanted it all to myself for many reasons: I was hungry, I had gone out to buy the chicken, it had taken me ages to make the sandwich, and my hands had really been sticky and gooey because I had to touch the skin and meat. And, do you know what, he bloody took and ate half of my sandwich, didn't he? Anyway, sometime later that afternoon he returned to the bedroom laughing to himself. I asked what was funny and he laughed at me, 'I can't believe you. Honestly, are you that stupid?'

A large, 'What?' yelped from my mouth. I mean, what the hell had I done to warrant being called stupid. 'The chicken was upside down, Mun. You were picking at its arse. Didn't you think to turn it over to the breasts? Seriously? I mean the bottom of the chicken looks different to the breasts. You do know that right?'

Well, I was shocked, horrified and upset that I had been picking the chicken's arse and that I had eaten it. I was only a couple of slices of a breast kind of girl, who would use a knife and fork to cut the chicken. Why hadn't I realised or thought to myself, even better, realised when I saw the chicken that it was upside down. And, I had the shock realisation that on this occasion, I had been a wee bit stupid. So, I sunk into the mattress whilst looking up at him with the duvet covering me and sympathetically asked, 'Please don't tell anyone. I honestly didn't think to turn it upside down. I just thought it was a chicken with little meat.' Whether he did or didn't tell anyone, I personally don't know to this day. But what I do know is that for some time after, he reminded me often of chicken Sunday to my distaste.

His caring side was there, and he shared it on a few occasions. I miscarried one Christmas and he came in the ambulance and stayed in the hospital overnight with me. He only left my side in the morning to get a taxi home to drive back and to pick me up. And that afternoon, once home, whilst I cried and cried, he held me in his arms until I fell asleep whilst he watched sports on the television. But sadly, those moments were few and far between, and he made me feel so lonely and desperate sometimes to try to make things work.

So, I did try my best to make it work, especially with a baby. And in his own way, I suppose initially, he did too. He encouraged me to try to get a local council house within the area to rent when I, we, found out that I was expecting and had passed the three-month mark. I filled all the forms in, scoured each estate within our valley, making a note of their names and then listing where I would like to be placed in order of preference. He even advised me to flirt with the housing officer as his friend had told him how his 'Mrs' had, and it helped them to get a house. Now, the housing officer was an elderly man with receding combed greasy grey hair, whose comb-over truly defined this balding man's hairstyle. Now, flirting is something I find hard to do unless legless with incomprehensible speech and smiles, but I was pregnant with a bump. It is expected and natural that a partner would find their pregnant partner attractive, but a housing officer who was hitting retirement in looks and whose sexual attraction came to zero on my sexual Richter Scale was a 'No' for me. I mean, come on, maybe for some women and men it would be an easy thing to do, but for me, I could never ever do it. Even if I had tried in my initial meeting with him, then it would have been me standing looking at him and then shaking my head saying, 'No, I can't do it. I can't do it.' It was just bloody wrong, so bloody wrong. I mean, good luck to those girls who did and could, but for me, it was a huge, massive, and gigantic 'NO!' So, due to me not even trying to sway extra points on the housing waiting list, we started to look throughout the valley for a house, any house that we could afford a mortgage for. And find the cheapest house within the area we did; a mid-terraced cottage for the pricey sum of £65,000. We are going back a few years now, so what you would see as cheap, I saw as expensive.

It was only when the house went through and somebody suggested it was not in the best location, being in a triangular shape to a rugby club and a pub, that I had to concur with this significant fact and yes, it bloody was not in the best bloody location for Sperm. Whilst I stayed with my parents as the pregnancy progressed, he worked on the house, which indeed needed some love and tender care after being neglected for so many years. And he did work, however, he worked sporadically in between social visits to these ale houses, other ale houses and God knows where else within the area. I was not in a position to see him every day and night. I worked up until the birth as a tutor for my local borough council. I worked morning, afternoons, and evenings during the week and on a Saturday morning and Sunday afternoon. I worked all the hours I could, and I had to, not by choice, but I had to go back to work three weeks after Sah's arrival as I had not worked in the UK to meet the requirement of maternity pay. I was in an exhausted, emotional state, continuously trying to juggle motherhood, work, to be positive and happy, when inside, I was not with him. I had to provide financially for my daughter and for the home we would build, but it was us two, Sah and myself, and he was not there. He would use the excuse of working on the house in the evenings and at weekends, but he was not always there. I would cry out of pure frustration, as he did not understand our needs as a young family to spend time together. My words did not get through to him, no matter how many times I tried. When I did go up to see him one Sunday, I found hooped earrings on the mantelpiece. His reply to my questioning, 'One of the boys put them in my pocket for a laugh when I was out last night.'

Our sex life had become non-existent months before Sah's birth, and when I tried to instigate any touch, it was not returned. However, twice I went up to the house, and as I proceeded to look around the house, he would follow me. I sensed he was close, but then out of nowhere, I would feel a repetitive thumping on my leg with a stick-like object. When I looked down, I could see that he had pulled his willy out, and was holding and pulling at it to make it bigger. I swear! He would tap me as if to say, 'Come on, I am horny, fuck me.' He would raise his eyebrows and have a huge grin on his face. I just looked at him and thought to myself, *what is wrong with you? Where is the bloody romance? Jesus!* It was not romantic at all, and our sex life remained non-existent even with such invitations. I can laugh about it now that the years have passed, but at the time it upset me. It upset me so much emotionally and physically, and I questioned what was wrong with me. Why was he like this with me? What had I done wrong? We were just not the same anymore. A major event happened when I was about seven months pregnant, which seemed to propel the unhappiness further. It was late one Saturday night and I felt restless. I had not seen him since the previous day, and I felt so uncomfortable and lonely. I needed him to hold me and to tell me that it was going to be ok. I walked down to the local pub on the square and arrived there a little after 10pm. I had never done this before and did not listen to my parents' concerns of walking the streets at this time while pregnant. I waddled my way slowly down the main road at a gentle pace and breathed the fresh, crisp cold air. I knew his habits, like clockwork, and I saw him in the busy pub in full conversation with someone, I think, who had been at school with him. However, on this occasion, I bumped into an old friend who I hadn't seen in years. He was an old college friend who would use me to make girls from different villages jealous. He would pick me up and we would drive around for hours. I would give him my boyfriend problems and he would try to make the girls he liked jealous by having me in the car with him. I couldn't drive and liked the cruising, but not the evil looks I used to get from some of his beauties who we passed in the council estates and parks.

I passed Sperm on my way to the bar, and he did not even notice my presence in his drunken state. On getting my cola, I went straight to speak with my old friend. We caught up within minutes and he certainly could see my baby bump, so I pointed to show him Sperm. It was odd because after a few minutes of catching up and laughing he was ushering me to stand in a certain position, whilst I was speaking to him, and he had a strained expression. When I knew something was wrong and looked around, over my shoulder to the right, the man I loved was snogging someone, no one special that I can make a comparison to or justify why he did it, but still he progressed to kiss/snog this woman who he had been speaking to as I had entered. I was pregnant, for God's sake. I stood there shaking with a gobsmacked face. He denied it for over six months even though I had seen it with my own eyes and my old friend had stated so during a phone call the following day, as I doubted/questioned myself. But, when you love someone and certainly when you are pregnant with their baby, you want to believe in them, whilst simultaneously knowing the undeniable truth. My old friend's words during that telephone call were, 'I think too much of you to lie to you,' (silence – pause) 'you did see that. I am so sorry, but I won't/can't lie to you.' And when he did confirm it, he was shocked and thought that he had already confirmed it previously. So, when I shouted, 'Six months, six months it has taken for you to admit to it!' He simply said, 'Oh, I thought I had told you.'

The final realisation that the relationship was coming to an end and the major push factor came one night when he forgot Sah was in bed alone, propped up on a V-shaped pillow. Sah was just over six months old, and we had only moved in recently when late on a Friday night, I had got up as I heard him come in late. He couldn't stay in on our first weekend together as he had plans, so why was any other Friday night different, or Saturday night to any other night of the week? I mean, on her first birthday as my family and his family celebrated, he simply rushed in from work to pick up his kit as he had a game on.

Well, on this night in question, Sah was in our bed and supported by a V-shaped pillow as I watched her. I moved her to the middle of the bed, propped up by further pillows that secured her. I left her in the bed and quietly came down the stairs to the living room. His hunched over body stood leaning on the kitchen top and the aroma coming from his alcoholic smelly farts and breath, which were stale and old, suggested that he had drunk too much and was intoxicated. I proceeded to make warm milk in the microwave to help me get to sleep. He said roughly, 'I'm going up,' after devouring his Indian meal and I told him to watch out as Sah was on half the side of the bed. I stated that I would put her in her cot when I came up. 'Ay, ay,' was his response without looking at me. I was in the kitchen when I heard a thud against the bedroom wall upstairs whilst Sah yelped a cry. I ran upstairs so fast and put the landing light on to see into the bedroom. I was horrified and held my right hand to my mouth. He had got into bed, tugged the duvet over him with some force and propelled our baby girl out of the bed flying. I jolted to pick her up and held her tightly whilst also looking to make sure she had not hurt herself. She had been asleep and the initial shock of moving with the duvet and resting on the floor had resulted in this cry I had not heard before. She was fine and had snuggly fallen back to sleep in my arms as soon as I had picked her up. I shouted, 'You stupid fucking idiot.' He had not even moved. He turned around and said, 'What?' I was crying at this stage in anger, fright and I shook my head and went into the other bedroom and lay on the spare bed. I watched Sah as she slept, unaware what had transpired, and held onto her right index finger. My heart broke. It was beating and felt so heavy as it pulled me down with the reality that this was no way to live with someone. I didn't have any trust in him personally as a partner and now with this, did he even have the correct initiative and understanding to look after someone and something so vulnerable and valuable as our daughter? He could not look after himself, me even, so how could I rely on him? If at all.

The next morning as he got ready to go to football training, I told him that this could not go on and that when he got back I/we wouldn't be there. We were moving back in with my parents. Living together had only lasted a few months. An unhappy few months, where I was alone, and it should have been such a happy time. It was not. Everything I did was not good enough. I would cook meals that he would spoon around with and not eat. I will never forget the comment, 'I work hard all day to come back to this? I am going to have a pint in the club.' Or on a Saturday morning when he would say he was going to the garage to get a newspaper and then go missing until 2 am the following morning when the pub or clubs had closed. I would try to reason with him, and he would reiterate, 'You're living in Hollywood, you are. Life is life, this is where we live. You need to stop dreaming.' And so, I did. I/we would never have the happy ending that I knew we were not entitled to with him, but sadly, I expected and wished we had if things had been different. If he had only loved me. My heart was used to sinking now, but it wasn't fair that Sah's would too.

We were two hugely different people, opposites do attract. He gave me an ultimatum on a Saturday night, weeks after I had returned to my parent's house. He had done nothing to make me want him back, and his visits to Sah were limited, but he confidently said, 'It is me or your parents'. I couldn't believe it. The shiver I felt was from the cold air around me whilst we smoked a cigarette each outside the pub in a doorway (and not from this ridiculous request). The disgust on my face with the change in my tone affirmed, 'There is no competition between you and my family. Where would we be if it wasn't for my family?' We both walked in separate directions. I walked to my parents' house where my little girl slept, and he back in for another pint or five.

That first weekend after we'd officially split, I was adamant we wouldn't get back together. I told him I never go out and that he was never in. I asked him to stay away from the main pubs as it would just be so hard to see him out and he smiled and said, 'Ok'. I hoped he would heed my request as it was true – I worked and lived for Sah and had not been out in bloody months. I was having a fag outside one of my favourite drinking establishments. There was a urine smell near the entrance due to the male and female lavatories being located near there. From behind the bend, Sperm and his friends walked past me from the direction of a nearby sports club. Not one from the group looked or acknowledged me, and I felt intimidated and guilty of what I did not know. I was upset, hurt and I simply did not deserve this. No one deserved this and why they felt a need to do it, I do not know. But it was unfair, and I pulled whatever strength I had left in each step I took as I returned to continue my night out. And I knew this was a forced action because anyone in their right mind walking past the entrance would have winced as the smell can be very bad at times, and it was at this time.

I returned to where I was sitting. As I sat there, I knew the sounds and images of laughter and chatting made me physically aware of where I was, but I felt as though a part of me had left my body, as I felt lighter, and as I stared around me, I felt weak and just a ghostly figure of what and who I used to be.

The next ale house was past the chapel and a few steps away. I walked to the bar, and they turned their backs to me as I approached the bar. I had my drink, and as you can imagine, it had not been the most enjoyable experience of buying one at a bar. I returned to where friends stood when one of his little young friends, a ginger, approached and walked towards me with a smile. As I said, 'Hi,' he clenched his fist and punched me in the stomach, not hard, but enough to knock me back and make me look up at him. I wanted to run home and hide under the duvet to block what my reality had become. I should have known as he once commented that his ex-girlfriend would not dare show her face in his town, so this should have given me an inkling as it was said with glee.

Legally, I wanted visiting and access rights to my daughter in black and white for Sperm, and I believed firmly that Sah should see her father. Every child deserves that no matter their parents' personal feelings for their ex-partners unless something seriously is wrong. Sah's dad was just like Peter Pan, liked by all who knew him for being a laugh, a fanatic about sport and the socialising side of it. But, behind closed doors, things are and were quite different. Solicitor's papers stated that he had access every other weekend, and I should know as I was the one who initiated it on countless occasions and paid for it. It never happened, a weekend with the boys or his daughter? I think you can infer what was important to him.

On the odd Saturday that he did pick her up, he should not have driven, let alone walked to get her, in the state he was in. I refused him once and told him, 'Go home, sleep it off and come back later.' He proceeded to walk away as I did, and Sah continued to play outside by the gate. However, it happened so quickly. He returned suddenly, and being the tall stature that he is, he scooped down, picked her up and walked off with her. By the time I ran out, he was driving off in his car with me frantically screaming, shaking, and running. I got in the car to follow and drive to his mother's house, where I thought he would be. His car was not there. I returned home and called the local police station, and explained what had just happened. The officer asked me to explain who this Sperm was, obviously giving his true name and identity, and I stated that you are bound to know him as he played/plays rugby, football, cricket, and that he drank in the cricket club with other officers and played golf. His response to my horror and dismay, 'Oh, I know Sperm. Hell of a nice boy. Don't worry, your little one will be fine with him.' The call ended and I held the phone in my right hand, looking into it and questioning what the fuck was going on in this world and even the police … well, as I told you, he was one of the boys, wasn't he?

Sunday nights were the worst after my family had paid him over seven thousand pounds to get out of the mortgage of the house, and more importantly, out of my life to allow Sah and I to live in the house. Things between us just got worse. On Sunday nights, he would be drunk, and the messages would start coming after 9 pm. He usually went out drinking on a Sunday early afternoon, so by this time he was well on his way. 'Send me a pic of your tits.' 'You horny – fancy a fuck?' Sometimes there would be a bang at the door and he would be staggering there. 'Let me in, please ... I can't go home.' I was soft and sometimes I would give him a blanket and tell him to be up first thing, as I did not want Sah to get confused. But it got to the stage where I would stay down my parents' house at weekends so that I did not have any 'shit' as my mother put it.

My parents both said 'God, you can pick them.' I would then repeat, 'Well, Mammy, it's your fault. You're the one that told me that I pick the good-looking ones who are no good.' My mother retorted, 'Go for someone's personality as looks aren't everything, I told you. Remember that nice one I liked who you were at school with and saw when you were seeing that one at university? He was a lovely boy.' Yes, he was indeed a lovely boy, good-looking, kind, caring, opening the car door for me to get in and a lovely puppy. I had gone through secondary school with him, and we even shared the same form room for four years. He had always been ok, I guess, but he shared the same facial characteristics as other family members with the only difference being their hairstyles, lengths and colours. I had returned from university for a weekend and we kind of hooked up and saw each other whilst I was home for Easter, but it was complicated as I had a boyfriend at university, so it was never serious at my end, and he knew that as I had been honest from the start with them both. Now, may I state before you get the wrong idea of me that this behaviour was out of character, but my university boyfriend had broken my heart literally by having a Christmas romance with a single mother ex-colleague whilst he returned home for the holiday, and then he had the audacity to invite her to our university for a dirty weekend whilst I was at home recovering from an operation. Well, I obviously found out, broke up with him and after months of tears, depression, and the loss of something that I had loved so much, well, we got back together. I loved, loved, loved that man. However, I could not forgive or forget. I was immature and did not handle the situation well, and my only adultery throughout my life, if that is what you call it, happened upon my return home that Easter. It was fleeting, enjoyable and I was honest with all parties. It also showed me that I was not ready mentally for a serious relationship with anyone. I mean, the belief of an eye for an eye was simply outdated, and I had not received this memo until years later. Do I have regret over the loss of my first true love whilst at university? Of course, but even though I knew I loved him I knew I had to walk away from him as the hurt has been deep and cutting. To this day, my mother states he is the man that made me the happiest she had ever seen. Whilst fleeting in time, to this day I still think of my Viking northerner and what became of him with a wicked smile and great fondness. If he was my soulmate, then I was happy to share what time we had together but wish the experience hadn't hurt so much. We cannot change or reverse what has once happened so long ago, and we must live to accept the consequences of our actions emotionally, psychologically, and physically, because it affects us, a broken heart, in the long term in all these areas.

However, with this Easter dalliance, I couldn't tell my mother that he was a no-no because when we made love, I didn't even know he was inside of me. Let's just say that it didn't hit the sides, and as I laid listening to his groans and his up and down rhythm whilst thinking, *What the fuck is happening?* I mean, you need to feel it right to feel something, well anything really. It just would not have worked out physically because of his chipolata sausage and my desire for a jumbo one. I was pretty honest and open in most things with my mother but telling her this fact would not have gone down well, to be honest, but at the same time it would have been funny to see her facial expression and shock as to what her daughter was saying.

* * *

I had previously lectured at universities in Tokyo, Australia and New Zealand, and taught in schools abroad, and as Sah would be approaching nursery age I thought to myself, *'I have no life here - whatsoever!'* I worked in a job that I loved, but it was not contracted. I taught wonderful students who, for whatever reason, had missed the educational opportunity that most of us have and always will take for granted, in centres and the probation service where I taught literacy and numeracy to high and low-risk offenders released into the community. I taught people like murderers, a paedophile, armed robbers, and the like.

Due to human rights, I was never told who had done what, but some of them would open up. I never felt scared as I was continuously filmed and monitored, with an alarm button on me. I only felt uncomfortable when I had a paedophile in the room. It is strange how the subconscious works, but I knew it was him – he had a discoloured beige anorak on (I am not saying all anorak men can be defined as this) a distant manner, greasy combed hair and eyes that were deep and although not black in colour, the darkness penetrated through, and he always gave me a shiver and a sense of heightened self-protection. He basically was a greasy, strange-looking, combed-over man who personified darkness.

Through time and professionalism, I got to know them as they got to know me. I never disclosed where I lived and where I was from, however, they would divulge their personal trials and tribulations. I would listen sympathetically whilst thinking to myself, *Jesus, your lives are really fucked up.* They too got to know me and if I wasn't my usual jolly self they would ask if I was okay. They helped me monetarily by giving me advice on how to claim bank charges from my past and even showed me web pages to make it easier. They knew I was single and off men, and many had said if they were younger, they would have liked to have had a go and been with me, and as I smiled and shook my head up and down, inside, I would say to myself, *No bloody way! My parents would have a bloody fit.* Daddy's last comment before he was to meet 'Sperm Donor' for the first time as he sat in his solid pine Victorian farmer's armchair next to the Rayburn Cooker was, 'What bright spark is this now? God, you can pick them!' I did not want to prove Daddy right, but then, on the other hand, I could have proved to my mother that I could pick someone with a good personality as some of them were very entertaining. But it was a big 'No' without feeling any guilt whatsoever. Boundaries are set for a reason, and I was a professional with respect for myself.

A few of my probationers, who I had got to know over the months and were committed and progressing well in their personal and private lives since leaving prison, knew I had an ex-partner and that I was seeing a solicitor about visiting rights for my daughter. I suppose discussing and divulging snippets of my personal life made me more human to them, as life isn't perfect for anyone no matter what people try to personify. Mine certainly wasn't and I made silly stupid mistakes just like everyone else, including you, I am sure.

They knew I didn't go out partying and that I enjoyed a glass or two, or I should say a bottle of Lambrini. My neighbour used to call me 'The Lambrini Girl.' They also knew the reason why I would rather entertain myself at home. I didn't want or need to be confronted by Sperm Donor's facial expressions as he ogled and looked at me as though I am and was the shit of shit. And to make it worse, it wasn't only him doing this to me. The people who I had become accustomed to socialising with and who I thought of as friends had now, because of the end of my relationship with Sperm, had also changed towards me. Once they would have greeted me with a 'Hello' or 'Hi,' but now I was purposely ignored and felt to be made uncomfortable in my hometown and places I had frequented throughout my life. Out of all of his mates, only five spoke nicely to me, and to this day, they still continually do so.

So, I spoke with my parents, who Sperm had referred to as being 'evil.' What I do know is that if it wasn't for them, I don't know where I would have been, or for that, Sah. Her father's promise of letting her want for nothing when we told my parents I was pregnant was like everything else he promised in life - hopeless. Being a single parent, hell, a parent at all to a young baby/child is hard and continues to be hard. And without them financially, emotionally, and physically I would have been desperate, and possibly in a situation where I had to stay in an unhealthy, emotionally damaging relationship with my daughter and her biological father.

I started applying for jobs via the great TES (Times Educational Supplement), the be-all and end-all of teaching jobs, nationally and internationally. I was well travelled, and my brother and his wife were lifelong international teachers, so I had their personal experiences and those of acquaintances for advice and support. My curriculum vitae went out, and the first interview I had was for an international school in Kuala Lumpar - the interview was held in London. With some interviews, candidates are reimbursed the costs of travelling, but with this one I had to cover all costs. My confidence had shattered into pieces over the previous couple of years, and as the interview was in the morning, I decided to travel up the night before and stay in a hotel, as I tend to get very lost in London and I needed to control the situation with calmness. I arrived for the interview in advance and sat down accordingly to meet whoever would interview me. My nerves were surprisingly calm – always the best form to be in control of a possible, and more importantly, a life-changing event.

The interview was in a hotel room, and I met the headmaster/principal. 'Sit down,' he informed me, and I adhered by sitting opposite, legs crossed and clasping both hands on top of my right knee. He proceeded, 'I'm Welsh, you know, from North Wales.' I thought to myself that it was a good omen to have a fellow Welshman. I became more positive with this realisation. Well, was I bloody wrong? 'You're my wild card, you see.'

No, I didn't bloody see.

'Your CV's ok but … you have moved around a lot.'

Erm, where is he going with this? I bloody thought to myself.

'You're a single mother?'

I replied a simple, 'Yes.' I gave the reason why I wanted this job, and it was simply to work in a good/outstanding school where my daughter would be provided with a formidable solid education.

'Hmm,' he said. 'Well, I'll be honest with you. If you think you're going to go to Kuala Lumpur to find a man and live happily ever after, it's not going to happen. You will be a single mother and the western men/American men out there like the local women. They won't look twice at you.'

I wish there had been someone videoing my reaction and facial expressions at this point. 'Excuse me? If you think I want a job abroad to get a man – then you are very mistaken. My God, if I want a man I will go to my local pub on a Friday or Saturday night and not travel across the world. And to be honest, I don't want a man after the shit I have been through, thank you very much. I want a good life for my daughter and myself. And furthermore, I am a bloody good teacher, and you would have been very lucky to have me.'

Pleasantries and questions ensued, and I left in a professional manner, but inside I was seething. He is no longer the principal/headmaster, and I hope wherever he is and whatever he is doing, that he has matured and is no longer the knobhead I remember meeting at that interview.

It wasn't until I spoke to my brother and explained what had been said that he informed me that I should have walked out.

'What? Do you mean to tell me that I can walk out of an interview?'

'Yes, of course you can. I have on many occasions.'

'Well, you never told me that before.'

'You never bloody asked'.

'Oh,' I answered.

'And to be fair, he was right in telling you that the men wouldn't be interested in you. They like tight vaginas.'

'Are you being bloody serious now?'

'He shouldn't have told you like that, but he is right.'

I retorted, 'And the worst thing is I paid for that experience. A hotel, the train, food, and it felt like a bad interview for a dating agency. Stupid Welsh bastard.'

'Well, you live and learn. You'll get something, but it may not be what and where you want.'

I thought to myself, *God, he is a happy bugger, isn't he*?

'Let me know if anything else comes up. Got to go as we are having a barbeque and friends are coming over.' I ended the call with a ta-ra as jealousy ran through me as my brawd's barbeque would be in the sun, by the pool with lush smells of flowers, the sizzling of the meat, the sound of music, laughter, and glasses being filled and drank with delicious cool alcoholic drinks. Whereas, I look out of the window and see grey clouds, rain, feel the heat from the gas central heating which has been on since waking up and the smell of past cigarettes smoked from the downstairs bathroom, as it's too bloody cold to go out for a fag. *God*, I thought to myself *where is* I'm a Celebrity Get Me Out of Here *when I need them?* I shook my head and muttered to myself in groans at the comparison of what our lives had become.

I reiterated my interview experience with the probation boys, and they were not happy at the thought of me leaving as they didn't like change. It was on one Thursday afternoon a week later at the end of a session when one of them was lingering back, and I sensed he wanted to tell me something. I was packing all the files up, as I too had to leave, when he casually said whilst sitting in his chair in a relaxed manner once everyone had left and I turned to face him,

'I know you are going through a lot and that you are stressed. I can see it. If this bastard is making you want to leave the country, you do know you have options.'

I looked at him curiously. 'Options?' I said with a frown.

'Yes. I know of a bloke in Burry Port who charges 500 quid. That's all he will need, the cash, a picture, places he goes to and times. It will be sorted with no questions asked. For extra, if you don't want the body found then that can be done too.'

I didn't know for a fact, but I hope he sensed that I was in extreme shock.

He continued. 'There is also someone in London, ex-IRA I think. He charges 10,000 quid and it will take a bit longer, but that is another option. You will save with solicitor's fees and then not have to go away. Think about it?'

My response was immediate, 'Oh, thank you so much. It is very kind that you are thinking of me. I must admit that I do hate him, but I don't hate him enough to have him gone for good. And anyway, I don't think my daughter would appreciate it if I had her father killed/assassinated. It could cause major complications in our relationship, like, for example, if I get locked up for years.' He got up and nodded sympathetically.

As he approached the door to leave, he ended this conversation, which I can only say was one of the weirdest and maddest I have ever had, with, 'I just want you to know that there are options. Think about it, and if you change your mind, we can discuss it further, but not here. Ok?'

I repeated, 'Thank you so much.'

'It's just that you're a nice girl and we like you here. You deserve better.'

'I know I do. Have a good weekend and see you next week,' I replied with a smile, and he returned it. He left the room and the door closed. I immediately put my hands on the filing cabinet and leaned on it, thinking to myself, *Jesus, did that really happen? Thank fuck they do not have any audio on the bloody cameras, or I could be having lessons here too.*

It wasn't until I was home that evening having dinner with my parents at the table, with Sah in her highchair, as we did most evenings, that I got to discuss my interesting day. I got in as it was being served and sat down with immediate effect after giving my beautiful little girl lots of kisses. We had always eaten together as a family all my life, and it was a time where we all caught up with our daily news and experiences.

My mother always initiated the discussion with, 'How was your day?' Daddy wasn't one for many words at the dinner table and would only interject seldomly.

'Well, Mammy, you're not going to believe this.' I reiterated the conversation I had of how a man who I taught in probation knew someone that would charge 500 quid from Burry Port, or an ex-IRA man in London for 10,000 quid to get rid of Sperm Donor. As I was speaking, Mammy had placed her knife and fork on the plate. Daddy kept chewing on his food, and when I finished with a repetition, 'Can you bloody believe it only costs 500 quid and there is someone down in Burry Port that does this, and an ex bloody IRA man in London for 10,000? I didn't think it could be so bloody cheap. Hell, I've spent more than 500 already on solicitor's fees.'

My mother's reply was shock and disbelief, 'Well, 500 is cheap, isn't it? Wes, what do you think?'

'Olive,' he replied, looking up at us both. 'I have heard that there is someone in the Llanelli area down the Pic.'

'Who told you that, Wes?' She questioned anxiously, with possible annoyance that this was something else my father had forgotten to tell her late on a Friday night when he returned after having a pint or two with his friends. 'You never tell me anything. Whenever I ask you, 'any news?' you say, 'No, nothing'.'

'I can't bloody remember,' he answered with annoyance.

She turned her gaze to me and asked, still not touching her food, 'Well, what did you tell this man?'

'I simply thanked him for thinking of me, but said I hated Sperm, but not that much to have him killed.'

'Well, what on earth is this world coming to? Honestly! I don't want you and Sah to go, but I think it is best for you to get out of here. The sooner you leave, the better. At least then you will have some peace and be able to get on with your life.' She picked up her knife and fork and continued to eat whilst commenting, 'I don't think I could do it. I wouldn't be able to live with myself. And I know I would never survive being locked up. Well, I am in shock. Don't tell anyone. I don't want the police coming here. Ok? Because if something happens to that … that …. wanker then I think this is the first place they will come. Isn't it, Wes?'

She looked at him as if for him to interject some fatherly advice. However, he looked disapprovingly at her with a 'Language!' expression. He then looked at me and simply stated in a calm and peaceful manner, 'From now on, shut your mouth. Don't tell anyone anything. You say too bloody much.'

'Ok, Daddy,' I answered like a little girl should answer her father, even though I was now 33 years old.

We continued eating when my mother, who I could tell had been mulling this over in her head, commented, 'I thought when people go to jail they come out better … not …?'

I quickly answered, 'I know, isn't it fucking mad?'

My father disapprovingly looked up at me and stated, 'Language! No bloody swearing at the table. Now eat your food and shut up.'

'Sorry, Daddy,' I retorted shyly, and we continued to eat our food until each plate was consumed and Sah had finished her fruit dessert. Our evening of watching television, crap on television, soon commenced with some arguments as to who watched what, but I slept well that night with dreams of a different reality after my discussion with my probationer that day. And it felt good.

My second interview was in London again, but this time with an international employment agency that represented a company which required teaching staff for its international school for its employees in the Middle East. Now, my brother had informed me in our previous chat about this position, that if I was successful I was a lucky bitch, because it was one of the best-paid teaching jobs to get in the world. Before the interview had even started, the recruitment manager, a South African blond lady, had looked me up and down and said firmly in her lovely, elegant accent,

'Oh, he is going to like the look of you. I know his type. He likes this kind of dress code. Good luck.'

The interview went well and the chap, or more appropriately titled headmaster, was lovely. I firmly stated that I was a single mother, and my priority was and always would be my daughter and second, teaching. He agreed with me that this should be the case. I had a cup of tea, and it was like meeting someone at a coffee shop and getting to know them.

On the way home, on the train, to Wales, I phoned my family and texted my friends, stating that the interview went well and that I had a good feeling as it hadn't been like an interview at all. Before departing the office, the South African lady said that she would be in touch in a couple of days. I then proceeded to thumb a taxi down to get back to Paddington. I knew I wasn't far from the train station, but London scared me. I was a little Welsh girl from the third-largest town in Carmarthenshire, and there was no comparison between anything where I came from and the capital city of England. It was a nerve-racking experience every time I had to come up for an interview with the busyness, and the hustle and bustle of hundreds of people surrounded by large buildings. But there were two things on my journey home that always lifted my spirits. Firstly, the crossing of the Severn Bridge and the 'Welcome to Wales' sign with the beautiful greenness of the mountainous and hilly Welsh countryside filled me up and made me smile. Secondly, the Welsh sign of my hometown as you drove down the steep hill to Rhyd- a -man. My English sister-in-law would say as we would drive past the sign as we entered this pretty, little shitty town, 'Oh, look. We are entering Rhyd – a – man', she would exaggerate, which evidently was a surprisingly good description if you observed the behaviour of individuals, both men and women, at the weekend. But, to me, it always meant that I knew I was home, and whilst I loved my home, and it would always be a part of me, I still couldn't wait to get the hell out.

I was at the local Tesco in town on a Friday afternoon. It was exactly 2.10pm. I was walking back to the car after getting groceries for my mother when my mobile rang. I recognised the number immediately, South African lady.

'Hello. I am pleased to inform you that you have been successful in your application for teacher. Congratulations.'

I stopped walking to fully comprehend and felt as though I was invincible and that my luck had changed. I thanked her and she informed me that paperwork would be sent to organise the contract and visas. When the conversation ended, I jumped one large jump and clasped my right fist, like a rugby player who had just scored a try to win the match from England. And, with my fist in the air I said, 'Yes! Yes! Yes!'

With a spring in my step, I walked joyfully, no not joyfully, but ecstatically to my old banger of a car. I hoped no one had noticed my display as it could have looked odd to some, I suppose. I sat down in my driver's seat of Frantic Fanny, yes, the name of my car, and not because I have one, but my life had been frantic, and I did have a fanny. I phoned Mammy with my news, and she too was happy.

'Well done. I will put the kettle on. See you soon. I will also phone your brother to tell him. Wes, she got it!' She put the phone down, I drove home, and there was an air of peace within myself that I had not felt in such a long time. Change is good, and it was coming our way, and I hoped for the better.

The weeks that followed were filled with paperwork and a request from my new employer to get official documentation that I was the carer for Sah, as they didn't want any issues once I had started my contract, or my employment being disturbed with any legal action of parental responsibility. Basically, that I had not kidnapped my daughter and fled abroad, so not to allow her father to contact Interpol. I contacted the solicitor who had dealt with me previously in relation to Sperm Donor, and she had no idea what they wanted. She then sent me to a retired colleague, who after discussion with her colleagues, found that I needed a Parental Responsibility Order from a court. She was of a small, petite stature, with immaculate make-up and blow-dried shoulder-length greying hair and was an intelligent and formidable force to be reckoned with considering her age. This meant that Sperm and I would both have to agree for him to give me full parental responsibility at court. Now, I can honestly say that I have never been to court or had any desire to go to court. The nearest to court I had ever been was either walking past the local one by the police station or seeing them on television programmes or films.

I had been honest with Sperm from the beginning about the job interviews and accepting the job. I can't say that he was particularly bothered. However, when I informed him that I would be on good money, so there would no longer be any need to give me child maintenance for Sah, which I had to fight for initially as he wanted to give me £15 a week. I thought this was a ludicrous amount considering the amount he spends on alcohol and cigarettes daily.

I contacted the Child Support Agency, and they were wonderful in legally giving me what Sah was entitled to, £40 weekly, which helped me to buy clothes, food, and toys for her. It was withdrawn from his pay. He wasn't happy at all, but I knew how he worked. I knew if he could save money, then he would be happier even though legally when we left the UK and not him, he was still legally obliged to support Sah. By offering this, he would be easier to deal with, but I then stated if he wanted to see Sah twice early, during the summer holidays and at Christmas or Easter, he would have to provide one flight yearly, a return flight at that.

He was sent solicitor's letters and a court date was arranged. He was advised to get his own solicitor, but oh no, he didn't need legal representation. Some of his friends had also separated from their girlfriends/spouses, so I am sure he had lots of free advice from his buddies - like the £15 child maintenance.

I ensured on the day of court that I was to pick him up and drive us both to Llanelli Magistrates' Court. I knew how unreliable he was and wanted to ensure he did not fuck this up, as getting another court appointment at a later date could possibly mean the loss of this job. I had to have this document; it was as simple as that.

I picked him up from his mother's, which is where he was lodging, and we drove. It made me feel sick to be near him after all the nasty, negative things he had said to me and the way he had made me feel about myself. And not only that, how he was with Sah. She had deserved so much more from him emotionally and physically. I thanked God that she had my father as her father figure, as hers was sadly lacking.

We arrived and met my solicitor, who asked him where his legal representation was. 'I haven't got any. I am not wasting my money, and to be honest, it sounds simple,' he arrogantly replied.

'This is very unprofessional as you should have your own legal guidance,' she said and went through what would happen and explained everything that he already knew.

'About this flight I have to pay for. I am not having that.'

'What?' I shouted as I turned to face him. 'You knew about this! And now here you are saying this before we go in?'

'No,' he smirked. 'You wanted the free flight, not me, and you want to take my daughter abroad, not me.'

The solicitor firmly stated, 'We are about to go in and you must be in agreement, or they will not agree, and I don't know when we can have another date. You must be unified as if there are any differences, the court will take this negatively.'

Venomously I stated, 'I am not backing down. You knew this and I have stated that you do not have to pay maintenance for Sah whilst we are away.'

'Well, if I have to pay for the flight, I will most probably end up paying more than the maintenance.'

'Don't be bloody silly. A return flight can be found for about £400.'

'Well, I don't know that. Where is the evidence to show me? I need to see it.' He quipped with a smirk.

I tried to remain calm, but he knew my triggers. I shook my head and thought to myself, *What a fucking bastard.*

Let's just say that the court hearing was not as straightforward as I expected. It was intimidating and after discussions and me firmly not backing down, an agreement was made. I was proud of myself as in so many instances I had kept quiet and taken it, so to speak. However, the old feisty me was slowly reappearing and it was about time.

The court papers were created, and we both signed them in a little room and then my solicitor proceeded to take them back to the magistrate. I didn't think that Sperm Donor could shock me anymore, but he did, and it was the most degrading thing that he had said to me yet. He sat back in his chair, stretched his arms out and then relaxed and looked at me, 'I think I deserve a blow job for just signing my daughter over to you. Don't you?'

My shoulders and heart shrank in disgust. I couldn't say anything, and if I had, what could I have said? With paperwork signed and me thanking him and being so grateful for finally having this document, we left for the 20-minute ride home. It was one of the most uncomfortable journeys I had ever had with him.

As we approached his mother's council estate, he turned to me and said, 'Fancy a quick pint?'

There was a pub not far up the road by the railway, but I honestly couldn't believe the nerve of this prick. He was still surprising me.

I shook my head as I replied, 'No. I want to get home to see our daughter.'

'Alright, was only asking,' he replied as I firmly stopped the car and waited for him to get out.

We didn't say goodbye and I had no pleasantries. I drove home, walked in to see a beaming little girl who I picked up and held in the air, kissing her cheeks.

My mother turned to face me in the kitchen and said, 'I can tell that went well by your face. I will put the kettle on, and you can tell me all about it.'

When I spoke to my brawd about the whole bloody ordeal over Skype, he told me, 'Ye, you should have given him a blow job, and then pretended to have a locked jaw. Bet he would have loved that?'

Now, you have to remember that my mother was part of this discussion and we both made facial expressions of disgust with Mammy then stating, 'Don't be so disgusting.'

'I am only saying, Mammy. He asked for one, and if she had used her head, she could have given him one with a bit of bite.'

'Jesus, I couldn't have his bits in my mouth and pretended to bite it with a locked jaw. Firstly, knowing my luck, he would call the police and accuse me of penis assault or something daft like that. Secondly, I don't want his dick near me. You have actually turned my stomach now, so thanks.'

'Well, he certainly would think twice about asking you to do that again, wouldn't he?'

My mother stopped the conversation with a 'That's enough talk now on that. Your father will be in later from the garden, and I don't think he would be impressed with discussing biting that prick's dick off and pretending it was due to a locked jaw.' The topic of that conversation did thankfully end, but to this day, that thought still turns my stomach and possibly always will.

The weeks progressed with paperwork being completed, the house being packed up ready for rental, packing suitcases, saying goodbye to friends, colleagues, and students alike. I did believe that visitation would have increased between Sperm and our daughter, but sadly it did not. In fact, on one occasion it got nasty. He turned up still pissed or on what from the night before I didn't know, and I firmly told him that he was not driving with our daughter. He needed to go and sort himself out.

He started shouting, 'You can't stop me from seeing my daughter.'

I retorted, 'I am not stopping you from seeing her. If anything, I have encouraged you to spend time with her and have letters to prove it from the solicitors.'

'Oh, you and your bloody solicitor's letters.'

'If anything should happen to Sah in your care, and I mean anything, when I know you are not fit to have her, I would and could never forgive myself. She is my life and if anything should happen to her – well. I guess she is lucky to have one parent that is looking after her.'

'What the hell is going to happen to her? Do you think I would hurt her?'

'No, not on purpose but look at yourself. Sleep it off and come back in a couple of hours.'

'No, I am seeing her now. You can't stop me.'

With this comment, my father came to the front door and said firmly, 'Listen now. She is not giving Sah to you now. Go home and sleep it off.'

With that Sperm put his right arm out to punch my father in the face and my father ended up going on the pavement being held by Sperm. Words were said and Sperm backed off before finally turning to me and stated,

'This is all your fault. All yours. I shouldn't have let you wind me up.'

He left in his car, we descended into the house in shock, and I phoned the police. Enough was enough, as I feared reprisal for my father once we left the UK.

A policeman came, a man who did not live in the area and listened to us. I knew he wasn't from the area as he was handsome and smart, and I had never seen him before. He went to Sperm's mother's house, but there was no answer, and his car wasn't there. He came back and said if anything else occurred to phone immediately. Nothing happened thankfully, but that evening I went down the local with £40 to give the landlord to put in a kitty for my father and to also say, 'I am moving away, and can I ask you to keep an eye on Daddy when he is here and goes to the toilet. I am not going to go into it, but my daughter's father, who you know, well, things aren't good, and I don't want him having a go at Daddy.'

'Don't worry. I will keep an eye out.' I was grateful as Daddy, like us all, had aged and Sperm was tall, big, and strong in comparison. I would be so far away, but it eased my concern, somewhat, a little.

The weeks flew by and the time quickly came for us to leave and start our adventure and new life abroad. We said our goodbyes and even though it was sad, it was for our best, and more certainly mine. We were dropped off at Swansea bus station by my emotional mother and proud father. Our journey to Qatar started on the National Express Bus, number 201. It was a long journey and Sah's second flight, but she behaved so well throughout, and my worry of her being an annoying child for other passengers was unwarranted. She had periods of sleeping, watching a movie, and colouring in and thought nothing of the experience.

We knew we would be met at the airport and proceeded through the gates where Sah was now very alert with her senses awakened in this new country. However, she suddenly stopped in her tracks and raised her right arm and pointed with her index finger. Now you must remember that she had just turned three, but I wanted the ground to open and swallow me whole.

'Look! Chocolate people. Can I eat?'

I quickly said, 'Sh,' and bent down putting my right index finger to my lips. I whispered, 'You can't eat them, Sah. They are people just like you and me. They are just darker because the sun is so bright and hot here.' I am not sure if she understood my definition, but she definitely understood and acknowledged that she couldn't eat them with a simple, 'Ok, Mammy. No eat.'

Part 2

First meeting – not love at first sight.

We settled in well on the coast in the small man-made city. We had a lovely three-bedroomed ground floor apartment which was very spacious and had huge areas for Sah to run, hide and play. We didn't have a garden, which I knew I would miss, but there was a swimming pool not too far away and a beach a small drive away. We lived on a compound with all the other workers of the company which included all teaching staff, engineers, managers, etc. It was a manmade city for the workers and had a shop, a restaurant with delicious, subsidised food and an international feel, as the workers were indeed from around the world and of all ages, both young and old. Within the first couple of days, we had been introduced to an Australian girl named Sheila.

Now, upon our first meeting at the swimming pool, we had hit it off and she seemed bubbly, naughty and fun with a wicked sense of humour. That very evening there was to be a party at a colleague's house, another Welsh single mother, and as I had no transport, Sheila had offered to pick us up and take us to the party. Sah and I could have walked but being a desert country and not knowing where we were going to, well, it seemed like a good idea to take up this exceedingly kind offer. I didn't fancy walking the roads in the blistering heat of 40 degrees with a three-year-old, questioning every three minutes, 'How long? We there? Carry me?' You know what I mean?

So, at the party, Sheila had exclaimed in front of another colleague 'We are going to become best friends.' In this conversation was a fellow Aussie teacher, Spencer, who was a cross between a punk and grunge dresser with a very strange Trans English Australian accent, and he retorted, 'But Sheila, what if she doesn't want to be your best friend?'

By this time, I had had a couple of drinks and whilst in the conversation and oddly observing how they were discussing me in the third person, Sheila replied, 'She doesn't have a choice.' I laughed as when travelling you do meet interesting and different individuals from around the globe, but from that time on we became close friends, who had giggles, shopping trips, and more importantly, we were a rock for one another.

Mine and Sheila's department shared the same portacabin, and one Thursday morning at work, she popped her head into the office and said, 'Fancy getting out of this shithole after school and going shopping to the city? I can take you to the Kia Garage where I bought my car from, so we can also get you some wheels. You up for it?'

I didn't have to think twice as I and Sah were reliant on the goodwill of people to be able to go and buy food to live and survive and not starve to death. I had previously had a contract with a hire car company, and it had come to an end for two reasons. I honestly thought I had a shit car until driving with Sheila to the city one day and apologising continuously that, 'Sorry Sheila, this car is so slow. It's shit! It has no power and ...' before she started laughing with a 'You are so funny. Change gears. Have you been driving all this time since you got the car in first bloody gear? Are you serious? Ha that is so funny.'

To my amazement, that journey was the quickest journey we had had in weeks, and I learnt that an automatic had gears like a normal car which needed to be used and were not just for decoration. Sheila was concerned about the damage caused to the engine and whether it would cost me, whilst she simultaneously laughed at my ignorance and stupidity. But, after a car accident which was not my fault, and neither was the considerable damage caused by the dish dash man that went into me whilst towing a small fishing boat, I decided that the car should go back because of my mother's belief that bad things come in threes which she had passed on to me. And realistically, it had been stressful driving pre-gear change, and the car accident had been the last bloody straw. And don't even get me started on the police in Qatar. What a bloody mad experience that was.

The police officers automatically blamed me until the driver admitted that it was his fault after some time of laughing and chatting whilst I was upset, emotional and pretty pissed off that our five-minute journey to the pool would not take five minutes, but a couple of hours. The arse licking that went on with the police officers and this dish dash man was sickening, so he was obviously known to them and thank God he admitted it was his fault, otherwise there could have been a whole lot more shit. And he had the cheek to ask me back to his place for a drink and was happy and jiggly in his hip movements when inferring that his wife and family would not be there. Dirty, dirty bastard! And Sah was with me!

Sheila had sold the trip to me with her immediate, 'We can also go to the liquor store and stock up if you want?' She had a drinking license, and this was a definite concrete plan.

'Yes please!' was my firm answer. 'But you do realise that Sah is coming with us?' Sheila was fantastic with Sah and laughed, sang and played with her. She sometimes made my daughter look like a clown with the makeup she put on her, but we all had fun together, and as always, this wasn't a problem for our Sheila.

'Make sure you bring her booster chair, and we'll leave at 4 pm. Ok?'

I smiled and said, 'Will do. See you later, Cariad.'

We finished our working day and got home. I changed Sah from her school uniform into something free and comfortable and proceeded to get her booster chair ready for a little trip to the big city. Sheila, as always, was on time, picked us up and we proceeded to drive off, but made a pit stop to fill up her engine with juice. As Sheila poured petrol into her car, I undid Sah's belt, and we proceeded to go into the garage shop to buy some liquid refreshments and snacks for all of us to enjoy on the journey.

As I queued, an Arab man was paying at the service desk. It is easy to distinguish Arab and non-Arab men as he wore a white dish dash, a long white robe and a headscarf (keffiyeh). He had a wallet brimming with notes and was having a laughable disagreement with the cashier, as the cashier had returned too much loose change. 'Where am I supposed to put this? You don't have notes? What am I supposed to do?' He laughed to himself whilst muttering something in Arabic, with the cashier continually uttering, 'Sorry! Sorry!' He turned to leave, and as I was standing directly behind him in the queue, we faced each other. He smiled at me, then turned and smiled at Sah, and I returned a polite curl of the lips back, whilst Sah stood there looking up and confused as to who was this man in a dress?

I returned to the car with Sah and re-sat her in her chair, giving her the purchased pop and snacks. I could see that Sheila was still meandering in the shop, so took advantage to have a quick smoke before the long journey. I informed Sah that Mammy would be back soon, and she smiled and simply said, 'Ok Mammy.'

I ushered quickly to the left side of the garage and lit a fag. Sheila would not tolerate smoking in her car, which is fair enough, but I simply needed a quick puff. As I lit, inhaled, and exhaled in the heat, the man who had shortly before been in the garage in front of me complaining about his change walked towards me. He stopped about a metre in front of me and with his right hand, he waved it and said, 'No! No! No!'

Then, I followed his hands opening, spreading, and raised to the air and made a 'BOOM!' sound.

I was very puzzled and said, 'What?'

'You speak English?' he questioned.

'Yes,' I simply replied.

He replied as I had his full attention. Well, he couldn't really ignore me as there was only the two of us there. 'You should not smoke here. Why do you? You want everything to go up? Boom?'

I retorted simply, 'I can't smoke in my friend's car. I wanted a fag, that's all.'

I thought to myself, *I just want a bloody fag in peace for a couple of minutes for God's sake.*

'A fag?' he questioned. I couldn't see his eyes as his shades covered them and I quizzed, he can't honestly think I am looking for someone who is gay, as a fag in Welsh tongue can also mean gay.

'One of these,' I stated as I held up my now depleted cigarette, which had been wasted during this conversation. I had now finished my cigarette with the last large inhale. It was rather awkward, to be honest, so I simply stated, 'Thanks for letting me know I could have blown the garage up.'

He replied, 'You live here?'

'Yes?' I nodded in confirmation and proceeded to leave and past him.

'Where are you going?' the cheeky bugger asked.

I turned to say, 'To my ride to Doha. There.'

'Ah, I see,' he confirmed. I pointed to Sheila who was now sitting in the car watching in amusement, as she could see my facial expressions and quick pace to return to the car. I jumped in the car and did my seat belt.

'Who the fuck is that?' she quizzed as she looked at me.

'Oh, don't bloody ask. I went for a quick fag; he came over and basically gave me a row for smoking and said I could blow up the station.'

'Far out. But he does have a fair point. We are on a petroleum site, and this is a petrol garage. So, in theory … ye, I suppose it could happen.' She laughed and called me a 'fucking idiot,' in her nice Aussie way. She turned the ignition on and by now dish dash man was also in his car. He was waving at me, so I looked at Sheila with each of our eyebrows raised and did the polite thing and waved back. Sah, too, was also waving as we pulled away. Sheila started singing, 'You have pulled, you have pulled.'

I retorted, 'Fuck off, will you? I don't want a bloody man and especially one in a dress. He looks more feminine than me in his whites and me in my blacks.' Sheila laughed and we proceeded to leave the garage and headed for the capital Doha, a 50-kilometre drive.

It took about 30 minutes to drive on the very modern three-lane highway that connected my developing place of work and home to the cosmopolitan city. It was always a mesmerising journey as you would drive past sand dunes that endured for what seemed like miles and pass the odd camel or two. It felt like normality to go to a shopping centre such as Villaggio Mall, a shopping mall in the west end of Doha with over 200 shops (American, British, French, and German) and buy food that was fresh, homely to what I and other British ex-pats took for granted, and could not be purchased in the developing shop, and I mean shop, where we lived. The only difference here was that there was a canal that meandered within the shopping centre, and it had a beautiful Venetian theme. It was truly mesmerising, whilst being mindboggling, and one heck of an experience to shop here.

Sheila had the High School Musical CD playing in the background and she loved it. I had become accustomed to her taste. We had only been driving for a couple of minutes when the Arab from the station passed us and was waving again.

'Oh God,' Sheila muttered. 'Did you get his name?' she questioned.

'Fuck off,' I replied.

'Well, he is a rich one, that's for sure.'

'How the hell can you work that out?' I questioned. 'His number plate is a giveaway and the car he is driving. Look at it. It is an Audi Q7. Don't think I have seen another one here in Qatar.'

I questioned, 'What?'

'Oh, you can tell you are new here. The lower the number plate the more wasta. He could be royalty and within the 300th in line to the throne. The higher the number plate the more wasta.' She went on to explain that wasta translates to line of authority, influence, political (or other) power, connections, or a combination of those. She explained the English translation and expression: it's not what you know, but who you know was the rough equivalent.

She explained, 'The rules are more flexible if you have wasta or know someone with wasta. Wasta, I think, means you can smooth or speed up business, bureaucratic issues, and other official procedures. I suppose it could also get you out of jail or deported if you have the power of it.'

'Jesus, Sheila, you are one intelligent girl.' I replied, and to be honest, she was a bright, intelligent girl and beautiful Aussie, of Aboriginal and Scottish descent. I had noticed colleagues misjudged her bubbly personality for the intelligent girl that she was.

Then, she continued, 'Also, that car he is driving is a beast. Wouldn't like to think about how much it cost.'

The car was indeed a nice red colour and big in size. Cars to me have no significance; as long as they drive from A to B and vice versa, well, I am happy. Growing up as a child, we were not accustomed to having great wealth and cars that personified that wealth to the masses. That was inevitably the reality for most of the families I knew living within the valley, as unemployment was high due to the mining closures and neglect from the years of a Maggie and Tory government. I had been brought up in an area classed as having social deprivation, but it wasn't felt as most families were in the same economic situation, and we were bloody happy.

We continued our journey, and Sheila and Sah sang songs from the CD, which I didn't know or wish to know, if I am honest. It wasn't my thing at all.

As we rode, Sheila stated, 'That's odd.'

'What's odd?' I quizzed, as the only odd thing on this road was the sight of camels which I had now become accustomed to.

In a serious voice she continued, 'That Arab, I am sure he is following us,' she whispered quietly as if not to worry the wee little one in the back seat.

'What?' I responded in a high-pitched voice, as I hadn't heard anything so silly and paranoid. I had never been followed in a car, and I found her comment entertaining. I wanted to laugh, but I knew by Sheila's face, she was dead serious.

'I am being serious. This is the second time we have passed him. He is driving too slowly. That car can go fast. Really fast. It doesn't make sense. It's as though he is playing cat and mouse with us.' She pondered and we continued.

Then, there was a beep of a horn and the Arab waved as he passed us. I raised my eyebrows and Sheila and I eyeballed each other.

She waved and then sternly said, 'Wave.' I looked directly at her, and she repeated, 'Wave!'

In parrot fashion we smiled and waved, with even Sah joining in. 'I knew it,' Sheila confirmed, 'He is playing cat and mouse with us.'

'I think you are being a bit paranoid now, Sheila. Seriously, you're funny.'

'I am telling you. What the hell did you do to this guy?'

'Bloody nothing. Seriously!' I replied sternly. Sheila confirmed confidently, 'I will lose him once we get into the city.' I laughed, and she replied, 'It's not funny.'

We hit the city and did lose him after a couple of roundabouts. 'Right, he's gone. Thank fuck for that.' As she stated that triumphally she continued, 'Oh no, we haven't. He's coming up behind us in the third lane. Shit, what are we going to do?'

'It's all right. We will lose him further on, or he is simply going in the same direction as us,' I pacified her, still thinking she was being paranoid and a wee bit over the top.

We continued driving. Sheila continued to be anxious and I didn't really understand why, to be honest. I just assumed that as an individual, I was more relaxed, whilst she was more observant. We hit a large roundabout that would take us in the direction of Villaggio, but we hit a standstill as the traffic was bad. His car appeared and was aligned directly to my right.

Sheila, facing straight ahead, said, in an uptight manner, 'Don't look now. He's there and he's looking directly at us.'

With that, what does a person do when they are told not to look at something – look. He was all smiles and gestured for me to unwind my window.

Sheila spoke trying to be a ventriloquist with little movement, 'What is he doing?'

'He wants the window down,' I replied.

'For fuck's sake, I told you not to look.' I was looking directly ahead and trying to disguise the fact that we were speaking by playing with my hair to the right side of my face.

'Right, let's both look at him,' Sheila suggested and like two morons, in synch, we looked directly at the Arab man and smiled and gave a quick wave.

He continued to smile from ear to ear, motioning for my window to come down.

'Oh God, do it and see what he wants, or he could be following us all night. Jesus bloody Mary and Joseph.'

'Are you Catholic?' I questioned as we had never really discussed religion.

'Am I fuck!' she replied as the window went down.

Then a little voice from behind questioned, 'Mammy, what happening?' as she danced to the music in her car seat.

We all anticipated what was going to happen nervously and I simply replied, 'Oh nothing, Cariad. Don't worry.'

The window was now down with a touch of a button. All eyes were on this man in a dish dash, who happened to be riding next to me in a very posh car.

'Hello again,' he said smiling.

'Hello,' I simply replied, *thinking where is this going?*

'Could I invite you to my house for a coffee? I live near here.'

I turned to face Sheila whose facial expression with her eyes wide told me a firm 'no', and I agreed. 'Oh, I am sorry, but we are going shopping.'

Sheila popped her head and agreed, 'Ye, that's right we are going shopping.'

You could see that he had not expected this answer. 'That is a shame. Really.'

The traffic started to move slowly, a crawl, in fact, but we were still aligned with his car.

'Excuse me?' he continued. 'Could I give you my business card? I would like to show you the true Qatar.' He started to look for a business card, presumably with some fiddling and opening of things within his car. 'I am sorry, but I don't have any… I run out. Do you have a pen and paper?'

I looked at Sheila, and of course, she was organised and had a pen immediately as she knew exactly where it was. She also had an envelope that she passed to me with a perplexed facial expression and enlarged eyes that looked as though she wanted to piss herself and was desperate for the toilet.

He uttered the numbers and I wrote them down.

'I hope you call me. By the way, my name is Abe. What is yours?'

'Emily,' I replied whilst thinking, *what is happening here?* 'I'm Emily, this is my friend Sheila, and my daughter is sitting in the back, Sah.'

'It is nice to meet you, Immi.'

'Okay,' I answered wondering, *did he just really call me Immi?*

Thankfully, the traffic began to crawl more quickly as we approached the roundabout.

'I hope to hear from you, Immi. Call me?'

I smiled yet again so falsely that I thought to myself *if this is acting it is not that hard and I am rather pretty good at it* and said, 'Bye.' We then proceeded to go our separate ways.

Sheila personified, 'We've lost him, Immi,' pronouncing the Immi strongly.

'That was bloody mad, and you were right. He was following us.'

'This is my second year and last in Qatar. I have never experienced anything like that. I have heard of people being given business cards, but not stalked, asked for coffee and then offered to see the 'true' Qatar. It must be your Welsh charm – Immi. So, you going to call him, Immi?'

'No, don't think so. He's not really my type. I like blondes, to be honest, and you know what they say about black men ... once you try black you never turn back?'

'He's not really black, though, is he?' Sheila retorted.

'Well, he's darker than bloody white and do you know he looks like a curly-headed Ali G. The resemblance is uncanny now I come to think of it.'

Sheila questioned, 'Who the fuck is Ali G?'

'Oh, he is a British comedian who does outrageous and satirical comedy. You should watch him as I think you will find his sense of humour very funny.'

We both laughed and we reminisced about our journey to Qatar that very Thursday evening, not in a funny way, just funny weird way.

Boredom and a phone call made under the influence of vodka: mistake or not a mistake? That is the question!

Weekends in Arabia are different and begin on a Thursday, and the new week starts on a Sunday. On Friday, I had cleaned the house, gone swimming with Sheila and Sah, and settled down that evening to watch a DVD copy that was purchased cheaply from the local shop. I forgot to mention that I had copious amounts of alcohol to drink, which I had purchased the previous night after being stalked by an Arab man in a dress. I was looking at the envelope with the mobile number thinking should I, shouldn't I? I hadn't had much adventure since just before having Sah, and certainly not after having her.

Being from Wales and teaching English to immigrants from Thailand, Russia, and Poland also entailed taking them on class excursions. I knew personally how advantageous it was to have someone local from the area to highlight scenery, historical buildings and things that are celebrated privately and that are not known unless you know personally about them or are from the locality. I had had a lot of fun taking students in convoys to Dryslwyn Castle, situated on a majestic hilltop location above the Tywi Valley near Llandeilo, Dynevor Castle, whose park also exhibits the grand Dynevor House with deer and white cattle grazing, which are beautiful sights that are often neglected or taken for granted.

Or Carreg Cennen Castle, a castle within the Brecon Beacons National Park, whose caves are suggested to meander under the hills to Llandeilo and Llandybie and were warranted in the turbulent past of our ancestors, as a means to inform of oppressors, mainly, the English invaders. Then, there is Merlin's lake, scientifically unproven, but a myth and legend that is passed on the way to Milo. Even a visit to Brynamman Cinema, which dates back to 1926, built through contributions taken from the miners' wages, restored to its historical elegance and half the price of other costly cinemas was enjoyed, and all had an educational focus. Plus, I got paid to do what I enjoyed. Bonus!

So, alcohol-induced I thought, fuck it. This man could educate me, and I then could educate others and see things my students would have possibly missed if it hadn't been for me. I took a deep breath and pressed the digits. It rang and then an answerphone message kicked in. Did I hang up? Don't be so bloody silly. The alcohol was indeed giving me the confidence.

'Hello, this is Emily. We met at the fuel station, and you stalked us all the way to Qatar… No. No. No! Hi. This is Emily. We met on Thursday night at the garage and in Doha you offered to show me Qatar. If the offer is still open, I would like to be shown your country. Many thanks, Emily.'

I ended the conversation with a deep sigh and continued to drink and watch films. I later staggered to my bed and fell asleep without a care in the world. I was living my new life with no regrets. Well, that was the aim anyway.

I didn't hear anything back and honestly, didn't think much of it. Sheila did ask me if I had called, but I was cool and laughed it off. For all I knew, he could have given me the wrong number, and I wasn't really bothered to be honest. There was no sexual attraction or chemistry on my part, and it is always nice to make interesting new friends. It wasn't as though that fateful night on the highway I had met my soulmate by any means. Then, one evening the next week, at around 7.30 on a Tuesday night, the mobile rang. It was in the kitchen, and I had to run from Sah's bedroom as I had been nursing her to sleep, and she was now fully out with the fairies. I didn't recognise the number and proceeded to answer. 'Hello.'

There was a pause and then, 'Hi, Immi. It is Abe. Is everything ok? You are breathing heavy, no?'

I was in complete shock, and I just had to respond immediately. 'I am fine. I had to run to get the phone, that's all.'

'I am sorry now I am phoning, but I have been in the desert camping and there was no signal. I only came back to Doha today and so now I phone you.'

'Oh, that's alright. Don't worry about it.' What could I have said? Don't you know it is bloody rude not to reply sooner? Fuck off. It's too late now. It was just a surprise, especially after the delay in response.

The conversation flowed well. It lasted about an hour which is something I had seldom done. I learned that Abe had studied yacht building in America, and that he had also lived in North Wales for some time. He had purchased a farm and bred Arabian horses. He also spoke some Welsh which was very funny. He said his mother had missed him so much that she flew to North Wales to spend time with him, forcing him to return home, and how the roads were very small. He had also described his experience of having to go to court due to a traffic offence, which was something I had never experienced before. I enjoyed the conversation and I told him about myself and Sah, where we had been and why we were here now. Finally, we made arrangements that Friday for me to drive to Doha and we would spend the day going into the desert. He told me to bring swimming costumes and he would organise everything else.

The week progressed until the Friday morning. Organised, we left in a borrowed car, and I phoned Abe when I got to Villaggio. He said he lived five minutes away near the palace and would drive. He did come as he had stated, and he parked next to me in his posh car. His window went down and he had shiny glasses that radiated his pouty lips.

He smirked, giggling, 'Hello, Immi. I am happy that you are here. Yes, very happy. Your journey, ok?'

I smiled, 'Hi Abe. Yes, the journey was fine.' He instructed me to follow him, and I did for a couple of minutes down a dirt track to a compound with large, ironed gates, whilst Sah was happy in her own world. The gates opened and I followed him in. It was a compound of about eight houses and a swimming pool that was not yet completed. We got out of the car and Abe was in his dish dash dress again, which made me giggle a bit, and I think that he could have put some pants on for me, you know?

'Welcome to my house.'

This was a strange welcome, but cultures are different, and the only thing to say was a simple, 'Thank you.' Two oversized Arabic wooden doors that were adorned with intrinsic carvings and were regal with large circular handles opened, and we entered. The speckled cream marble floored house, which was sparsely decorated with big heavy dark brown wooden furniture, was very Arabic. The sofa was of an American style that could seat about 12 people and the TV was a plasma screen, large at about 60 inches. He took me into the kitchen, which again, whilst being decorated nicely, you could tell it was not used. There was an Indian boy, well man, in his early 20s whose head was bowed in the kitchen as he stood by the fridge. Abe said something to which I didn't understand, and the boy nodded. Then, he turned to me and said, 'Immi, this is Maahir and if you need anything then you ask him. He is my servant. I have told him he is also to serve you, ok?'

'Yes,' I answered. 'You look shocked at the way I speak, Immi.'

'No, not shocked. I know a lot of families have help and it is the normal way of life out here. Whereas it is alien to me.'

His eyes narrowed and his eyebrows shrivelled, his voice became deeper, and he questioned, 'Alien?'

'What I mean, Abe, is that we do not have servants back

home in Wales. Only the rich like the royal family and famous people do. We do things for ourselves, without help. It is possible, you know?' He nodded and I hoped he had understood my meaning.

'Know this, I am good to my workers, and I look after them. I help their families back in their countries - home. And I am very very busy, Immi, and need help. Do you want some tea or something?'

'No thanks, but we will have some water please. It's too hot to drink tea.' Sah and I drank some water and then we left in Abe's car.

He opened the boot and put in a very large cooler bag, stating, 'Refreshments for when we stop. I think you will like, yes, I know you will like.' And he laughed as we drove off. He had Arabic music on the radio, which aided and fuelled our Arabic adventure with Abe, the man in the dish dash. We spoke continuously and as we drove, Abe would tell me of his memories as a child before Qatar became developed. 'You see this here, Immi, when I was child there was nothing. It was beautiful and you could see for miles. Is it miles you use or kilometres?'

'Miles,' I confirmed.

'We lived a simple life and were happy. There were many, many children to play with: brothers, sisters, cousins. We lived from the sea and bartered with fish and pearls. But look now - concrete everywhere.' I envisaged what he had stated as I looked through the window. I felt from his words that he missed the childhood that he had experienced through the words he spoke. I understood his fear that present and future generations would have no understanding of the past life once lived, a hard and difficult life, but one that was truer and more honest.

The wealth in Qatar visibly is overwhelming, everywhere you look, from the architecture, shopping malls, gardens with wonderful displays of flowers and trees to the roundabouts adorned with water fountains and statues within the Arabic desert. After driving one hour from the city, we arrived at a gate just off the main road. 'This is something you are going to like, Immi. Qataris know of it, but not many others. We will have fun, wait and see.' He smiled and chuckled like an excited child. Sah was asleep and we continued onto a path that was now sand, and the road seemed like a mirage in the distance. 'You are going to need to hold on soon, I don't want to scare you, but you will be amazed at the size of the sand dunes. Don't be scared, but I can't wait to see your face.' I just looked at him and thought *what the fuck?*

Sah had woken up asking, 'Where we Mammy?'

'Oh, we are going on some sand dunes.'

'What sand dunes?'

'Mountains of sand,' Abe replied. And then he slowly stopped. 'Now, I want you and Sah to hold on. Ok? The fun is about to start.' There were no other cars as we looked around. He then started to edge forward in an upward climb to a stop. 'It's about to start,' he excitedly exclaimed, and with that, we edged forward to what looked like a cliff of sand below.

'Jesus,' I shouted as we edged to the drop, and we fell. Sah laughed uncontrollably as I dripped droplets of sweat in sheer fright. The next 20 minutes consisted of us climbing and dropping sand dunes, some larger than others, with screams of sheer panic and laughter, until we started to descend lower to the view of a beautiful beach in the near distance.

We parked, got out of the car and Sah ran into the sea, paddling and kicking the water, whilst Abe got the cooler bag and a blanket. We were the only ones on this beach, a beach that was beautiful as the opulent blue waves brushed the seashore, and the warm dry air surrounded us. I pulled Sah's dress off to reveal her bikini and with her bucket and spade, she played. Abe set up the blanket, wine and food in easy reach and view of her. 'Immi, come and sit. You like?'

'Abe, I am shocked. This is beautiful, truly beautiful. You even have wine glasses, and the wine is chilled,' I commented as I sipped it.

'I hope you like it. I thought very hard and worked very hard getting this together.' More like he gave orders and instructed.

'Well, thank you as it is all very beautiful.'

We had a wonderful day, and Sah and I both laughed with Abe. She played joyfully on the shore, splashing in the crystal blue, warm, salty sea and buried her toes in the sand as the sea was coming in. She often laughed, jumping up and down when the waves came in and wet her. We all walked up and down the beach with our feet being massaged from the continual movement from the waves, and it was one of the most serene and beautiful afternoons I had had in a very long time. It was wanted and most definitely needed, with no regrets or expectations.

After spending what seemed like hours, but in reality, was a short space of time, it was time to depart as we had to get back to civilisation before it got dark, and we didn't want to get lost in the desert. It hadn't dawned on me that we were indeed in a dangerous situation, as I didn't really know the man or anything about him, only what he had told me during a telephone call. Sheila was aware that we were seeing him, and I told Mammy about it. My father had told her not to worry as I was old enough to do what I wanted. But, as a precaution, I had given my mother Abe's mobile number just in case, you know, because I honestly wasn't used to going on such days out or dates like this. But there was something nice and innocent about him. He didn't brag about things, but spoke softly, gently, and sometimes our conversations would get lost in translation. However, it was a comfortable and nice feeling. And, when I thought about it, I had been in a few relationships over the years with a couple of prize pricks and really didn't know them at all when I came to think about it. So, it was nothing new really in the scheme of things, except that now I went out with my daughter. We were a pair, and that had to be accepted by whoever we met and came into our lives.

As we drove, he asked if I would like my seat warmed. I looked at him as if to question, *how the fuck are you going to warm my seat for me?* He saw my perplexed face and said, 'I will show you. You see, this car has heated seats and I press this button and the seat will warm.' *My word*, I thought. Sheila was right, this was indeed a posh car as I had never, ever heard of such a thing. I sat back waiting for something to happen. And happen it did. As the seat warmed up, so did the stench of urine that had peeped out in excitement, or pure trepidation as we hurdled the sand dunes. The smell got stronger and stronger. I tried to cross my legs in the hope of preventing the sour smell from circulating to no avail. As I sniffed, the smell got stronger and stronger.

I held my right hand in my left hand as I leaned against the window. I honestly didn't know where to look, and I sat in sheer embarrassment and shame. I prayed he had a poor sense of smell and that he couldn't smell what I could. I looked for the window button and pressed it down hoping that the warm air would somehow disguise this stink attached to me. It made the smell worse. *Oh God*, I spoke to my inner self. Then, I could see Abe moving in his seat.

'Do you want a pee pee?' Abe asked as he turned to me.

'No, actually, I don't need to go,' I answered with my cheeks heating up and illuminating the sheer embarrassment I felt. How the fuck can I deal with this? Quick thinking Em, come on, think. 'Abe, I am lovely and warm now. Do you mind putting the heater off?'

'Yes, of course.' With the switch pressed and a few minutes passed, the smell subsided. However, my humiliation had not. In all my years, I had never smelled so bad, especially on a first meeting with someone. I slumped my shoulders and looked out of the window to hide my shame.

Thank God Sah was asleep, as I know if she had been awake, I would have had a repetitive, 'What smell Mammy? Can you smell Mammy?' If first impressions counted, I had surely put Abe off even with a simple friendship. Was he now to remember me as Welsh Fishy-Fanny Emily?

We got back to Abe's and said our farewells. Sah gave him a big hug which was strange, as I didn't prompt her to do so. She did it because she wanted to. Abe was pleased, smiled, and complimented her back by picking her up and spinning her around. 'Beautiful Habibie, beautiful.'

I said goodbye, no hugs or kisses, as it just didn't appeal to me and especially after the embarrassment of the pee-smelling incident. I still couldn't see through the dish dash and had never been into transvestites, not that he was one by any means, but it was and would be too weird. I mean, I am used to unzipping pants and not putting my hand up a dress. That just didn't do it for me.

Abe instructed that I was to follow him, and he would take me out of Doha onto the road that I needed to follow to get back home. I thought it was extremely sweet, and to be honest, I wasn't used to such sincerity. As we both drove our individual cars through the busy roads, Abe would weave in and out, smiling, waving, and making the journey entertaining for Sah. We came to the roundabout that would take us directly home. However, Abe continued the journey with us. I did think that this was a wee bit strange, but then questioned, maybe he will pull off further up the road. And this is how the journey continued.

I decided to call him. 'Hi Abe, I know my way back now, and you really don't have to take me all the way home. I don't want you to travel further than you have to.'

He answered gently, 'It is ok, Habibie. I want to make sure that you are safe. I will come back with you to the gates. Ok, bye.' He hung up on me, and I assumed that he would indeed leave me at the gate. Then, from nowhere, I remembered that during our day, I had mentioned that we were returning home to go to a house party at my Welsh colleague's house. I was looking forward to it because our Sheila would be there, and we were sure to have a giggle. I hoped to God that he was not intending to come to the party with me. I honestly cringed at the thought of us, Abe and me, walking in together, into a party full of British ex-pats, ranging from their 20s to 40s. Oh God, I could imagine Sheila laughing and all eyes questioning, 'Who is he? Why is he here? Who brought him here?' with all eyes on me and this man in a dish dash dress.

We came to the security entrance, and I stopped whilst Abe continued to follow me and was directly behind me in line. I smiled at the security men, who were always very nice and proceeded to get out of my car. I approached Abe and his beaming smile confronted me. 'Abe, are you coming to the party with me?' Horrified, I questioned.

'Yes, Immi. I have nothing else to do tonight, so will come. Yes?'

How about being bloody invited, I thought? Oh God, how do I get out of this? 'Oh, ok, Abe. You never mentioned coming with me/us to the party. I need to go home and shower quickly, ok?' This was an absolute must as I had to get the stink of old granny's piss off me.

'Yes, I understand. I will follow you. Yes?' he squinted, with his right eyebrow raised.

Oh, my word. How the hell am I going to manage this? What are the others going to say? Fuck, fuck, fuck!

We got into my apartment, which I thought was clean and tidy, considering I worked full time and had a busy child. We entered through the regal wooden Arabic doors, well, they looked regal to me, well posh. Abe looked around the living room, kitchen, and bathroom as if he were viewing a house for sale, while I stood in the hallway. *Bloody cheek* was what was going through my mind.

Then, he returned to me whilst Sah ran to her bedroom and said, 'Nice. Very nice. Do you have a cleaner, Immi?'

'No. Not at the moment, but I hope to employ one soon. A maid who is also a cleaner, cook and general nanny. A general dog's body."

'What? You want a maid with a dog's body?' His frown protruded.

'No, it's a saying. Basically, someone who will do all I ask, within reason.' *Oh, my word, I am bloody teaching English to speakers of other languages at work, and I don't really want to bring my work home,* I thought, before I said, 'Listen, we have to have a wash and change. Please make yourself at home. Open the fridge, make yourself a drink, and put the TV on. We won't be long. Ok?'

'Oh, ok. Thank you, Immi. Will you be long?'

'As long as it takes.' I turned around and followed the corridor to Sah's bedroom. I picked her up and said, 'It's shower time, shower time,' as I jokingly chucked her up in the air, slightly, and entered my bedroom. I quickly locked the door to ensure there were no unwanted guests or pests entering my bedroom.

We quickly washed our hair and our bits, well, more importantly, my wee smelling bits, dried ourselves and changed into our evening wear. Blow drying our hair wasn't needed as it would dry quickly with the heat. Sah had a lovely white floating long dress, and I had a floral maxi dress. We both looked smart with our hair brushed straight and then into a high ponytail. In all, we were an impressive 20 minutes.

I unlocked the door, and we walked to the lounge where Abe sat in front of us, in his dress with his legs open wide. Thank God it was long, as it would have been horrific if Sah had seen a brown snake hanging down. That would have been an interesting conversation to have with a three-year-old - NOT! We walked towards him, and he got up and walked towards us, clutching what looked like a large, straight vodka. How many drinks had he had? I questioned internally what his plans were for going home, as surely, he wasn't going to drink and drive home?

Abe bent down to Sah's level, and may I add with good balance as there was no slippage from the drink, and he patted her on her head. She looked up to him and smiled. He then raised his slight frame and looked me directly in the eyes.

'Beautiful, Immi.' He then proceeded to come close to my face and as I pulled my face backwards to avoid his closeness, he turned to kiss me on my right cheek and then, on my left cheek. His breath was warm and smoky from the cigarettes he had smoked throughout the day and reminded me of an old man's stale breath. He then stared into my eyes, I looked down to Sah who looked strangely, as she had never seen a man kiss me, not even on the cheeks. I looked at her and raised my eyebrows and not my smile and thought, *what the fuck just happened? Was that our first kiss? Someone please get me the fuck out of here!*

'Right, I will get our shoes on and then we can go.'

'I will drive us, Immi. I want to drive you and look after you and Sah.' I stared into bewilderment with a frown on my forehead creasing and I questioned to myself, *is this normal for out here? I am really not used to this and not amused.*

We departed my complex of flats, with me ushering Abe to get into the car before anyone noticed us, and more importantly, Sah and I with a man in a dress, in a posh car. Abe was coherent with directions: right, left, straight on/ahead, and turn. In no time, we were there.

Sah ran in excitedly, anticipating that other children would be there to play with. I looked at Abe who was locking his car, and then he coolly walked towards me, until he was directly in front of me. He lifted his right arm slowly and let it drift, stretching until he touched the top of my fingers. He then progressed to interlock our fingers, and pulled me closer towards him, with the result of me being able to smell his Arabic tobacco stale breath again.

I pulled back from him. Within myself, I was shaking my head and looking back and forth at Abe, to hope and pray that this wasn't happening in that:

1. I was going to a British party with a Qatari in a dish dash dress; and,

2. The man in a dress is getting amorous with me. What the fuck!

I opened the door and walked in, hoping to do so anonymously, with Abe walking behind me. I had successfully and purposely lost his grip. I was very chuffed and relieved with this. However, Sheila, being her usual self, loudly shouted to all, 'Immi is here.' With further observation, she lowered her tone and I lip read her continuation, 'And, what the fuck, she's with dish dash.'

I waved, blushed and I knew Sheila would recognise my genuine discomfort. I approached the host, a Welsh mother, who was fun and thanked her for our invite, meaning Sah and I. I then quickly apologised for the literal personal invite of a man that I didn't really know. However, the more I got to know him, the more I questioned my liking of him. I obviously didn't say this, open and loud. I simply thanked her for allowing my friend Abe to the party too and walked off, straight in the direction of Sheila, with Abe in tow.

The pleasantries predictably happened with 'Hellos' and Sheila watching my facial expressions closely and exploding to ask me questions. Colleagues approached, obviously being nosey, as this was the first time most of them had had a physical conversation with me. They got to know Abe better than I did with all the personal questions they were asking him. I just listened at the side, whilst having a giggle with Sheila and learnt ever so much. And he was being very nice: polite, agreeable, and amusing with these conversations, like a well-groomed gentleman who made funny mistakes with his English when speaking. I couldn't believe that the British colleagues I had worked with, for a short time admittedly, were just so false in their very beings. The personal questions that they asked him concerning his business, interests etc were not from caring or concerned individuals, but just royally bloody nosy people. It was a sad depiction of what some people represent and how like-minded individuals come to nest together. They had not bothered with us since our arrival. Of course, we had a very British, 'Hello,' and, 'Where have you come from?' or, 'Oh, you're Welsh? Where in Wales?' And since these initial introductions, there had been nothing more. It was sad really, and hurtful to see the difference in the way some people treat and respect others differently. There was no need for it, but whether you want to acknowledge it or not, it made me aware and distrusting of these individuals going on.

Whilst Sah played with her friends, the adults drank copious amounts of alcohol to their heart's desire. That is except for Sheila. I had noticed that she was not always confident in situations like this. I assumed it was due to her knowing these people for two years longer than me. I was already making assumptions about the individuals I had met. Well, you do, don't you? I theorised that she wanted to be aware and in control of what she was saying and doing: Self-protection, I suppose, and in a sense, I believe it was.

The time flowed and Sah cwtched up with the other kids in a bunk bed and fell asleep. (I have always found it more romantic linguistically to say the Welsh 'cwtch' instead of the Anglicised 'cuddle'.) At approx. 5.30 am the sun started to rise. Abe and I had been outside most of the evening chatting, giggling and just being stupidly drunk. Sheila had long gone, and gradually everybody had left, until it was just us there. The colours of the sky were majestic, lifting from darkness to an emporium of vibrant colours, as the sun began to rise on the horizon. It was breathtakingly beautiful, and we both turned to watch this spectacular vision. I was sipping my vino when Abe said,

'Immi, thank you for tonight. I enjoyed. Truly. Very good.' And with that, he pulled me towards him gently and kissed my lips. I could feel my cheeks rising in heat, but he just kissed my lips and sucked them each time as he pulled away. It was an ok kissing experience, and as we kissed more, he entered my personal space until both our bodies, and more literally, my maxi dress and his dress were touching. By this time, our arms caressed each other. Then Abe moved his arms to gently cup my chin. He then proceeded to French kiss me, and whilst I can say it was by far not the best, or worst kiss I have ever had that I can remember soberly, it was oh so very different. His taste of tobacco, and the softness of his big, plump lips as they sucked my lips were not a turn on, and there was definitely no feeling of bubbles fermenting down there with tingling, as to the possibility of having a good old Arab seeing to and session.

But, as a woman in her early thirties, I was desperately in need of some tenderness and kindness. I had been through a lot. Was I being a bit desperate, or was I just following my fate as I was meant to have met Abe? If I were being honest, it would have been nice to blow the cobwebs off, and to pump some life into my non-existent sex life. I had never been one for one-night stands, as I believed that they were an abuse and use of sexual gratification that was impersonal and unclean. I mean, you don't know the hygiene of people; how often they wash, what they put into their bodies and how often they brush their teeth. Masturbation was a much cleaner option, I believed, safer and cheaper after the two occasions I did have a one-night stand, as I felt used and abused, without feeling. It was depressing to me, and I just didn't feel comfortable with a wham, bam, slam and then goodbye.

We kissed on and off for an hour. He held me in his arms and let me rest my tiredness on his body. The time came where I needed to hit the sack. We walked in and told the host, who was still up drinking and full of energy, that I was going to get Sah and carry her to the car. Fair play, as she suggested that I leave her to sleep and pick her up after I had had a kip. *Bloody fantastic,* I thought, as it was always me and Sah. I knew she would wake up and want to play, and at least here she would have the company of other children. I knew she would annoy me whilst in bed by lifting my eyelids individually and asking, 'Mammy! Mammy, you awake?' until I gave up and caved into her will no matter how exhausted I was.

Abe and I drove back to my place. I know, I know, you are right. He was over the bloody limit, but living here was different as we had our own security on the compound. Most people I knew drank and drove because traffic was quiet all the time, to be honest. Anyway, we got back, and I asked Abe what his plans were. He seemed to wake up and began jumping up and down, as though warming up to go on a jog. However, he was still wearing his dish dash. 'I stay with you, Immi. Come!' With that, he held my arm and pulled me to my bedroom. Like a matador to the bull, he stood in front of me, ready to strike.

'Abe, I am sorry I have to go to the bathroom,' I screeched as I quickly pulled away from his grip and slid to the bathroom. I locked the door and sat on the toilet. *Fuck! Fuck! What do I do now?* I squeezed between my legs to drain any remaining alcoholic urine from my bladder, in anticipation of the thought that he would be entering me, entering an unknown suction pump that had not been touched or stimulated in years past. My second anticipated sex job was to wash my derriere. A flannel soaked in water, some nice body/fanny wash, a quick rub and dig into the crevasses, a fresh swill and repeat and drip dry, before patting dry.

'Immi, I am waiting. I am horny, horny, horny.' I turned to face the door. I questioned myself, *did he actually fucking say that he was horny, horny, horny. What the ...?*

'I will be there now. I just have to brush my teeth.' I meowed quickly back. With the last tooth brushed, I knew that this man was now in my bed, most probably in his dress, he hadn't washed except for tipping 2 litres of drinking water over his head whilst we were in the desert. I then envisaged a stinky, sweaty cock and balls that had slowly been fermenting in this heat. All I could think was *no, no, no. I cannot do this. No fucking way. I really don't want a smelly sweaty cock coming near me.*

I reluctantly washed my toothbrush clean and placed it back neatly in the cup that I kept it in. I turned to face the door that would allow me to enter Abe. I walked slowly like a virgin walking hesitantly with each step, knowing that each step took me closer to him.

'Immi. Immi,' he requested.

As I opened the door, I faced him, dress off, showing a very hairy dark chest. I had my black lace nightdress, Marks and Sparks, so it wasn't cheap. I had whipped it on after my fanny wash. He was arched up on the pillow and leaning on his left arm.

'Hello, Immi. Very, very sexy, Immi.' He exclaimed as if this is what was needed to bed a Welsh Brit. This was a first for me, and if this was Arabic seduction, fuck, they were centuries behind. I jumped into bed and lay on my half of the bed, with my head back.

I yawned, 'Oh, I am tired now, Abe. It will be nice to sleep.' Well, with that, he pounced on top of me, wetting my face with his juicy kisses and trying to enter me by wriggling around on top of me, jiggling his penis into a hole set in darkness.

I wanted to laugh, but firmly said, 'Abe, you are not going near me unless you have a condom on. Understood?'

'Ah, yes. Do you have one, Immi?'

'Oh, Abe. I am sorry, but I don't.' I lay snug back into my mattress, thanking God.

Abe jumped out of bed, 'I will go to my car. Yes, I have some in my car.'

As he proceeded to walk out of the room, out of the apartment and outside in the open air, most importantly, naked, I had to yell, 'Abe, what are you doing? Put your clothes on!' He turned around with a big smile, grabbed his dress, chucked it on over his head and sprinted to his car.

I lay back, hoping and praying, 'Please no condoms, please no condoms.'

Now, I never have much luck. As my mother put it, 'Emily, fach, I don't worry about your brother, but you, you seem to get all the bad luck. I wouldn't mind if it was shared, not that I want your brother to have bad luck. But it would be fairer.' It always made me laugh when she called me 'fach' as it means 'small' in English and I had been taller than my mother since I was a teenager. But, I think you know where this is heading. Abe returned incredibly happy.

'Immi, look what I found!' He was like an excited child and had swagger in his walk. He skipped into bed, removing his dress, whilst I lay thinking, *oh, fuck. He found one and who the hell keeps condoms in their car? It's the Middle East, so I had wished that it/they would have melted in the car. And where in the bloody car did he keep them?*'

Anyway, we kissed, but he didn't touch me down there at all. He put the condom on, got on top of me, pushed it in, and pushed up and down 10 times, sighed, and then pulled it out, and lay next to me. He didn't even kiss me.

'Immi, that was good. I work hard. See I am wet with sweat. Touch me.' With that, he grabbed my right hand and touched his forehead. There was no sweat, and as for working hard, well put it like this, yet again it didn't hit the side, and even though I didn't touch it once I had a feeling that he wasn't even of average size in comparison to all the other men I had slept with. *Or,* I questioned, *was this an Arab thing?* As I lay there, I wondered whether the thing I had just experienced was the way they did it over here. I remembered that when I was backpacking across Israel, I had been told that in the Haredi Burqa Sect women are covered from head to toe when they have sex. Maybe his in and out, in and out with no foreplay before, or kissing during was like the Haredi Burqa Sect, however, without the covering. Whatever the experience, I lay in bed perplexed, exhausted from the long day, and fell asleep next to Abe who had taken ¾ of my bed, and lay in a star position. He was lucky that I always slept in the foetal position, or he would be having a lot of thumps and nudges throughout the night.

Whilst there was no hugging or kissing during the early morning, not that I minded as I don't particularly like morning breath, I woke at 11 am to get Sah. To say I was tired was an understatement. Abe drove me to pick her up, and then he returned us to our apartment. We spent the day hanging out and playing games. It was nice as I had never had the opportunity to do this normality with Sperm Donor as he was never around. It was nice for both of us, Sah and me. I made him food, my speciality, which was lasagne. Abe's face was a picture, and whilst Sah and I tucked into it with a balsamic herb salad, he played with it and said,

'Mm. What is this again? Lasagne? Yes, I have eaten this before. But this … mm... This taste different. Mm.'

With that, he thanked me and said he had to leave as he had business. Sah and I said our goodbyes, and he picked Sah up firstly and kissed her, then he put her down so gently and turned to me. 'Goodbye, baby. We will speak soon.' He kissed my right cheek with no spit or suction and left. I knew I had to be up at 5.30 am for work, so I quickly got ready for bed with

Sah. She was as exhausted as I was, and quickly fell asleep cwtching into my right breast as I held her close. I looked up at the ceiling and thought to myself, *'What a fucking weekend. Sex? Was it sex if I didn't feel him inside of me and I didn't, you know, climax/cum or whatever you call it? Well,* I thought, *at least if I see him again and want him to leave, I could just cook for him.* I quickly fell asleep not even contemplating what work would be like tomorrow. Fuck! Fuck! Fuck!

The next morning arrived and as I suspected, they were waiting for me in the staffroom. As I entered for the morning meeting, the different groups – the cool gang, the abnormal ex-pats, and the ex-pats who thought they were better than everyone else sat there. I had new looks that I hadn't had before, so I believed I was right in my assumption that I had been spoken about and was the new topic of gossip.

Sheila was sitting smirking in between the groups and simply said as I approached, 'Immi. Immi is here?' She chuckled, and I could feel a smirk rising and the need to tell my dear friend everything.

The humanities teacher, a nosy northern lass who liked to gossip, questioned slyly, 'It was lovely meeting Abe. Where is he?' Now in my old age, I have learned to read people better. It has nothing to do with a gut feeling, but with all the shit and experiences I have endured since forever. I was more equipped psychologically, or so I believed. Self-delusion is a nice thing to have sometimes. So, my answer was short and sweet. I knew she was a catalyst, and everyone else would sit there being nice but have their big bloody ears wagging for any snippet of information.

'Well,' I said casually, 'He's not here sadly.' This was followed with a smile and a small wink from my Sheila. I had always been a firm believer that it was rude to ask personal questions when I knew it was purely for gossip. My life was nobody's business. Sheila was my friend, and I trusted her implicitly, more than the others who had lived as ex-pats for some time, earned money that they could not spend, had maids and drivers to do their basic needs and socialised in friendship groups that were false, a pure necessity, and not from choice. Sometimes if somebody was sitting in the staffroom and got up to leave, they would be the topic of conversation amongst the others, and I hated this. And what made it worse was the fact that the worst ones were the churchgoers, hypocrite Christian minions who personify righteousness and who will return to this tale in due course. I had no time or empathy for such relationships. I knew that I would be the topic of conversation, but thought, *Fuck you. If your life is so sad that you are using me as a conversation piece, then possibly, get a fucking life!'* Obviously, I didn't say this out loud, as it would be rude, but it was what I had experienced, witnessed, and felt personally.

The proceeding weeks and months encompassed spending time and hanging out with Abe at his compound in the city. We drank copious amounts of alcohol and watched and listened to Arabic music. I wish I could say that we made beautiful, sensual love, but sadly, Abe had his way, and I had my way. They were truly opposites. It was very Neanderthal, on top, in and out and shake it all about. But we, Sah and I, were very happy. I didn't mind that we were not in each other's pockets. I enjoyed the peace and quiet of the week, as it allowed me to spend time and have fun with Sah and Sheila at the swimming pool. I had the best of both worlds, or so I thought.

One weekend, Abe had returned from a business trip in Dubai, and we hadn't seen each other in five days. Excitement thrilled me as I drove to meet him on the Thursday evening after work. We met, hugged, and kissed. The kiss was long and wet, and like many kisses we had, I had to wipe my face after.

We sat, and one of Abe's friends arrived. As always, Abe had company - privacy was usually only in the bathroom and bedroom.

Sah had been asleep upstairs when suddenly Abe had remembered something. 'Habibie. I bought you some gifts. I am sorry. Now I remember.' I never expected anything from Abe, as previous relationships with Western men had not equipped me with gifts other than on special occasions: St Valentine's Day, my birthday or Christmas. It was true indeed that I loved gifts, but since having Sah, I had been ignored by loved ones, and it was so refreshing to have a heartfelt item, as a gesture, with the realisation that he had thought of me.

Abe ran upstairs on the curved staircase, and immediately returned with a black plastic bag with a gold logo of a shop in Arabic. He handed the bag to me, a normal size, plastic, dark carrier bag, and kissed me in the middle of my forehead. 'Open it, Immi!' I did and pulled out the contents. My brow raised and eyes opened like two saucers. He had indeed given me a hijab; an actual hijab with its full body covering and veil.

'You like it, I can see. It will make me so happy if you wear this, Immi. Go and put it on please, Habibie.'

I nodded my head like a nodding dog on the dashboard of a car, my lips glued together, and I had to make a false smile of happiness, arching my eyebrows. 'Ok,' I nodded in disbelief as I walked upstairs with my new present. 'Oh God,' I muttered to myself in the bedroom. 'Really? Really?' I couldn't believe that out of everything he could have bought me, it was this.

I took off my clothes slowly, manoeuvred the material over my head and pulled it down over my voluptuous breasts and hips. I am a size 12 – 14, so not huge by today's standards, but curvy, or as my daughter says, 'lumpy,' and I had to concede that this was indeed a very flattering look. It was rather elegant, I was rather elegant, and as I moved in a circular direction to observe every part of me in the mirror, I felt majestic in the cut and regal. Now the headscarf was a no-no. After numerous attempts and my cheeks starting to heat from my frustration, I concluded that I didn't have a bloody clue how to wrap this thing around my head.

Now, I knew from my travelling that this costume/uniform/code of religious dress, or whatever you want to call it, was used to keep the female, my body, covered in the presence of people and the opposite sex. The attire is typical of Arabic countries and inherited from the Bedouin culture. You know what I mean, and if you don't recognise it in today's age how certain cultures dress, i.e., men in white dresses and women in black, then I seriously question, 'Where the hell have you been living?'

So, the day had come that I was indeed to carry forward these ancestral traditions by dressing in this way. *What the fuck!* I walked down the stairs to a standing ovation. I did have the veil on, the scarf that covered my neck and the top of my head, and the long-sleeved robe, the Abaya. It had colourful embroideries around the collar and on the sleeves with shimmering gold and turquoise. It fell to the floor and as I took each step, I thanked God that he also hadn't given me a niqab, which covers the mouth and nose, and only leaves the eyes exposed. I addressed my physical shape, and I didn't have one, which was a blessing in disguise, but seriously, again, the words, *'Get me the fuck out of here,'* sprang to mind.

Abe was so happy and boldly stated, 'Immi, look at you. You are beautiful, beautiful.'

His friend nodded his head and repeated, 'Yes, yes, yes,' in agreement. Abe and his friend instructed me and helped me to manoeuvre the scarf around my head, and even though it did feel a bit odd at first and I wanted to shake it off like a horse shaking its head to get the flies away, it was surprising how you become used to wearing something.

So, Abe and his friend thought I looked beautiful in it, well, they bloody would, wouldn't they? That's what they were used to seeing their women, mothers and sisters wearing in their country and the surrounding Arab countries.

As time passed, Abe requested and encouraged me to wear it in his company, and I did. And, to be honest, I didn't mind wearing it. It was so easy just to pull it over my head and body, with or without some knickers, sometimes, and to get in the car and go shopping without time-wasting and hunting for clothes that matched. Yes, I used to wear nice lipstick, mascara, and a bra was certainly a must. It was a novelty at first and flattered my curves. I didn't have to worry about hairstyles, just a brush and bobble to tie it back, and then the headscarf. And yes, I did fiddle with it and constantly readjusted it.

When with Abe, especially shopping, I would get some odd looks from westerners and Americans, but I was comfortable in my own body. Hell, growing up I didn't care what people thought and I would happily walk around naked in my own home until my father would always shout, 'For God's sake, Emily, put some clothes on.' If people judged me, then that was their choice and their freedom to do so.

When Sah first saw me with it on she thought it was fancy dress and got rather excited. I looked like a witch in her eyes, except without the pointed hat. If it didn't upset her, then I honestly didn't care a flying fuck. Was there an ulterior motive for Abe buying me these clothes? At first, I didn't question it. I had had many relationships where I had had to question ex-partners, and I didn't want confrontation.

However, one day, before we left to go shopping, I came downstairs in normal clothes; a skirt just below the knee and a black t-shirt that was fitted. Abe stood by the solid wooden doors, doors that look as if they came from a Welsh castle, centuries ago, and he raised his eyebrows and asked, 'Immi, why aren't you wearing what I bought you?' I honestly didn't think, as when I worked or was with friends, I was Welsh Emily.

'Sorry Abe, I forgot,' I answered as I proceeded to walk to meet him at the entrance.

'Immi, please put it on. It makes me happy to see you wear it. I get jealous when you do not wear it. This way, they know that you are with me.' I shook my head and looked up to the sky shaking my head, ran upstairs quickly, changed and that was the end of that.

I also wore it sometimes whilst camping. Weekends often entailed camping in the desert or driving Abe's three-seater jet ski around the coast. This was something we all enjoyed as Sah got to drive it, and the further out to sea we drove, the rougher it got. Sometimes the jumps were frightening, but Abe had lived most of his life on this coastline, and his profession of building yachts allowed me to trust our lives in his very capable hands. If we went without Sah, which was not often, he would bring some food and wine for us to drink on an island not far from Doha. It was very romantic as sometimes it would only be the two of us with the ocean surrounding us, with the city in the distance and the American base.

When camping in the desert, we would go in a convey with Abe's family and friends. We would always meet in the same location at the entrance of gates that came off the main highway. There would be an array of 4 by 4s and pick-up trucks, and we would follow one another, play on the dunes and the continuous terrain of sand that could be seen for miles. Sometimes, we would enter Saudi Arabia, but Abe was always very clever as if we did stop for a while and the others continued, he would always be able to find them. Whereas everything looked the same to me. Whilst the dunes were fun, sometimes they could be terrifying. I would hold onto and grab the handle as we climbed steep dunes, and as we approached the summit and the steepness and depth of what lay beneath us, I do have to admit that I did shit myself (not literally, of course), but sometimes. Sah just assumed that the bumpy rides were fun like a rollercoaster, whilst I would hold on for dear life. Why is it that as we age, we become more afraid and apprehensive of things, whereas once in younger days we would be unfazed? One thing was for sure that whilst it was frightening, it was also exhilarating at the same time and so much bloody fun.

Depending on the superiority of the royal that was in the convoy, sometimes we would arrive to a fully functioning camp that had already been set up. They were in the dunes off the Saudi/Qatari desert, far from any signs of permanent human habitation, and on the coast. The camps offered a historical glimpse into what it might have been like for a Bedouin family trying to survive in the harsh desert landscape before the development of its people and culture from the western world.

A typical evening would include a barbecue dinner with fish that had been caught by the Indian workmen with rice and pita bread. I didn't have a clue as to the name of the fish, and I know that it doesn't sound like much, but boy was it tasty. And sometimes, if we were lucky, we would also have freshly caught lobster and crab. It was heaven. Abe would always be the gentleman and debone a fish for us or pick the good meat from the crabs and lobsters for us. We would be seated on Arabian carpets and rugs, whose colouristic design was a feast for our eyes, a kaleidoscope of colours from pale pastels to opulent reds, whose different textures from wool to silk gave a touch of luxury and style. Beauty and elegance were further exaggerated with the large Arabian floor cushions scattered around the inside of the tent. The interior and centre was a simple pole tent, followed by other shorter poles that were positioned to make it look more like a circus tent. It was a high-quality tent that was robust enough to withstand the wind from the Indian Ocean and a large structure capable of seating a hundred guests. It stood magnificently against the swooping backdrop of the rolling sand dunes, with fires that were alight outside. And, on special occasions, if there was a certain sheikh, there would be a caravan on the beach. Now, caravans are a common sight in Europe, but to see one on a beach in Qatar was unique, and Abe had told me that this caravan had been specially designed with air conditioning. It was nothing like the caravans I had enjoyed as a child, and whilst we could peep in through the door, we were never invited in.

On one occasion, whilst we were cushioned around the central left of the tent, a man came in with a stringed instrument like a guitar. He started playing and then singing along to melismatic tunes, and even though I didn't understand a word, music transcends understanding, and the whole audience sat, listened, and we were mesmerised by the beauty that was before us. It drove the whole audience into a submissive relaxed embodiment where movement was only witnessed with someone taking a beverage (alcoholic, of course) or a puff from a hookah, a type of water pipe used to smoke shisha. It was beautiful, and I felt privileged with ecstasy to have experienced this.

Every want and need was compounded by the Indian men/servants of the royalty. This gentleman, who sang so beautifully, was a famous musician from Doha, who had been driven from the capital to join us. Once his singing had ended, he would be transported back, with a payment I would not like to hazard a guess of.

Whilst the majority would sleep within the tent, we always retired to our own three-man pop up tent. Sah loved it as she was treated like a princess by all. The royals and the privileged had children, many, but Sah was a blonde, happy, beautiful bony girl who wanted to get involved with the fishing, cooking, and dancing to the music, and they treated her well. She was a more friendly and open spirit who was adventurous and not confined to the apron of her nanny, and was encouraged as much as possible to live, laugh and be happy. The workers also enjoyed her company, as she didn't see them as workers, she saw them as playmates. Some of them had left their families and not seen them, or would not see them for years, so I believe they saw this child as a friendly child, with innocence and a wandering need for love, affection, and attention. They gave it willingly to her, and she loved them for it.

A harem of ladies would also be present, mostly brought from Doha, and whilst they were all Arabic, they came from an array of Arabic countries, such as Morocco and Syria. They were there working a day job, but they aspired for a better life, and being beautiful, attracted wealthy men who were married and wanted entertainment. They were treated well with beautiful clothes, hair and makeup that made their beauty shine in the light, wore big pieces of jewellery, and had a strong feminine Arabic smell. Abe had educated me that it was traditional for the first wife to be a family relative, possibly a cousin and this would sometimes be arranged when the child was young, even when still in the womb or before birth. It allowed for the wealth to remain within the family. I had questioned Abe, 'So you were never forced to marry your cousin?' He laughed in his response and stated, 'No. There was talk, but I ran away to America to study yacht building.' And that was the end of that conversation.

So, the wives and children would be in their palaces in Doha, or weekend getaways with their convoy of children and maids, whilst the men would be playing away, literally. They had so much power, money, and wealth that they could do as they pleased. For example, entertainment on the beach would consist of an array of toys such as speed boats for water skiing, two and three-seat jet skis, and sometimes a camel would appear in all its attire: a handmade camel saddle with halters and rope. Being the only white and western woman there, I would hear a symphony of voices telling Abe to make me have a ride when a camel appeared. I felt like a clown in a circus, and Sah encouraged the barrage of voices by squealing in excitement whilst jumping up and down, 'Go Mammy!'

Now my camel riding days had been long over, and I hadn't done it for about 10 years. In my early twenties, I had worked in Dubai and single friends of mine (all ladies and about three of us) would go to a nearby Bedouin camp on a Friday, or sometimes Saturday, depending on our personal needs to escape the hustle and bustle of the city and retreat to the old ways in the desert. It was also enjoyable in other ways too. If you are a woman and have been lucky enough to ride a camel, so to speak, you will get what I am on about. Yes, camel riding has a massage effect and when you're single, off men, very dry, well needs must, and we would have one hell of a laugh.

Now since having Sah, my adventurous days and let me be blunt here - they were over. I was no longer the free-loving, try anything for a laugh girl in fear that I could hurt myself, as I questioned what would or could happen to my daughter if something happened to me. For me, in my younger days, riding a camel was awesome, and I enjoyed the massage from the movement of the camel and the seat as my body rocked oddly. But the surreal exhilaration of being on a camel as I made slow, methodical movements across the sand, made me feel the rhythm of massage. Oh, and don't get me started if the camel trotted. Well, put it like this, we were all incredibly happy ladies, and I, for one, always lit a ciggie after it, and sat back with a smile on my face.

Each evening, after camel riding, the experience included a Bedouin buffet too, which was delicious and, whilst simplistic in its preparation, delivered a beautifully fragranced and colourful array of dishes that included meats, salads, vegetables, and bread. But that was then and now I thought to myself whilst inhaling and exhaling consciously and carefully, *You can do this Emily. You're still young, in your early thirties, and there's still life in this old dog.* Now, did I have the proper camel riding ensemble? Bloody hell, no. I was on the beach in my swimming costume, and my legs were not covered. I did not have shoes on as I was hoping the sand would exfoliate my hard skin and save me from paying someone to do it for me. I had no protection on my head, only for a layer of sand that had accumulated through the gentle breeze, playing in the sea and on the beach. I had a tight swimsuit on from Marks and Sparks that sucked me in to make me look thinner, and I kept repeating mentally, *PMT. PMT - positive mental thinking!*

So, the time had finally arrived for me to get on this camel. I had a good look at it, and I wasn't sure if it was a boy or a girl, so that is why I called it 'It'. 'It' was fit for purpose, had the humps, the eyes, nose, neck, body of a camel and was natural to its environment. Now, thank God I had waxed my nether regions that week because you get on to a camel when it is sitting down. I had to situate myself on the camel by raising one leg in the air and then propel on onto its hump with the help of the Bedouin man who oversaw this camel. His help in all this was pushing my big, rounded bottom up and over, so that I was sat on the saddle and did not hang off.

I am very facial and talk to myself continuously, and throughout this experience, I muttered to myself quietly, 'Jesus… what the ….,' whilst Abe observed stating, 'Beautiful, my Immi.' He was pleased as punch, whilst I questioned if he needed bloody glasses. It was not an attractive sight may I say honestly, but it was welcomed with cheers and laughter from my audience. I held on to the saddle handle tightly. We hadn't moved, but already I was clinging on for dear life. Then, the time for movement had arrived. A camel rises its back legs first, propels itself up then the front legs raise for an equilibrium. The back legs rose under instruction from the Bedouin, who I had named quietly introvertly to myself as, 'Black Teeth Dirty Man in Whites'. This was a fair and good description, and I also questioned could any woman kiss this man? I shuddered at the thought. Then, with a big 'ohhhhhhhhh Goooooodddddd' my body moved at a 90-degree angle as my head aimed for the floor as the back legs rose. My heart pumping furiously, and with one more move, the camel raised its front feet one after the other, and I was straight in the air on top of 'It'. As this was happening, Sah's joy and excitement had turned to fear from my facial expressions, and the words and sounds that escaped my mouth.

Instead of jumping she was now screaming, 'Mammy, Mammy come …. down.'

I tried to pacify her with, 'I am alright, Sah. Look it's fun,' and my eyes were like saucers with my forehead risen so that it touched my scalp.

We walked for what seemed like ages, but in actual fact was about five minutes up the shore and back. The sun was on me, and I could not escape it in the expanse of my environment. I was white, and I knew I was burning. Black Teeth Dirty Man in White spoke no English, so with sign language, I explained that I wanted to return by using my right hand and index finger to say, 'Please may I return to where we just came from?'

The audience in the distance had left to continue whatever they were doing. However, upon my return they re-emerged to witness the sight of me getting off this camel. With adrenaline running through my body like a great athlete, I conditioned myself to believe that I was going to get off this bloody camel with grace. Did I hell! The camel got down with its front feet first and yet again I was holding on for dear life going

'Ohhhhh shit.' And then with a last motion of its back legs folding, it was sat comfortably on the sand. Now getting off should have been easy for someone who is both flexible and elegant. I was neither, and my bottom and upper legs had become cemented to the saddle, and the Black Teeth Dirty Man had to lift one leg up and push me off. If Abe hadn't come to hold on to my arms, I think I would have somersaulted in the air and onto my face.

The audience had found the whole thing very amusing. My brow and body had sweated profusely throughout this ordeal and now it was Sah's go.

Abe called her over and said, 'It is your go now.'

Horrified, she shook her head and replied, 'No, no, no.' She ran away, shaking her head before anybody could try and persuade her.

Abe then looked at me lovingly and spoke softly as if for no one else to hear. 'Habibie, did you enjoy that? I organised it especially for you.'

Now, I have been brought up to be kind and appreciative, so with a big smile and thankful to be on my feet again I simply replied, 'Yes, thank you.' I then proceeded to drink a strong vodka and coke. There was no ice, but I didn't bloody care. I also had a cigarette that was lit for me by an Indian, as I was shaking so much that I couldn't light it. I then proceeded to walk into the sea with my legs still shaking and feeling like jelly and wipe away the last 20 minutes of my life. I basked in the sun and sea, and I then concluded as I soaked in the tranquil, temperate sea that my camel riding days were over.

It had been a hell of a day, and after a few more drinks, I asked whilst we sat on the dry, hot sand and watched the sunset, 'Why am I the only western woman here, Abe?' because I was. The ladies of the night visited, hence my name for them, because it was the only time I saw them. They seemed nice and smiled at me, but our speech was limited to greetings.

His answer was honest. He explained that Muslim women were easier as they shared culture, customs, and language, whilst western women were independent thinkers, did not understand their differences and did/would not accept being a mistress. Abe had always assured me that he had never married, and I trusted his honesty. I mean, why lie? I am always a firm believer that if there is no trust in a relationship, whether with a friend, family member or in a sexual relationship, it will never be a true relationship. And, if a relationship starts with a lie, it will end with a lie. I trusted Abe, respected him, and it was, I hoped and believed, vice versa. We both had imperfections, but we were both happy and thankful that we had met. I looked forward to my future with him and the experiences we would share, both in the short and long term.

It is custom, as Abe had once told me over drinks in his kitchen, in detail, that an arranged marriage is sometimes organised before the birth of a child, as the baby develops in the mother's womb, or after the birth of a first, second or third cousin. His argument was that this united the tribes and kept the wealth within the family/tribe. The second marriage is for love, whereby the man can choose freely, and the marriage is not determined by duty or for the need of the family, but from personal want, desire, and individual choice. The third wife was to continue breeding once the first and second wife were too old to have more children and was usually a young virginal wife that would continue the line.

We had had a lot to drink, so my reply was, 'Oh God, if I had to marry one of my cousins, well it's disgusting. I could never imagine kissing or even sleeping with one of them. Oh God, that is disgusting!' My facial expression was one of disgust and my body shuddered.

But, he continued, 'Immi, it is our way, and we accept it.'

Christmas Celebrations in the UK

Christmas Day, the great annual festival commemorating the birth of Jesus Christ, celebrated among billions of people around the world, had finally arrived. My family have celebrated it more since Sah's arrival. Like most people, presents were exchanged, and food was eaten to the extent that most of the day we would be positioned on the sofa, moaning with full tummies at the rubbish that was yearly on television. Sah was far too young to understand the religious importance; however, she did make the connection between a man with a beard and a very fat tummy, wearing a hat, who brought presents once a year to all the good children of the land within 24 hours, whilst riding his sleigh with his reindeer. Very magical indeed!

Christmas Day started much earlier after Sah's arrival, and this Christmas would be no exception. Gone were the days of going out for a Christmas Eve pint or two to welcome in the new day. We had returned home to the UK to celebrate with my parents as Christmas was never the same in the sun. I had experienced it twice, once in Australia and once in Dubai, and it just wasn't the same without being home and sitting down with my parents for our dinner.

I am unsure at what time it happened, but Sah opened my right eye with her tiny fingers whilst I was sleeping. 'Awake Mammy?' she whispered as I was immediately pulled away from my dream about Russell Crowe - what a man - with an extremely uncomfortable dry eye that was being penetrated by the clumsy and small, thin-fingered girl who now looked enormous in my vision.

'Oh Sah, leave my eye alone.' With a nudge, I released her grip on my poor eye.

'Has he been, Mammy?'

I bloody knew I shouldn't have watched that late film last night. I moaned excitedly, or that's what I thought, 'Come on then. Let's go and check to see, shall we?'

Deep down, I hoped that she would say no. Did she? What do you think? It was still deathly dark, and I couldn't see in front of me. I was grateful that Mammy had left the heating on, as otherwise I would have had goosebumps all over me and pointed, hard nipples from the cold. Sah jumped out of bed once I had put the light on. She always slept with me on Christmas Eve as she was scared in case Santa took her. She was adamant that he had previously been tempted to take her on his sleigh for a ride. The complex imaginative minds of children amused me at times, and Sah was no exception.

The door creaked open, and I prayed that we wouldn't wake my parents up as it was still too early. Daddy had only retired three weeks previously after getting up every morning for work at 6am, and the day would be too long for them. I slowly and quietly turned on the landing light, followed by a 'shh' motion to emphasise we had to be quiet. We crept down the stairs trying to avoid the wear and tear of the creaks that now enveloped the old staircase. To try and avoid the creaks and manoeuvre down the stairs, I looked as though I was participating in an odd dance. Sah was lucky that she was light on her feet. I had always been referred to as being like a hippo on the stairs, may I add, not due to my weight but my heavy feet.

I approached the living room door. I pushed the door open, knowing that all the presents had been neatly packed and positioned on the sofa. I could see the luminous clock that dictated the time was 2.30am, and it was then that I realised that I had been in bed for less than an hour.

'Sah, he hasn't been. I think he is in Europe now and coming later.' With that, she galloped upstairs and was in my bed before I was halfway up the stairs.

I jumped in, and she was waiting for me to cwtch her. 'Now cuddle in and I will wake you up. Now remember, if you are awake, he won't come.'

With that, she replied, 'Ok, Mammy. I love you.' I held on to her as she snuggled into my 38DD pups in her foetal position, and we both closed our eyes. This was going to be a long night and day.

It was like deja vu when at 6.45am Sah awoke again. I woke being shaken, but this time with one eye being opened and a little voice questioning, 'Mammy, has he been?'.

Now, I knew he had very bloody well been by now. *Right! Positive Emily, happy Emily, it's Christmas, Emily,* I kept telling myself. 'Let's wake Mam and Grandpa up and go down to see if Santa has been. I think I heard him.'

'I heard him. I saw him. He waved me,' Sah replied.

'Did you really see him, Sah?' I questioned, smirking even though I was sleep-deprived.

'Yes, Mammy,' came her confident reply.

'Well, you're lucky. I never saw him when I was a little girl. Aren't you lucky?' I smirked as I knew the truth. *But then, I thought, she just lied and looked me in the eyes. I hope she isn't bloody following in her father's footsteps.*

As we stood at the entrance to the door, my mother, Sah and I, you could see the anticipation and wonderment on her little, rosy face with her eyes wide and penetrating. 'Ok, on 1, 2 and 3, we are going to open the door. In sync, we said, '1, 2 and 3.'

As we walked in, I put the Christmas tree lights on and it illuminated the room so that Sah could see that he had indeed been. My mother and I both looked at each other and smiled at Sah's merriment, whilst I envied my father for sleeping in.

The next hour consisted of 3 cups of tea, helping Sah rip the cheapest wrapping paper that I could buy off her presents and then watching her ignore the presents that I had bought and play with plastic bubble wrapping instead. She played more with that than all the presents bought for her. It made me chuckle because, despite the cost of the presents, they remained boxed up, and would be recycled for her birthday presents.

Like many families, we sat together with Sah to eventually encourage her to play with her gifts. I dressed her up, girly and pretty, and by midday, the enormous meal was nearly cooked and on its way to my awaiting large bowel. It was delicious as always, and took a short time to chew and swallow whilst I slurped my Lambrini. My mother had one glass and poor Daddy none, as he was driving me to Swansea Bus Station to catch the 201 to Heathrow at 2 am on Boxing

Day. I think it was the first year that I had never seen him with a can in his hand on Christmas Day. *Fair play,* and *poor Daddy*, I thought.

In the early afternoon, Sah went to spend time with Sperm Donor and his family. I thought it was important for her to spend time with them, as they were her family too, and no matter what my personal ideology was of them, I knew she needed them. It was her right. It also meant I could pack, get organised and relax somewhat before our journey back to the sunshine and Abe, whom I missed more than I had anticipated.

Sah returned at 6pm, so we all had the evening to enjoy and an excuse to eat more chocolate. I had planned what I wanted to watch, and Doctor Who was a bloody must. Sah and I sat down cwtching on the sofa, and we sang the music as it started, not eloquently. We were hooked after watching 10 minutes of it, when my father sat down, took hold of the remote control, and made the bold statement, 'I am turning this crap off!'

'Daddy, we are watching this, and it's bloody good.'

'It will be on again,' he confirmed.

Now, I had looked forward to this episode because I thought David Tennant was a bloody good Doctor Who, if not the best. Sorry other Doctor Whos, as you were rather good, and whilst I have enjoyed all of you as the Doctor, well, it was a travesty when David left, even though Matt Smith did a good job.

'Mammy, Daddy has turned the television off and we were

watching Doctor Who,' I childishly shouted as Mammy cleared the kitchen up.

Her voice echoed back. 'It will be on again, Emily,' she answered.

'Oh, this isn't fair.' I shouted. 'You wait, Daddy. You'll be old one day, in a wheelchair. You will want to turn the television programme over and I will have the remote control. I will hold it in front of you, and we will see how you like it.'

'Emily. I heard that. Don't be so bloody nasty. It will be on again.' My mother retorted. I suppose I had been a little childish in my reply.

'Yes, but when? And I am not even here to watch it. It's so unfair!'

'Oh, bloody watch it then. If it stops you moaning. But I am watching everything I want to after it. Watching bloody crap like this. Jesus!' With that, my annoying, childish behaviour had saved the day. We did get to watch it, mostly in peace, with a couple of, 'Watching this crap!' comments, followed by sighs, coughs and fidgeting, which made me giggle inside a bit, not the fidgeting as Daddy had been complaining about for some time that his hip was cold, and his right leg was uncomfortable. It made me realise that it doesn't matter what age you are, everyone likes to get their own way, and the child inside is always there and can appear at any time and age. We, Sah and I, thoroughly loved it along with millions of other people across the UK, I am sure.

I wanted Sah to have a nap and it had been a long day, so I dressed her in her Christmassy PJs, she kissed us all goodnight and I also said, 'I am going to try to have a kip too.'

'What?' my mother exclaimed. 'You are going to bed too?'

'Yes.'

'Oh. Alright. What time do you want me to call you?'

'Right. We're leaving at 2am, so about 12.30. I will have a quick cuppa and then we can go.' With that, we said our goodnights, dashed upstairs, brushed our teeth, and Sah cwtched in and fell asleep quickly.

I tossed and turned, and for some reason I could not settle. I could hear a commotion downstairs, so I put my dressing gown on and went downstairs after what seemed like a long time, but it was only several minutes.

I opened the door and saw my mother walking into the kitchen and questioned, 'What's going on?'

My mother complained, 'Oh, it's your father. You know he has complained all day about his hip and how he couldn't get comfortable, well, you know what he is like?'

With that I looked at my father. He got up and unsteadily made his way through the living room and was bumping into things as he walked. He was perspiring slightly and looked an off-grey colour. He kept repeating, 'It's bad.'

I smirked a little as Daddy had never been a good patient. I remember growing up when he would go out with his colleagues from work, and he would come back with a bad cold, flu even, as he tried to climb the stairs to go to bed, with my mother telling my brother and I that he was ill, and certainly not drunk. I watched him lopsiding from right to left and sensed something was not right. Inside I thought selfishly, *shit. What if he is too ill to take me to Swansea?* But you know that feeling that seldom comes, but when it does you cannot deny it and it scares you? Well, I got that feeling with a chill, and I was worried, really worried.

I stood with my mother in the kitchen, who always kept herself busy. 'He's been complaining about it for some time. I have told him to go to the doctors, but you know what he is like.' With that statement followed a cry and howl of pain, and we both rushed to the toilet where my father was now.

I opened the door first to find my father on the cold tiles on the bathroom floor. 'I can't get up,' he repeated. 'Help me up?' His face was contorted with pain and now perspiration was clear on his forehead. He was grey. I looked at Mammy and said firmly, 'Mammy, call an ambulance now.'

'What do you mean? Call an ambulance?'

'Mammy, just phone an ambulance now, ok?' My voice was more pitched, and I loved my mother to bits, but it was clear that my brother and I followed my father academically, as he had the brain, and she even admitted this for each year of my life, especially when we had homework.

My mother questioned my father, 'Wes, do I phone for an ambulance?'

He struggled on the floor to focus, but with what sounded like a whisper, he concluded, 'Yes, call them.' He was visibly in pain, internally. Whilst at university, I worked at two residential care homes, I have also watched copious amounts of *Casualty* and *Holby City*, and whilst I am not medical and hate the sight of blood, so you can imagine how I am with the monthly cycle, my gut was telling me that this was serious. Urgency was needed. My mother phoned the ambulance service and described in depth what had occurred. She was in the kitchen whilst I stayed with Daddy, and I placed a coat on top of him to keep him warm, as he was on a cold floor and made a pillow out of another coat.

'Help me up, Emily.' I understood why he wanted to get up, and I advised him that he should not move. 'Bloody help me up,' was his answer and order. I obeyed him, knelt down and put my right arm under his and raised him with effort. Although Daddy was not a large man, to be honest, we were the same height, but he was thinner than me. I put this down to me being a woman with curves and a smallish beer gut from drinking too much Lambrini, and not having enough sexual exercise, or at least the exercise I was used to. I managed to lift him. I walked with him to the living room when my mother came in and said, 'There's an ambulance coming from Tumble. They will be with us as soon as possible.'

It appeared that whilst we thought we had waited for ages, the truth was that it hadn't been that long for my mother and myself, but for my father it was a different story. My father wanted some water, and again I gave in to his needs, although I knew it might not be the best for him medically. Nil by mouth was the medical terminology. I quickly filled a glass with water and helped him sip it. His facial expression said it all, and there was nothing that we could do but just wait. The man I had always looked up to was now weak. It scared me, as even though with all my knowledge and degrees, I couldn't help him. My mother was scared too, walking back and forth continuously. She opened the door without the paramedics knocking, as we had heard the arrival of the ambulance. Outside was so quiet and eerie, after all, it was Christmas night. Two ladies in uniform came through, and I felt sorry for them that they had to work Christmas night, but also so incredibly grateful. They asked their structured questions, and by this time, Daddy wasn't speaking. I asked them what it could be, and they gave different examples of different illnesses, such as a kidney stone. They stated that they would be taking him to the hospital, and sadly they would not be able to take another passenger because there was no room in this old ambulance that they had. It seemed to take them forever to get him onto the stretcher, but they told us before moving him to kiss him goodbye. He whispered because now the pain was great, 'I think this is it. This is the end!' I firmly told him not to be so silly, and we would follow him down in an ambulance.

My mother was like a peacock, standing upright but looking in all directions, emotionally and physically. How Sah didn't wake up, I still don't know to this day. Mammy was now a wreck as the doors of the ambulance closed. It was Christmas Day, and there was no one on the roads. Usually, if such an event occurred, neighbours would be out. However, there was no one. After a minute or two, the ambulance drove off.

We returned to the house, silent as it was. The turmoil of what had happened was now clearly visible on both our faces. My mother wasn't a strong individual, and her eyes moved from left to right continuously as she tried to process that her husband, my father, was no longer at home, but alone in an ambulance not knowing what was wrong with him.

'Emily, you can't drive to the hospital as Sah is upstairs. I will get my phone book and see who can drive me down. My uncle was our first choice; however, he had had a whiskey or two. Then, our neighbour's daughter and son-in-law popped into my mother's head. Luckily, they had not been drinking and were down quickly. Their son, Sam, also came down to keep me company, which was very kind as he was a twenty-something and it was Christmas night.

What transpired next was my mother leaving for the hospital. I said that I would try to follow. I phoned a friend as I knew her husband didn't drink and luckily, she offered to come to the house and sleep downstairs to save disturbing Sah and unsettling her. My uncle walked over with his two replacement knees, and I ushered him home as he couldn't do anything.

My mother called the mobile to state that they were leaving Glangwilli to go to Morriston Hospital. In the pit of my stomach, I knew deep down that this was not a good sign, and I had a feeling and premonition that nothing was going to be the same again.

It is still hard to recount what happened on the 25th of December 2009, but one thing for sure is that our lives would indeed never be the same again. I had managed to get a lift to the hospital and after some time of waiting for news of my father's surgery I called my brawd, my brother in Vietnam, who had phoned earlier in the morning to wish us Christmas greetings, but this time I would be waking him up in the middle of the morning.

'Hiya, Rob, it's Daddy. He collapsed earlier. He is in hospital, and they are operating. He has had a pulmonary embolism; his main artery has collapsed and it's not looking good.' I was so matter-of-fact because of the adrenaline and trying to be strong and supportive as my mother sat and broke her heart.

'What?' a sleeping voice replied.

I repeated the words in robot fashion. However, it started this time with a 'Listen carefully. This is serious!' It also ended differently, 'They are operating now to stop the internal bleeding.'

'What is Daddy saying?'

A stupid question, I thought, to be honest. 'Rob, he is in surgery. You need to start thinking of coming home as soon as possible.' He didn't hear my plea for help.

He ended the conversation with, 'Phone me back and let me know what's happening.'

I looked up the long corridor, and there was no one there. Not a single sound could be heard. It was peaceful but cold. I wiped the tears that had escaped and caught my breath, glancing forward with each step I took as I returned to the waiting room that we had been placed in. We waited five hours before two doctors came to speak with us. Throughout our time in this little room, my mother repeated, 'He's strong. He's going to be alright. You wait and see,' as she wiped her nose and the tears from her eyes. I held on to her left hand and smiled to comfort her.

The doctors were professional and matter of fact. They explained in layman's terms, thankfully, that Daddy had a blockage in his main artery and the blood could not pass, so the artery was blown up like a balloon until it had burst. They operated in total for seven hours and stated that if my father had not been so healthy, they would have lost him. They stated that on his way to Glangwilli Hospital, they had lost him, and they were unsure how much damage to his brain was caused due to the lack of oxygen. They also stated that they were not sure what damage was caused to the other organs as the blood had no escape and that basically, it was a waiting game. But they assured us that they had done everything in their power and that he would be brought onto the ward. They were calm, sympathetic, and reassuring, but we now had to wait. Daddy came through and was unrecognisable. There were tubes and machines all around him and he was on a bed of ice. My mother broke down immediately and I held her.

I sat her down and touched Daddy's freezing hand and stated, 'Mammy, I am going to call Rob.' She nodded and I escaped this terrible and awful reality that we found ourselves in. I left the ward with great trepidation. I knew the survival rate was going to be low, although I willed him to get better. I did indeed call Rob, and to great dismay again he just asked,

'What's Daddy saying?'

'Rob, Daddy can't speak. He has tubes coming out from him!' I answered in dismay. I explained what the doctors had said as best as possible. He understood. I reiterated the importance of him coming back as soon as possible, but he hadn't started looking at flights. I ended the call with a repetition, 'You need to come home. I will phone you and keep you updated.'

Upon my return, Mammy was sitting as close to Daddy as possible. She held his right hand and she was shaking. I stood behind her and held her shoulders. She asked if Rob was coming, and I answered that he was in the process of booking.

She repeated, 'Oh God, Wes. Come back, Wes. Come back, please, Wes. I need you.'

It was heart-breaking, and there was nothing that I could do to make Daddy better. We sat and waited. Time had no meaning, and everything else seemed meaningless. Nurses checked his vitals and smiled at us. We both could not drink anything, and sat praying, waiting, wishing, and willing that Daddy would come back to us. I knew he would if he could. He had only retired three weeks previously, from a job he hated, and he had so many plans to travel with Mammy and to do all the things that he had always wanted to do, as they would be financially secure.

I screamed suddenly, 'Mammy! Look! There's blood.' My mother shouted for the nurses. Blood was pouring slowly from his nose, ears, and eyes. I got up from my chair and wanted to run, escape from this nightmare that now would visually scar me for the rest of my life. The doctors and nurses worked as I ran out, telling my mother that 'I can't do this, Mammy. I can't, Mammy. I'm sorry. I am so sorry, Mammy.'

I practically jogged out through the corridor to the main entrance, as I had to get fresh air and breathe. I did breathe -

cold fresh air. I looked up to the sky that was still pitch black and the stars that could faintly be seen flickering majestically. I knelt holding my head in my arms, not believing that events had taken this road. I plucked up my courage and again, pulled myself together and returned to my mother.

A nurse asked if I was ok as I entered the ward, and I informed her that I would be now. My mother was still sat, holding onto Daddy with dear life.

'Emily, are you ok?'

'Yes. I am sorry, I just freaked out.' She smiled at me. I don't know how long we sat there, but then the doctors reappeared and asked to speak with us again, so we followed them to a private family room. I had an awfully bad feeling and held my mother up as we walked. I helped her sit down and listened intently. The male doctor informed us that the damage to Daddy's organs was too great, that he had suffered organ failure and the blood that had escaped was the blood that they had pumped into him. They also stated that when we were ready, they would turn off the life support, as this was now keeping him alive. I sank into my chair and my mother wailed, 'No, no, no!' All the scenes of television programmes and films I had watched and all the books I had read did not prepare me for what followed. We returned to him, sat, spoke gently to him, thanking him for everything and me personally, for being the best father I could ever have had, even though I hadn't realised or shown it.

The machine was turned off, and after some time, he silently passed. Mammy was motionless and I asked her if it was ok to go and tell Rob. She didn't utter a word, just gave a simple nod.

I walked down the long corridor that now had started to wake. It was nearly 7am and whilst I walked to the outside of the building, teary-eyed, passers buy looked at me, some in sympathy and others with work on their mind.

Rob answered quickly. I was in shock, and possibly didn't handle the next conversation as best as what I should have. I was 33 years old, and no experience or training had equipped me with the skills I now needed. 'Rob, about 10 minutes ago Daddy died. I am so sorry. You need to get back here as soon as possible.'

I heard a deep breath and the reply, 'I will book it now.'

'I have to go back to Mammy. She needs me.'

'How is she?' he questioned.

'You can imagine. I will call you later. I am so sorry.'

The hospital staff had been supportive and had booked a taxi home for us. We didn't speak. We were in shock. The stark realisation of what had happened over the previous hours were unparalleled: my father was gone. I looked out of the window, feeling sorry for the taxi driver, he had two women, two broken women: one who had lost her father, and a wife who had lost her life partner, best friend, father of her children and the man that had become her life. I also felt so guilty, God, I had made him watch Doctor Who when, in fact, he had wanted to watch David Attenborough. And the comment I had made about waiting till he was old to have control of the remote control. I knew Daddy was 65, but he was young and one of the healthiest men, fathers, I knew. The sun was rising, but we were enveloped in pure darkness, grief, and misery. I didn't know where to look or to turn.

The hours that followed entailed me phoning family and friends. Everyone was in shock and disbelief. Mammy sat in her chair chain-smoking, and whilst people knocked on the front door to give their respects, because in our town news travelled like wildfire, I became a shell. Luckily, Sah was not with us as my friend had dressed her and taken her to her house. My brain felt as though it was going to explode into pieces, and I knew I needed something to calm me down. I phoned a friend who I knew would sort me out with a magic weed that would numb me and enable me to exist for my mother.

I called him and when he answered I was unable to speak, just the words, 'Daddy's died.' With that, he said he would be down now, and he and his partner were. They offered to have Sah for me anytime and hugged me. I gave them some money for whatever they could find, I mean it was Boxing Day morning and the chances would be slim, but I was desperate to feel nothing and would be grateful for anything.

They indeed came through for me and I appreciated what they managed to do for me so quickly. I knew it would numb me and even though my bedroom stank, Mammy didn't say anything because I think she also knew I had to find a way to cope with this madness of loss.

Rob returned within days and he and my uncle, between them, sorted out the funeral and other things. It was a blur and some of it to this day still is, but the heartache is still felt. I have always said you can sympathise with people, but to understand truly, you must go through things yourself. I would not wish this on anyone, even though death is a natural part of existence, and as I type these words, the tears roll.

Sah was too young and didn't understand. Sperm Donor knew what had happened and didn't phone at all. I had to phone him to ask him to have Sah about four days later. His excuse was that he thought we were back in Qatar and his response was, 'Ye, I heard. Tell me, Em, what happened then?' was what he said. He had plans to come to the funeral too and I had to firmly state that he was not welcome, and certainly my father would not have wanted him there. I asked him to have Sah on the day of the funeral and he did, thankfully.

We tried our best to ensure she didn't pick up on what was going on, but Daddy's faithful dog, who slept on his tummy on the sofa when Sah didn't, knew something was wrong.

We had a long wait for the funeral, due to the snow and waiting time. I guess a lot of people die over the Christmas period. We were asked by the funeral directors if we wished to say goodbye to Daddy, as he was starting to discolour and bruise badly. I could not summon up the courage or strength.

Mammy brought up the subject of having Daddy home before his funeral, and that we would all leave the house together. Whether it was immaturity on my behalf and that of my brother, but I freaked out, and so did Rob.

I just couldn't cope with the fact that his dead, lifeless body would be here and not him. I couldn't. I just couldn't.

On the day of the funeral, Daddy would have been surprised and shocked as to how many people were present at the crematorium. Men of all ages adorned the inside on the first and second floor and outside in rows at length, as its seating was at capacity.

Consciously, I never confront the memories I have from Daddy's death to this day. You see, I am confronted with the nail in the coffin, so to speak, literally. As I write these words now, I am taken on a journey of distorted memories not in a logical time order. My subconscious, I believe, protects me from this day and when I think of Daddy, I have happy memories and thoughts. I am not immune from the events and dates which led to his death. I can be watching television and a programme that dramatises such medical situations or images of what my father looked like in hospital can take me right back there to what happened. His absence on his birthday and at Christmas is also felt, along with conversations of past shared family memories and things he liked, enjoyed, experienced, or would have enjoyed if given the opportunity. The wave of immediate emotion is immense, and tears roll and are hidden as not to upset Mammy. But do you know what? I am always pulled through.

I feel him sometimes, and I know this may be unbelievable to some of you, but I have found as I have got older, matured, and I had more life experiences, positive and negative, that I have become more open, spiritual, and braver in my understanding and ideology. And I now have the belief that even though he is not here in physical form today, Daddy lives on in me, and is and will always be a part of me of every single day and every waking moment that I continue to live in the life we have shared. We are bonded from my birth, as I am bonded to him, his father, his grandfather and all the past generations of both my parents. We do not just share our DNA, our experiences through our lives, but most importantly, we are bonded by love. A love that will always stand the test of time and will inevitably continue as we are all parts of each other in an endless and continuous cycle to be added to, and that death is just one part of this cycle of evolution.

I will not discuss that day in length. I just want to simply say that for the atheist he was, the hundreds of people that came to pay their respects to him on that day is a testament to the man he was. It is just a shame that only in death others can see this, and not the individual.

After the funeral, my mother willed Sah and I to return to Qatar before Rob departed, as she knew I wouldn't leave otherwise. She would have been right. I promised that I would be back in a couple of weeks at half term.

I had notified my school a few days after Daddy's passing, and they were supportive and sent a beautiful bouquet of flowers. Abe, too, had called and spoken to my mother. He had asked if I had wanted him to come over to Wales to be with us, but there was no way we could have coped with him coming to visit under such dire circumstances. He would pick me up from the airport in Qatar as pre-arranged.

Part 3

We - Sah and I - returned to Qatar. We had to. I was a mess and functioned on pure adrenaline. Everything was robotic and I didn't know how I was feeling, what I was thinking and how I was keeping it all together in between fits of tears, uncontrollable sobbing and out of body experiences of not feeling like me.

Upon our return to Doha, Abe, as promised, was at the airport waiting to pick us up. I had missed him, and to have his strength through this emotional heartbreak was wanted and needed. Just to have his arms around me, holding me, meant everything. As we left the departure gate, it was Sah who initially saw him through all the dish dashes. As I followed her through the crowd, I witnessed her running to him and holding on to his leg with both arms, gripping his leg tightly. He looked down smiling and stroked her hair like I would a much-loved pet. As we met, he held out his arms to me and we embraced. There was no kiss, but just two friends holding on to one another. The embrace was tight, and I thought if he let go of me, I might break into a thousand pieces. Even though it was just seconds, it felt longer.

Into my right ear, he whispered, 'I am sorry, Immi. He must have been a great man to have been taken on Christmas Day, a religious day. If I could bring him back, I would. I would give all I have, but I am sorry, I can't.' I exhaled and loosened my grip and kissed him on the cheek. I smiled and held on to Sah's hand. He pulled our suitcases, and we made our way to his car.

We got in and Abe placed the suitcase in his boot, and once he was sat in the car, he held my left hand. 'Immi, we are not going back straight away. I have something I need to do. That, ok?' I was bloody tired physically and emotionally after a long journey from my mother's home to Swansea Bus Station, to get the National Express to London, Heathrow. Then, a three-hour wait before boarding the plane, followed by a flight of over seven hours, and all with a busy three-year-old who constantly needed attention and entertainment. I smiled, inhaled, and Abe drove to the airport exit. I was too exhausted to speak. Sah had fallen asleep and was content in her own dream world, whilst I awaited to find out our destination.

We followed the coastal road out of the airport, passed the souk and left the busy weaving and fast-paced driving of the city. The journey only took approximately 20 minutes when suddenly we turned off to a dirt track that led to a small harbour. As soon as we parked, men approached Abe's car. Sah started to awake from her power nap. Abe pressed his window down and he proceeded to instruct the Indians in

Arabic. My Arabic still at this time was nil. After travelling and working in Japan, Holland (that was fun and absolutely bloody crazy), Australia, New Zealand and Dubai, I had not learnt basic conversational language in any language other than the French and the Welsh that I had learned at school. It was not through total laziness, but purely because I am not a linguistic and everyone speaks English. The men listened and followed Abe's instructions, then Abe got out of the car, and I followed. Abe walked forward to a large plain fishing boat whilst I got Sah out of her car seat. I was puzzled as it was mid-afternoon and the sun would be going down shortly, so I asked him with exhaustion, 'Abe, what are we doing here?' I quizzed Abe knowing his profession was yacht and boat building, whilst questioning that surely any business discussions could have been conducted by phone.

'Immi, I have asked my friend if we can take this boat out. It was my first boat and I sold it to him. I think...' (he paused) 'going out on the open sea will make you feel better. When I am sad, it helps me. It is a healer – yes – do you agree?' It was the last thing I could have imagined him organising, but it was so welcomed, plus, Sah had heard, 'We go boat!' So, that was bloody it. We were helped on, and positioned ourselves at the helm of the boat, ready for departure. The sea was calm, and the heartbeat of the engine pacified me. Sah played peacefully within the cabin where Abe drove and manoeuvred the boat from the shore into the majestic and turquoise blue Indian Ocean, with some assistance from Sah.

I stood there, letting the breeze surround me, and the waves, as the boat proceeded, hushed the turmoil that had been my life for the last month, to a place where I was at peace and thankful to be alive, here, at this very moment. I had time to breathe and digest the enormity of what had happened and how now, life would be very different for all of us. Suddenly, I was pulled back, and Abe was now behind me and he held my waist in his arms, holding me, letting me balance and lean on his very own vessel. The strength I felt from him propelled me to believe that the sadness and loss that ached in me like toothache, coming at times so strongly and then easing, would reduce in time. It would never disappear, but it would appease and subdue in time. I would learn to live with the loss, but I would never forget, as it would be felt continuously. I realised this and as I looked at Sah playing, oblivious to the life-changing events that had impacted us, it broke my heart that she would lose the memories she had of Daddy as she grew. She would never know the man that loved her unconditionally from the moment she was born. It was so sad, and there was nothing that I or anyone could do about it. It was life, but nothing could have prepared me. Nothing and no one could have prepared me.

The weeks that followed were hard. I had to go back to work, smile, pretend that everything was ok and concentrate when my mind was elsewhere. I was numb as each day I would work, then Skype my mother and speak with her, support her as a daughter, whilst simultaneously needing support myself. Sah was too young to understand as she had been shielded from the grief. When I did break down, which was often, she would simply come and sit next to me, place her arm around my shoulder and wipe my tears and kiss me on my cheek. Then, that would make me cry even more. As the majority of teachers were British, they were sympathetic, but the Arabic organisation was not. Upon my return, I was asked for evidence of my father's death. This evidence could encompass the death certificate and the funeral sheet specifying the venue, date, time, and hymns. To say I was shocked was an understatement, and to make matters worse, I had to ask my mother for this information. Once the information was received, it didn't matter as they didn't pay me for the time missed. When I complained, I was informed that a high percentage of staff had claimed to have lost a loved one when they had not actually. I was also told that the company does not understand why there was such a delay from Daddy's death until the funeral. It was Christmas, a bloody white Christmas, and we all know what it is like when snow hampers daily life in the UK when it comes, and that there is always a waiting time for cremation, especially after a national, public, or religious holiday. You decide what you think. And to make it worse, the secretary had to tell me as the headmaster and deputy head were too scared. And the way she came out with it, 'Oh Emily, I am going to tell you as everyone else is too scared and I really don't know why they don't just tell you. You deserve to know. You're not going to get paid, I am sorry, but that is the decision that has been made. I don't know why they couldn't have told you.'

When I told Abe he was outraged and disgusted. He offered to call the school and speak on my behalf. When I informed the headmaster, he said, 'No, you don't want to do that.' Abe had once promised me, in a somewhat serious manner whilst holding my hands that if anyone ever hurt me, he would hurt them back. He informed me that he could do this in two ways, firstly, by having someone arrested, and secondly, by having them deported. He said it only took a phone call, but I jokingly laughed it off. I had spoken to a colleague about it, and they told me to be careful otherwise I might find myself being deported, and again I laughed it off.

Life continued as it does. Days and weeks passed until the summer arrived. In between the holidays, my brother and I took turns to return during half term and at Easter. Mammy reminisced about her life with Daddy, and she struggled. We did our best, but nothing we could say or do would or could take her and our pain away, individually and as a family. Before returning home at half term Abe had proposed to me whilst sitting in his living room. I was taken aback, but he didn't want any misunderstanding between us. He simply turned to me, placed his drink down and said, 'Immi, I will miss you when you go home. I know, no, we know that we will be together. I will want to marry you and I would like to give you a ring, so when you go home it will make your mother happy.'

With an 'Oh God,' I accepted. We went to the Gold Souk and bought a beautiful engagement ring. It was a plain and simple design and cost more than I would have liked. When I called Mammy to tell her she was over the moon. I told her that it would be a long engagement, but she simply stated to us both, 'Some good news. Just look after my girls, Abe, and make them happy. That is all I ask of you.'

There was no celebratory party or anything like that as I wasn't one for show. I returned to the UK immediately after, and it had brought some joy to us. Whether Sah understood I still don't know, but she loved trying my ring on when we played together. It didn't ease our pain at all, but something nice had happened.

My brother, on the other hand, said, 'Emily, if Abe has the wealth and power that you say he has, well, why the hell is he with you when he can have anyone he wants? I mean, you are pretty, but I have seen a lot prettier girls than you.'

I simply said, 'Oh, thanks, Rob. Jesus.'

This was also followed by, 'If you do marry him and it turns to shit, then know there is nothing we can do to help you. You will be on your own. Think hard about it and be careful. The British Embassy won't even be able to help you, and we do not have the money.'

I retorted, 'You're a happy bloody bugger, aren't you?'

He summarised, 'You don't think about these things, and I am being practical and not having a go. Just be careful, ok, for both of your sakes.'

I was not stupid by any means; I mean, I had a couple of degrees and other qualifications. I had been accepted at university to do my doctorate previously. Yes, I agree, I didn't have much common sense and was too trusting sometimes, but this was not a legal contract and not binding in any shape or form. It was an engagement, that is all.

The summer holidays had finally come, and it was time for us to return to the UK to visit my mother, who I had missed daily. Abe was in Dubai on business. He had to oversee a yacht interior that was nearly completed but needed some further specifications. So, we drove to Abe's house where one of his friends was waiting to drive us to the airport, as he had prearranged it for us. Our arrival to the UK would be so different, as now only my father's memory would be in the house, and he would not. His presence and shouting, 'Make me a cup of tea,' and, 'Don't be so daft,' would be sorely missed, and even though I longed to be home, I also dreaded the realisation that now I was really going to feel his loss. It scared me. His presence, words and rules had annoyed me somewhat as I grew up, but now all I wanted was to hear his shouting to keep the noise down because he couldn't hear the TV, my mother shouting that he had returned from the garden with muddy shoes and walked through the house, him shouting for me to put clothes on, to give him the remote – things that would have annoyed me once – now never to be uttered and heard ever again, only in memories. It hurt.

We arrived home and within a day or two my brother arrived with his wife and son. My mother had lost weight to her already tiny arthritic frame, a frame that had once towered over me. She said that there was no point in cooking for one, so she ate sandwiches when I questioned her weight. Whilst she no longer confirmed that she too wanted to die, she was angry, angry with God, life, the British Government for taking Daddy's pension and with those that abused their bodies with drugs and alcohol and who survived. Daddy had worked hard all his life, and had given up on his personal dreams and aspirations to have a family and work hard to put us, my brother and me, through university. With anger comes negativity and hate, and a cloud hung over her. It was felt.

I honestly could not cope being back home with everyone. The act of trying to maintain normality with children who did not understand, who squabbled over simple things and the noise, the noise was constant. Everyone's stress levels were magnified and heightened. The simplest comment would cause a reaction. I was fine individually with my mother, but with everyone else in the picture I just needed to escape. So, that is what I did. I knew Sah would be fine with Mammy, had her cousin to play with and the possibility of spending some time with Sperm Donor, when he could, of course.

So, I headed back from the cold summer in the United Kingdom to the sweltering summer heat of the Middle East. My journey up to Heathrow and the three-hour wait at the airport was the first time in months that I had had to myself to inhale, exhale, and simply breathe. I had lost a part of myself since having my daughter, as most mothers do, and with the loss of my father, I had to learn consciously now who I was. I missed, in essence, the old me: the happy, smiling, naughty but nice, laughing me. She had gone somewhere between all the hurt, stress, and loss. I had gone, and I had to find, accept and grow to like and love the new me. And more importantly, to be kind to myself and understand that I was trying my very best in my personal madness. I was lost and knew I would find myself with time. For now, I looked forward to my escapism from my reality.

Abe had stated that he would be busy with work, but I was just excited and looking forward to seeing his apartment and the development of his yachts. I drank one or two vodkas with coke whilst I listened to the Black Eyed Peas and 'Meet Me Halfway' as we flew over Europe. As I listened to the lyrics, butterflies whirled in my tummy and I smiled as the words resonated deeply within me. I was travelling halfway around the world to be with Abe, where our two cultures would meet and collide in a good way. I finished my drink as the lyrics played, placed my black snug eye covers on for sleeping, sat back with a big exhale before getting comfy and snug under my blanket. One thing is for sure, I had a big smile on my face, I felt pure excitement and I couldn't wait to be awoken in Dubai, and to see Abe.

Abe was waiting for me as I left arrivals in his usual dress, with a big cheesy smile. I walked to him, and he kissed me on both my cheeks and said simply, 'I am so happy that you are here, Immi.' We left the craziness of the airport and drove. It was late and approaching midnight, and Dubai was alive with bright lights, taxis and cars escorting people throughout the city as the night buzzed with excitement. We drove and discussed what we had been up to, and the conversation was continuous. I noticed that we had started to leave the city as the hotels had gone, the towering apartment blocks were sparser, and the lighting was dimmer. I knew Abe's apartment was in the city, so I questioned where we were going. Abe had a habit of sleeping during the day and being awake all night and I was tiring due to the long day of travelling.

'I have surprise for you, Immi.'

I laughed and shook my head with a sigh, 'Oh Abe.'

Then, within 10 minutes he turned right into a car park where there were a few cars parked in the darkness. 'Immi, we are here.' He parked the car, and our immediate view was the beautiful moonlit beach. We had a perfect view, and I could see a few families with children scattered on the expanse of this beach. Some were eating, chatting, and relaxing in the ocean. It was beautiful and there were no western people, just Arabic families.

'This is the beach I come to swim at night. It is quiet and only Arabic people come here. It is our secret.' He said these words and then got out of the car. He then faced me and said, 'Come. Come for a swim, Immi. It is very, very nice. You will see.'

With a puzzled look I stated, 'But Abe, I don't have my swimsuit on.' He smiled with the reply, 'Then you need to put it on, Immi. It is simple, yes?'

Yes, I suppose it was a simple process, or I could just go in my bra and knickers. As it was dark and my underwear was a flowery brown design, I could just whip off my dress and walk into the sea. Abe instructed that he was going in, and he did. He proceeded to walk down to the beach, wave at the locals who sat around their little fires, whip off his dish dash and jog into the sea wearing his white y-fronts. His pants always made me laugh as they were like the ones my father wore. They were not a fashion accessory, but more a comfort soother with plenty of stretch to breathe. In fact, they were a bit like my granny knickers I used to wear in my younger years when my mother used to buy my knickers for me. She didn't believe G-strings were good for down there and referred to them as 'up your bum knickers'.

It wasn't until Sperm Donor saw me undress one day and start to pull them down that he pissed himself laughing and said, 'What the fuck are those, Em?' Followed by, 'How bloody old are you? You're wearing bloody granny knickers.' Well, it was this embarrassment that no other past boyfriend had commented on that pushed me to make more of an effort and forced me to buy my own underwear, even though I was embarrassed as my mother washed my knickers and put them on the line outside to air, and in full view of Daddy's garden.

I got out of the car, making no contact with anybody and focussed solely on Abe, who by this time was like a male mermaid bouncing up and down in the water. I graciously walked down to the shore whilst peeping in all directions as to who could see me, pulled my dress over my head, and walked into the warm Indian Ocean. Whilst the Emirati women sat in the traditional dress, I enjoyed the freedom in my underwear in the dark. It was so dark and visually beautiful as the moon shone bright, surrounded by stars that flickered, with a few small fires that lit the distant shore. As I submerged myself and descended into the warm abyss that surrounded me, I re-emerged, obviously very wet, but lighter in body and spirit as I was surrounded by warmth.

I swam to Abe's arms and positioned my legs over his to form a seat and held on to his neck. We kissed on and off before separating to do our own thing in the water.

I shouted over to him, 'Oh Abe, this is amazing. Thank you so much. God, I needed this.'

He answered, 'You are very welcome. I love this. Love, love, love this.'

In the distance, as I meandered in all directions, I could see Abe motioning as though he was doing something, as I could see his arms moving under the water and then he threw something at me. 'Abe, what did you just throw at me?'

He smirked, and his eyes were mischievous. He answered,

'My pants, Immi. My pants. I now have freedom. Freedom! It feels good,' he shouted.

'You are bloody crazy. Make sure that no one bloody sees your big hairy balls. You're a bloody crazy bastard.'

He retorted whilst swimming backwards, 'I know, and you love me. My horny, horny Habibie.'

I swam to get his pants and threw them onto the beach. I didn't want him exposing himself to any innocents on the beach and causing them psychological damage with a memory of him walking in the nude. And more importantly, this was an Arabic country where you could get arrested for less.

We departed the tranquillity of the beach and returned to the apartment, which had a beautiful view of the city. I wasn't used to being so high up in the sky, other than in an aeroplane. As I looked out, I ensured I was a couple of steps from the window just in case. We had a drink each, a shower to get the salty layer off our bodies and then went to bed. There was nothing physical that night, and it was not felt or needed. The bed was gigantic, and I woke up as I had fallen asleep, cwtched into Abe's chest.

We didn't rise until midday and then went out for brunch at a posh hotel that was near to us. It was delicious and as Abe had a busy day of work, he encouraged me to have a nice afternoon of shopping. I hardly ever got the chance to do this, so I looked forward to it after I had got rid of the trepidation of doing things by myself. I felt lost without Sah to run after. I walked to the cinema to see what was on, but as I didn't fancy anything, I proceeded to do some window shopping. Abe would call in between to check what I was doing, where I was and to inform me of how hard he was working, which always made me laugh. Our work ethics were very different and opposites.

By early evening, I had had enough and decided to get a taxi back to the apartment. I phoned Abe to say that I was back and to question when he would be home. When we were speaking, I could hear an Arabic female voice in the background.

'Who is that?' I naturally questioned.

'Oh, Immi. My niece phoned me as they have arrived in Dubai, and she is bored. So I picked her up to take her for a drive. Immi, she loves my car.' Something was said in Arabic, and I had no reason to question Abe and told him to bring her back if she wanted to hang out, as it would be nice to meet her. He made his excuses by saying he was in traffic and near to dropping her off. He also informed me that he didn't like the thought of me on my own, so he would send someone over to keep me company.

I asked, 'Will it be Mo?'

I had met Mo many times during our weekend visits to Dubai and even though our communication was basic, as he had little English, we got on. Abe and Mo were friends as Mo's mother had been Abe's wet nurse when he was a baby. My facial expression when he told me this was shocking. But, on the realisation that when Abe was a baby, Qatar was not developed and certainly without refrigerators, so I suspected this was the norm. But the thought of sucking someone else's boobies, well… But a friendship had been made from the sharing of this mother's boobies and now, when Abe was in Dubai for work, Mo helped him with errands and Abe paid him to help him out as he wasn't very wealthy. I remember when he told me of the wet nurse, I looked at his lips and thought, what else have your lips sucked and quickly shook my head with a frown forcing myself to think of something else. I mean, wet nurses were something from British history and decreased in popularity in the nineteenth century and not a few years ago.

'Oh, Immi. Mo is dead, I think?' was his casual reply.

'What?' I screeched.

'Yes, he was arrested for something. He had a weak heart and I think he is dead.'

'WHAT, Abe? This is the first I have heard of it. He is dead. You think he is dead.' I was disillusioned by the oh-so-matter-of-fact way he had just told me. I understood that we both came from different cultures, but to be told about it like that was shocking, to say the least, especially after losing Daddy so soon too. I came off the phone and poured myself an alcoholic drink. I sat down and thought, w*hat the fuck?*

It wasn't long after that there was a knock on the door. I approached and looked through the peephole in the door and answered, 'Yes, can I help you?' to a small rounded, dark Arabic Muslim man.

'Hello, Immi. My name is Mo, and I am here because Abe asked me to come. He will not be long.'

I continued to look this new Mo up and down. I replied, 'Oh, hi Mo. Thanks for coming over, but I am fine, thanks, and Abe won't be long.' I repeated, 'I am fine, thanks.'

'Immi, Abe has asked me to come and sit with you. He will not be very happy if I do not do as he ask.'

I just rolled my eyes and said to myself, 'For God's sake, I don't need a bloody babysitter.'

'Immi, are you there?' He questioned looking concerned as I watched him through the peephole.

'Ok. Give me a minute and I will let you in.' I then proceeded to open the door and let him in.

He was a bubbly, happy, smaller, and rounded Arabic man in comparison to Abe, who was tall and thin, and sometimes more serious with pouty lips.

I shook hands and I welcomed him in with a half-hearted smile. He clearly knew the apartment as he asked to go to the toilet and knew where to go. So, I questioned if he would like a drink, and he did. He asked for a vodka and coke, so I politely obliged. We sat down on the sofa, and I learnt that Mo number 2 helped Abe when he was in Dubai.

'Yes, I know Abe for long time. I help him when he need it. Abe very good.'

I was perplexed about Mo number 1 dying and with this new Mo number 2, so I instinctively phoned Abe to inform him that his guest had arrived, and to question how long he would be. Abe always seemed to be near, but there was always a delay in his arrival. I felt a little uncomfortable whilst trying to be polite to this unwanted guest. I did inform him that I was fine and that if he wanted to go then he could. However, his response shocked me.

'No, Immi, I will stay. Abe not happy if I leave. He crazy sometimes. You, see?'

As he grappled for words, he seemed nervous as he answered me, and it stuck with me before I answered him questioning, 'Abe crazy? Really? He can be funny, and he does like to party,' I answered seeing how this conversation would flow.

'Yes, we have many party here. We drink too much.' He answered with a smile.

Now, two men partying, Abe and Mo, didn't seem like a crazy party to me, so I casually asked, 'Who else was at these parties, Mo?'

'Oh, we have parties. Every night we drink, dance, eat. Fun. Very fun. Abe is very good.'

Now, I wasn't one to phone Abe before going to bed as when I was working, I was in bed early, and when I was home in Wales there was the time difference to contend with. So, the if and when Abe had been 'partying' I would have no knowledge of, as I was away with the fairies and not in his presence. I was not with Abe enough to know what he was up to and with whom. More investigation was needed.

'So, Mo, you don't mind me calling you Mo, do you?'

'Yes, Immi, that is fine.'

'Oh, good. Well, Mo, who was at these parties? I have met another Mo here in Dubai, but Abe told me that Mo was arrested and is now dead.'

He answered looking directly at me and said, 'Yes, I hear something.'

I continued, 'Yes, it is very sad. I had met Mo many times and he seemed very nice.'

'I hear something. But I not know.'

'Oh well, it is very sad. I am just happy that you are here to keep Abe company. I worry about him when I am not with or near him.'

With further polite conversation, I found out that Abe frequented nightclubs and then invited people back to his bachelor pad. He would also pick up girls as he drove by, flashing his lights at their cars to pull them over.

I smiled whilst I listened, but inside my guts twisted, my heart rate increased as the beats quickened, whilst the weight of the truth made my shoulders droop, and I felt the weight pull me down. I kept serving him drinks whilst limiting what I drank to see what else I could/would find out.

When Abe did finally appear after an hour later than expected, he waltzed in and kissed me on both cheeks declaring, 'Oh Immi, I work so hard today and I miss, miss you, my Habibie. Please get me a drink. I shower quick and then I relax. I am very, very tired. Yes, good. Mo is here. It good that Mo sit here and keep you company.'

Whilst Abe was in the shower, I took him the drink he had requested, and he queried if I had been happy with Mo.

'Well Abe, I don't see why you needed to send him here. I am perfectly fine by myself. And your niece, it would be nice to see her, meet her if she is bored.'

Abe changed the conversation by telling me, 'Sit down, Immi, and tell me what you have done today.'

'Well, I went shopping, as you know. But I think I want to know more about these parties you have been having. Sounds like you have been having fun.'

With a big grin, he smiled and said, 'My beautiful Habibie has missed me. I will try to spend time with you tomorrow.' He totally changed the conversation and then he said, 'Come here, Habibie and kiss kiss me.'

I got off the romantic stool of a toilet, walked towards the shower, and leaned my head in when he grabbed me and pulled me in kissing me all over my face with his wet face. I shivered and had goose bumps, and it wasn't a nice feeling.

On the one hand, I was seething with him for having parties here and for all the other stuff Mo had said, but he never divulged anything sexual, or was that because I was afraid to ask. I was scared at the same time, but hopeful that I may have translated and interpreted everything so wrong because of what I had gone through with Sperm.

I was confused as I looked at him and could only answer, 'You're bloody bonkers. What about Mo?'

He answered, looking directly into my eyes with his big dark black eyes smirking, 'Mo will be fine. He is comfortable and has drink.'

After our shower, we both dried each other and redressed in dry clothes. We returned to Mo who was busy drinking and watching television. We joined in and had an evening of drinking more vodka and chatting, Abe and I on the two-seater brown suede sofa whilst Mo sat on the single one. We all drank copious amounts of booze when Abe, with a smirk looked at me, then looked at Mo and said, 'Immi, Habibie. I want you to sleep with Mo.'

I looked at Abe with a huge frown and then to Mo, and back to Abe, questioning did he truly just ask me to bed his friend? What the fuck! So, I screeched, 'What, Abe?'

He repeated, smiling and in a comic voice, 'I want you to sleep with Mo, Immi.'

I looked at them to and fro again, but this time getting off the sofa next to Abe and standing backwards. 'What, Abe? Are you crazy? What the fuck? No! No! I can't believe you would say such a thing. What is wrong with you?'

Mo was sat back comfortable watching my every move with little expression, whilst Abe smirked with a big grin. I could see he found it amusing. 'Abe this is not funny. How dare you! How fucking dare you! Jesus, Abe!'

Mo shuffled in his chair and placed his hands on his knees before gently stating, 'Abe, ok. Immi does not have to sleep with me. It is ok.'

Abe looked at him disapprovingly and then at me. 'But I want Immi to sleep with you.'

I was disgusted, horrified, confused, and knew this was totally fucked up. As I looked at him, I questioned who this man was in front of me. Did I really know this man at all? I had my answer in front of me. I had had my answer earlier that evening with Mo if I was being honest. I was crushed.

Mo then stood up and I stepped backwards. He could see I was scared. 'Abe, it is getting late. I go.' I looked him up and down and then to Abe. He said these words sympathetically and I hope he was as uncomfortable as I was.

Abe retorted disapprovingly, 'I am very sad, Mo. If you want to leave, go.' I stood fixed. He left and I followed him to the door to lock it. He turned to say goodbye to Abe and stated that he would see him tomorrow. He quietly asked if I was ok which I answered with a nod. He answered softly spoken as not to arouse suspicion from Abe, 'He crazy!' I nodded and said goodnight and locked the door.

I took a deep breath and turned to walk and face Abe. He was still sat slurping his drink when I firmly stated, 'That was not funny, Abe. What the hell? Why? Never ever speak to me like that again. It is sick. You are sick. I am going to bed. Please leave me alone. I am very angry now. So, fucking angry!'

I walked to the bedroom door and then turned to Abe when he had finished, 'Immi, you are angry with me. I am sorry. I was joking. It is funny, no?'

Sternly I answered for the final time that evening, 'Abe, I am disgusted and angry. You treated me like a prostitute, selling me to your friend for fun. What the hell is wrong with you? I am going to bed and am going to try to sleep. I do not want to speak to you. Just leave me alone.'

I entered the bedroom and closed the door behind me. I brushed my teeth, changed into my nightdress, and got into bed. I curled up into a foetal position and tears escaped from my eyes. I was in complete shock, horror and for the umpteenth time in my life, I felt truly used, even abused in the most undignified way. I did not deserve this. I felt so alone and questioned what the hell I was doing here with a man, a man that had treated me like this and who had professed his love, then had wanted to prostitute me out to his friend and then joke about it. I had never felt so small in my life or so sorry for myself and for Sah.

I managed to fall asleep after repeatedly questioning myself, 'Why did he do that? Why?' but it was not a deep sleep as was expected. I did hear and feel Abe get into our bed sometime during the night. There was no bodily contact between us in bed that night, thank God, and if he had touched me, I think I would have punched him. I was so angry with him that my nasal breathing, along with my facial expression, would have scared anyone.

I awoke first thing in the morning, and I just couldn't stop thinking of what had occurred in the previous hours. I made myself a cup of tea and sat on the sofa thinking to myself that I have another three nights here. I couldn't wait to get back home to normality which I had shunned, and Sah.

Abe woke with a 'Good morning, my Habibie,' from the bedroom. I could hear him stretching and moving about in the bedroom, whilst I held on to my cuppa. He walked into the living room without a care in the world with a big smile and jovial. 'Oh, Immi. I slept very good last night. Are you ok, Habibie?'

I looked up at him and questioned, 'Am I alright? Are you serious? Last night you wanted me to sleep/have sex with your friend. So, am I alright? No, I am far from being fucking alright.'

He looked down at me and spoke softly. 'I was joking, Immi. And Mo is not my friend. He works for me. He does work for me when I am here in Dubai. That is all.'

'I really don't care a damn what your relationship with Mo is, to be bloody honest. What has angered me is what you suggested a few times. It was bloody disgusting and the lowest of the low.'

He walked over to me and sat next to me on the sofa. 'I did not want to upset you so enough now. It is finished. I was joking. Ok?'

I could see clearly that he would not take or accept any criticism for his unforgiving and demeaning behaviour. He kissed me on my left cheek and informed me that he had a busy day ahead. Considering it was midday already and knowing his work ethic of just instructing people to do his work, his actual workday would not amount to much. To say the atmosphere was frosty was an understatement, but with the realisation that I had a few more days staying with Abe I made the decision that I would be civil. If I left Abe to stay in another hotel, I knew I could make a situation for myself here and for when I returned to Qatar, so I needed to appease him and ensure that I did not do anything detrimental to myself and for Sah. I knew it was going to be hard, well, truly fucking hard, but I could not worry my poor mother. She had been through enough with Sperm Donor and me, and with Daddy dying. I had to tread carefully as we had all had enough hurt.

We were both hungry and went down to the lobby cafe for brunch, a basic snack to fill our tummies. It also meant that we were surrounded by others and not confined to the apartment. I wanted to ensure that the apartment would now be used only to sleep in. Our toasted sandwiches accompanied by a fruit smoothie was lovely, and then we made our way to Abe's car. As we walked, I instructed him that I did not want to see Mo for the remainder of my trip and Abe's reply was, 'Why, Immi?'

I did not have the energy and I was full of contempt for the man that was next to me. 'Because you have embarrassed me with your fun, and I do not wish to see him. And that is final.'

We got into his car and drove to a nearby small port where Abe wanted to show me the yacht he had been refurbishing. It would not be a long journey and whilst he drove, I listened to the Arabic music and looked out of my window daydreaming. Anything was better than reminding myself of the events of last night. As always, when we arrived there were men running around and following every instruction he gave them. After literally climbing onto the yacht via ladders, it was indeed impressive. It had leather and marble imported from Italy, which gave the interior a very luxurious and expensive finish. He had another meeting that afternoon and dropped me off at the Dubai Mall for a spot of yet more retail therapy. The heat was too fierce to walk in, so the cool air conditioning of the shopping centre was a relief. He wouldn't be back to the apartment until late, so I had a nice meal to ensure I was full before going back as I did not want to go out with him upon my return and just to sleep.

I got back about 7 pm and it was nice as he hadn't called to interrogate where I was, where I had been and what I was doing. I had peace all afternoon and anticipated that he wouldn't be back until very late, so I had a soothing bath, a large vodka and coke and relaxed.

It was about 8pm and I was sitting on the sofa flicking through channels on the television when the door buzzer went. I thought *who the hell is here now* as it couldn't be Abe as he had a card and could let himself in. So, I went to the peephole to see who was standing there. When I saw the image in front of me, my jaw dropped. It was Mo, not the dead one, but the one I really didn't want or need to see. I shook my head. I turned around, resting my head and body against the door, and said, 'Hi Mo. I am sorry, but Abe is not here. He won't be back for a couple of hours.'

He answered, 'Immi, I know Abe not here. That is why I am. I need to speak to you now. Immi, please let me in? I must speak with you. Please?'

I turned around to look through the peephole again, with annoyance, as this man was indeed the last man along with Abe I wanted to speak to or see.

'Mo, Abe isn't here, and he will be back later. Or phone him if you want to speak to him.' I gestured as politely as I could, given the mood I was in.

He pleaded nervously as I watched. 'Immi, please let me in. I do not want to speak to Abe. I have come to warn you. Police are coming. Please let me in.'

Again, I was perplexed as to what the hell was going on. I decided to let him in quickly because the mention of the police scared me. I answered, 'Ok Mo, I will let you in for five minutes, tell me what you have to and then I want you to leave. Ok?'

He answered with a masculine, 'Yes. Ok, Immi. I give my word.'

I opened the door with pure trepidation and let him in, closing the door behind him before I followed him down the corridor to the living room. He walked straight towards the single-seater and turned to face me. In a concerned voice he stated, 'Immi, you don't have long. You need to pack and leave. Police are coming to arrest Abe and if you are here, they will arrest you. Please, Immi, you need to leave now. Come please.'

I just stared at him in disbelief and thought to myself, *what next?*

'What, Mo? The police are coming here to arrest Abe? What has he done?'

'Abe has been crazy. He was nearly arrested in nightclub last week. There were air hostesses, British, and he liked. He was pulling to leave with him and she ... didn't want to. Others got involved, and I think English men. Abe had to leave. He got crazy. He has been driving and flashing many, many girls and invite them to parties. He has crazy parties with drugs and prostitutes. He is sick, ill Immi. He has a lump on his groin - I know this because the women have seen... feel it. They say he is sick too. They tell me, Immi. I see this. Please, come with me, Immi.'

'What, Mo?' Whilst my eyebrows were raised my shoulders sunk. I just couldn't believe what I was told, and I knew about the lump that he was describing.

'Immi. You saw what Abe did last night. He is crazy. Believe me? You have to leave before they come, or they will arrest you. I like you, and I do not want you to get in trouble. You do not want to be locked up here in Dubai. I do not want you to go to jail. Please trust me, Immi.'

'Mo, why the hell would I be arrested. I haven't done anything, and where am I supposed to go?'

He instructed me, 'I will take you to a hotel until you leave on flight to home country. Please, Immi. Get things, bag and we leave before Abe comes back.'

I argued, 'Mo, this is crazy. Why would I be arrested? What have I done? What has Abe done?'

'Immi, the police not know about you. They not know you coming. But they arrest you if find you. Hurry! Please hurry!'

I shook my head and tears started to run down my cheeks. More bloody tears! I could not believe what was happening. It was such a mess, such a bloody mess. I went into the bedroom and threw all my bits and bobs into my small suitcase.

From years of travelling, I always travelled light, and it only took a couple of minutes to whizz around, pack and bring my bag back into the living room.

Mo stressed whilst looking at his watch, "We go quickly. Please. No time, Immi.'

'I have to get my jewellery from the bathroom.' As I returned with my rings, necklace and watch, my mobile rang. I picked it up from the kitchen counter and saw that it was Abe. I whispered to Mo, why I do not know, 'It's Abe. What do I do?'

Our senses were both heightened, and he told me to answer it. 'What do I say?'

'Just act you are ok.'

I pressed the answer button and tried to pretend that Abe's prostituting me out never happened and that I was not going to be arrested by police that were on their way. 'Hi Abe.' His voice in a lazy manner answered, 'Hi, Habibie. You ok?'

No, I was not bloody ok. I was freaking out. 'Ye, everything is ok. How about you? Are you ok?'

'Yes, Habibie. I am very, very tired. I have been very busy today. Is Mo there with you?'

'Is Mo here?' As I said this Mo shook his head. 'No. I haven't seen Mo today. I have been shopping and have been back at the apartment for over an hour.'

'Are you sure you have not seen Mo today?' He repeated, with a voice more alert now.

I knew something was up. 'Abe, I am sure I would know if I had seen Mo, especially after last night. Remember? Why? What is a matter?'

'Oh, he called me today asking me for money. I said no. I give him money all the time to help him. You know his family is poor. I am sorry for them, but I cannot keep giving. I give when he helps me with work and things. But today I said no, and he became very angry. I do not want you to speak with him if he comes. Do not let him in and phone me.'

Inside, I was so confused, and I wanted to scream out loud. I could feel myself begin to shake as to the seriousness of the situation. This man was now a few metres away from me, and whilst he would not have heard all the conversation, I was sure he would have heard some of it. I was shitting myself, well not literally, but you know what I mean. I knew that the relationship was over by what had happened in the last 24 hours. There was no way of going back, but this was a new ball of shit I had been thrown, and I wanted to get out of this as cleanly as possible. I simply answered, 'Ok, Abe. If he comes, I will not let him in and call you immediately. When will you be back?'

'I will not be long. I will see you. Bye.'

That was the end of the conversation. I then walked to the kitchen and placed my jewellery on the counter. I looked at Mo and said, 'Abe is on his way back. He won't be long. He said that you asked him for money, and he said no to you.'

He walked to get my bag and walked towards the door ushering me to come with him. 'We go now, Immi. They here soon.'

I firmly replied, 'Mo. Please put my bag down. I will leave by myself.'

He pleaded, 'But where you go? I take you hotel. You will be safe.'

I shook my head and said, 'No! I will do this properly. I will say goodbye to Abe and go to a hotel by myself. Now, I would like you to go. I will leave as soon as I say goodbye to Abe.'

'Immi, please. This serious, very serious. You do not have long. I have go. I here too long. Good luck, Immi. I pray for you.' I could clearly see he was on edge, with possibly high blood pressure as his face was a reddish brown and sweat droplets were visible and clear to see on his forehead. I watched as he turned and walked down the corridor until he was gone.

I closed the door and grabbed my bag, and placed it on the counter next to my jewellery. I went to the kitchen and poured myself a stiff vodka and coke and drank it within three gulps. I proceeded to pour myself another one before sitting down on the sofa. I then phoned Abe to see exactly where the hell he was, as I knew time was ticking. My heart rate had increased, so as I called him and asked him where and how long he would be, he stated he was just about to park his car in the underground parking. I waited anxiously for him to come to the apartment, then I heard him outside and the door slowly opened. I sat facing it and watched him walk in without a care in the world. I looked up, holding my drink in my right hand, and took a big gulp before the shit could possibly hit the fan.

He stood still in front of me and looked to his left, where my bag was. He looked at me while jiggling his keys and then took his sunglasses off. He sternly said, 'Immi, what is this? Why is your bag here?' pointing to it on his right.

Softly I answered, 'I am leaving, Abe. I am going to stay in a hotel until my flight home.'

Puzzled he questioned, 'Why? You are leaving? You are crazy! Why, Immi?'

I thought to myself how dare you call me crazy boyo after the way you have treated me. My blood boiled.

'Abe, last night you wanted me to sleep/have sex with Mo. I have also been told by Mo that you have been picking up strange women when driving, having crazy parties and nearly got arrested for harassing an air hostess in a nightclub. Oh, and then there are the prostitutes.'

He looked at me more sternly stating, 'I ask you on the phone if you see Mo. You talked to him, yes? I told you he wants money, and we had argument. You are stupid for listening to him.'

'Stupid, yes, I have been stupid. I am in agreement with you there. But, in reality, I think it is you who has been stupid because the police are coming here to arrest you, Abe.'

He looked at me with anger. "What have you done, Immi?'

'What have I done? How dare you? I have done nothing. Nothing except be a stupid, stupid fucking cow. You should know that Mo was here when you called, and he said that the police are coming here. He wanted me to leave with him, and he wanted to take me to a hotel. But I thought that you deserved better than to come back to a note.'

'Oh, I told you, Immi. He is angry because I not give him money. He is poor and gets greedy. He is joking. Now end this. I am tired. I am going to have a shower and then go to bed. If you want I will take you to a hotel tomorrow and then it will be finished. Hallas.' He confirmed it as so matter-of-fact.

'You really do love me, don't you?' I had no more tears to shed and looked up to him.

He turned to face me and sucked his lips and with casual ease proclaimed, 'Yes, I did once, but not now. It is finished. Hallas!'

I felt my whole being crumble and sink into the sofa. I looked into the contents of my glass questioning why? Why did this happen again? Did I have a sign on my forehead saying, Fuck me in all ways? I really didn't understand, and I could hear him undress and jump into the bed without a care in the world. I sighed and, again, my life was like a glass half full. My daughter was in the UK with my family, and I was in an alien foreign country, lost in a whirlwind of madness from the unreal events of the last two days. I finished my last long mouthful, got up to place the empty glass on the counter, near my bag, before going to the entrance of the bedroom to take one last look at Abe. He looked relaxed, comfortable without a care and at peace. Then I heard it, 'BANG! BANG! BANG!' I jumped initially and turned to look at the door, and then back at Abe. Was Mo's premonition and warning bloody coming true? I hoped to hell that this was not what he had forewarned. I slowly crept with each step to the door to peep through the looking hole, as to who and what was the unexpected visitor. Another bang, bang, bang with increased strength followed with, 'Open the door!' I saw six Arab men and two Emirati women in their blacks, whilst the men were dressed in jeans and t-shirts. I scuffled back to the bedroom and shook Abe.

'Wake up. I think that they are here.'

He stirred, questioning, 'What is it?'

I answered quietly, 'I think the police are here, Abe. They are here.'

Abe jumped from the bed and put on his dress. He informed me to quickly shout that I was getting dressed, but they continued to bang the door.

'Wait a minute,' I shouted, 'I am getting dressed.'

The banging continued and what I glimpsed of Abe was him opening the balcony door. He went to the bathroom and wrapped toilet paper around something before flushing the toilet a couple of times. I watched as he moved quickly, organised, and confidently going from one place to the other, getting rid of whatever he had hidden in the bedroom drawers and the pockets of his clothes. I had no idea what the hell was going on or what he was getting rid of. I had never needed to go through the drawers and search the apartment as I had trusted him. Abe was composed, he instructed me to go and answer the door. I walked towards it, took a deep breath and with my final step before the door, I opened it.

I gently stated, ensuring that they could hear me, 'Ok, I am opening the door,' and as I did, the door was pushed open, and I was sent back against the wall. Within seconds, handcuffs were placed on my wrists as I was pushed and held facing the wall. The same thing happened to Abe, and Arabic was being spoken. They were asking me questions and I informed them in my shocked state that, 'I don't speak Arabic. I am British.'

Abe then piped up in English, 'She has nothing to do with this. Please let her go. This is nothing to do with her.' They laughed amongst themselves, whilst I shat myself, not literally. The male officers joked amongst themselves whilst Abe looked to the floor. He had no control, I could see that, and I had even less.

I was asked, 'Name?' Petrified, I stated it. The women positioned themselves behind me, whilst Abe had two behind him, and the others looked around the apartment.

I asked, 'What is happening?'

One answered, 'If you have done nothing wrong, you will be free?'

Now, I was puzzled as I hadn't done anything wrong, so the logical question from me was, 'What have I done for you to do this?' Something was said and laughter echoed from them. After the two had gone through the different rooms and supposedly found nothing they were preparing to leave when I interjected, 'I was leaving to go to a hotel. Can I take my things?'

Something was said and then my bag was picked up by one of them. My jewellery was still on the counter, so I questioned strongly, 'What about my jewellery?'

I was told by the one who spoke English to me, 'You can get when you come back. Ok! Leave!' They asked for our mobile phones and took them from us.

We were marched out, and Abe was in front of me. We all walked down the corridor, got into the elevator, down the floors and finally past reception. The people we passed on our journey and at reception looked at us in a way I had never been looked at before. I felt many emotions: hatred, shock, hurt, embarrassment, worry and I was absolutely mortified inside. I looked down at my feet trying to hide from the stares and judgments, but whilst my view was narrowed, I couldn't get away with the fact that my image would be etched into their memories forever. I was thankful that due to the lateness of the time, we did not pass any children on our dark journey to who knew where.

There were police cars outside the reception entrance, and I was placed in one and Abe in the other. There was no conversation whilst we drove, and I was scared, so very scared. I had no one, no one at all. I was handcuffed and guilty of something I did not know. I watched from the window the busyness of life outside of the car, and then at my handcuffed hands in front of me. The tightness made my wrists and hands ache. I could not believe the situation I now found myself in. To say I felt sorry for myself was an understatement. I had never been so scared, and this was the start of it. Why hadn't I bloody left when I had the chance? I should have learnt by now that doing the right thing just didn't bloody pay off always. I should have been quicker. If I had left five minutes earlier, I would have missed all of this. I just wanted to do it right, you know, for when Sah and I returned to Qatar. In that, we would be ok, and by being mature about it, well, it couldn't hurt could it to try and do the right thing? Or so I thought.

Prison hell

My prison hell began in solitary confinement, where I spent hours in a concrete box at my new destination in Dubai: Dubai Police Station Anti-Drugs Department. It was an absolute fucking nightmare.

Firstly, I was taken through doors and departments with the women, and then my fingerprints were taken with help from the officers, as I had never rolled my fingers in black ink before and didn't know how to do it. My mugshots were taken and to this day I do not know how they came out. I knew I was not supposed to smile, and I certainly was in no mood to, so I stood emotionless waiting for it to be over. I am sure my red eyes from my tears, my rosy flushed cheeks, damp hair from the heat and my sweat made me a model British citizen. Ye, right!

I was made to sit down outside an office, and I did not know where Abe was as we had been separated. There was a row of seats, and one of the female officers sat next to me. The handcuffs were still on as plain-clothed officers walked past. Some males were in the traditional whites, and some females were in their blacks. However, some females were in an olive-green uniform. It consisted of an olive-green shirt with a red band running under the left arm and looped through the left epaulette, a dark green beret with a golden badge depicting the logo of the police force, olive green trousers and black boots.

Obviously, the women officers wore a headscarf since this was Dubai. I could distinguish that the high-ranking officers wore a combination of a cap and rank badges on their collar, together with their light brown uniform. And in all honesty, the uniform was smart and suited the colour of the officers' skin.

I had no idea what was going to happen as I sat there. All the television programmes I had watched had not prepared me to comprehend the simplest ideology of what it meant to be held and locked up abroad. No one knew where I was. Yes, they knew I was in Dubai for a holiday and believed I was living it up and enjoying myself. I knew if they could see me now their hearts would break as mine was.

The door opened and a man who wore a white medical lab coat ushered me in with his right hand, so I assumed that he was a medical doctor. The female officer next to me got up and instructed me to with her right hand. I walked forward and into the office with the officer following behind. He sat down by his desk, which had files and pads of different papers, and it really wasn't organised. I sat down and the officer sat behind me.

The doctor smiled at me and said, 'Name?' He looked like a nice grandfather figure, and he had been the nicest person I had met since the apartment with his little smile.

I said my full name followed by my date of birth. I showed my passport, which I had in my bag, and then he instructed, 'Please now go to the bathroom and please give urine sample to be tested.'

I questioned, 'Can you please tell me why I am here? I haven't done anything wrong.'

He simply smiled and informed me with hand movements that he didn't know why I was there. He handed me the urine sample tube and stated, 'If you have done nothing wrong, you will be free. Now, please go.'

I pleaded and questioned, 'I have done nothing wrong here. Why am I here and why do you need a urine test? I don't understand.'

He explained, 'The urine test is to test if you have drugs in your system.' When he stated this, my heart sank because I knew there would be marijuana in my system from what I smoked back home in the garden. And I remembered what my brother had said whilst we sat there inhaling and exhaling, 'You need to be bloody careful that you don't get tested in Dubai smoking this here.'

I knew I had to be truthful immediately with the doctor and have the officer as a witness. So, I answered, not knowing what retribution this would cause. 'I will be honest with you. Before coming here for my holiday, I was in the UK. Whilst in the UK, I smoked marijuana. I smoked it every day and I know it will still be in my system. I have also been drinking vodka tonight and that will also be in my system.'

I looked behind me to ensure the officer had heard this declaration of truth. However, she looked at me blankly.

The doctor repeated whilst scribbling down something in Arabic. 'As I said, if you have done nothing wrong you will be free. Now please take the urine test. The officer will take you to the bathroom and please give a sample, then bring it back to me. Go!'

I took the sample and followed the officer. The bathroom wasn't far from the doctor's office. She led me into the bathroom and I asked her, 'How can I take a pee sample like this?' holding up my cuffs to show her.

She looked at me with her red lipstick as though I was nothing and told me, 'Turn around. Put there,' pointing to the sink.

I did, and then I turned around to face her. She unlocked my handcuffs, stood back, and turned around. I had had experience of peeing in a toilet in front of friends when I was a lot younger and toilets were sparse or busy in pubs or nightclubs, but never in a police station with a police officer who could listen to every drop. I had to really push to get what dribbles I could, knowing that it could potentially land me in major shit with the Dubai judicial service. While legal considerations are the same the world over, legal styles differ greatly from culture to culture, country to country. What is customary, appropriate, and acceptable in one country may be uncharacteristic or offensive in another, and whilst I knew of individuals who had been caught smoking weed in the UK, whilst I had been home, I had not driven as I didn't have a car. So, I theorised that I had not put anyone in danger whilst under the influence: so, to speak. It had simply been a method I used to numb myself from the reality I was in and make life more bearable. However, I didn't know what the hell to expect and was afraid as to how long I would be here and under what conditions. I was fucked, and unknown to them, my family was too. They just didn't know it yet.

After I had finished my business and had collected enough to complete the level needed for the sample, I turned the top to secure it. I pulled up my G-string, pulled down my dress and then coughed to alert the officer that I had completed what had been requested. She re-cuffed me, and we made our way back to the office. She held the sample and gave it to the doctor who was standing and waiting for it. The officer and I resat ourselves down, and the doctor then tested the urine in the tube. I couldn't see exactly the method he used, but after the test was completed, he then sat down and completed the paperwork. I was not told anything but instructed to leave by the officer. I knew my test would not come out clean; this I was sure of. I was polite to the doctor and said thank you and goodbye. I followed the officer down the corridor, through some doors and down some steps.

As I followed her, we passed cells. There were men in these cells, men who were Filipino, Indian, and Arabic. What I could see were individuals in each cell and even though my passing of them happened momentarily I could see their worn, stressed, and lost expressions. We turned right where there was a small table, radio, and a chair that sat opposite another cell. The officer opened the cell door and instructed me to go inside. The cell was then locked, and she motioned me to put my wrists through the gap where she proceeded to unlock my handcuffs. She then walked off to where I do not know, and I was left to massage my wrists and look around my 1.5m x 2.5m room with no windows, a bare concrete room with nothing on the floor and a toilet at the back with a sink. The door did not close correctly and was ajar, which was a necessity, as there was no natural light or window.

Initially, I paced the cell relentlessly, first walking back and forth along the length, in the middle and then the perimeter.

How long I did this for, I did not know as time had no meaning. I decided to sit down and lean against the right wall, so I would have a visual on anyone who came into this cell area. Slowly, I could feel my paranoia heightening, my heart rate increasing, and as I sat there, my mind started to do backflips. I relived everything, in no particular order, trying to make sense of it all whilst trying to calm myself down by holding myself and rocking.

There was no fresh air, and my throat was dry. I had not been given any water, so I made a polite effort to say on numerous occasions, 'Excuse me?' in the hope of attracting attention to no avail. I could hear echoes that screeched and travelled from others, possibly the men I had passed or those I had not seen and were not yet unmasked. The noises and words I did not understand and they did not make me feel any better. They were just a reminder that I was lost in unknown territory and alone.

I craved human contact while in my solitary confinement, and I am sure what had felt like hours was not that long. The vodka I had drunk previously was starting to wear off, and my need for a cigarette was wanting. I estimated that from my pickup to this cell must have been a couple of hours, but having no watch, clock, or window to look at left me anticipating that in the near future someone would come to see me. Then I heard faint footsteps that became louder until the other female officer from the apartment, and who I had last seen on my arrival at the police station, reappeared. She opened the cell door and looked me up and down. 'Come,' was her response to me as I looked at her, hoping this would be the end of this ordeal and that she had come to release me.

Was it hell!

I followed her through more corridors and doors until we came to another door and entered it. It was an office with desks and some male officers in jeans, shorts and t-shirts and others in their traditional dress. I was taken to a desk, told but not asked to sit down, and so I did. She then left me sitting there to face the wall and went to sit at a desk a few feet away.

As I looked around to see if I could make sense of where I was and what was going to happen, I looked in the direction of the female officer and asked politely, 'Excuse me, can I have some water to drink?' She heard me as she looked in my direction and then turned back to what she was doing.

One of the male officers looked at me, a large, rather obese one whose dish dash made him look pregnant, said something to a response of sniggers and laughter from others within the room, and a smile and smirk from the female.

As I continued to look around, only one male officer did not respond to the comment, but he left the room to shortly return with a bottle of water. 'Here,' he simply stated, and I smiled and thanked him before opening it and drinking it quickly, as I was so thirsty.

I could see that whilst he was Arabic, he was not a local. Firstly, he was very handsome, lighter coloured with a muscular frame and well-trimmed beard and moustache. He was not that far from me, and as he hadn't mocked me like the others, I hoped he could clarify what was going to happen to me. So, I questioned him, looking straight in his direction.

'Excuse me, but can you please tell me what is happening as no one else has told me. I do not know why I am here?' and with those words my eyes teared up, and I cried uncontrollably with tears following one another.

I could see that he saw my desperation, and he looked around before walking towards me and lowering himself to my eye level. 'I will tell you. Drugs have been found in your urine. You will be arrested, but you will go home. Listen to me. You will go home.'

He spoke softly and sympathetically before a comment was made by the female officer and he departed the room. She then got up and walked over to me with a file. She opened it and pulled a form out written in Arabic. 'Sign!' She pointed with a black pen before handing it to me.

I looked at the document and did not understand one word on it. I informed her calmly, questioning, 'What does this say? I do not understand it. What does it say? Please explain what is saying?'

I could see that this annoyed her as she turned to look at me irritated and repeated, 'Sign.'

I firmly said, 'I am not signing a document that I do not understand. No, I will not sign.' I placed the pen on the sheet. She said something for the other officers to hear, and then one proceeded to walk over to me. He was larger and what I could gather by observation was that he was another very obese Emirati.

He stated firmly, 'Sign this and you go home, ok? Sign! I try to help you.'

I looked up at him and said, 'Help me by telling me what this document says. I will not sign something that I do not understand.'

He then questioned, 'What is your name?' I quickly replied.

He continued, 'I tell you, Emily. Sign this and you will go home.'

I repeated, 'I am not going to sign something that I do not understand.'

The male officer and the female officer said something between themselves in Arabic and then English. They laughed when the man said, 'Good cop, bad cop.'

I looked at both with utter contempt and disgust. Then, the male officer said, 'You not going to sign, then you go back to the cell. We can do this for many many hours.' The female then smirked at me before returning me to the cell where she proceeded to lock me up. My denial to sign the document had consequences for me. I knew what they were doing was so wrong and couldn't believe that this was happening. I couldn't imagine this happening back home or any police station come to think about it. But it was another example of my naivety.

I don't know how long I sat cradling myself and trying to keep myself warm. It was cold in the cell, lonely, and I anticipated that I would be called back to the officers, as it was clear that they needed my signature. I came in and out of consciousness with pure exhaustion. I would sometimes stir as I was disturbed by the echoes that screeched and travelled through this part of the station I now found myself in. Echoes of pain, crying and banging travelled through this much I knew in my delirium, as it made me question whether I would be making these very noises if I did not sign the document they needed. Then, whilst lingering in and out of consciousness, the same female officer returned to take me through the process of trying to get me sign again. It was strange as she would speak nicely with the other officers in the room, but once she directed her attention to me, her complexion and heart changed to the blackness of the clothes she wore. I would repeat that I would not sign the document as I did not understand it. I even asked for a translator, to which I was told it would take too long. Then, she would change her strategy and smile at me, encouraging me to sign. I refused on numerous occasions and sat there exhausted and hunched, leaning on my elbows. I asked for water and was told to sign, and water would be given to me. I sat there thinking, believing, and knowing that this was just so wrong on so many levels - humanitarian, legal and ethical. 'Sign,' I was told and encouraged by another male officer, and I was tired as this had now been going on for what seemed like hours.

Then, the nice officer returned to the office who had given me water. He sat on the desk and asked, 'What is the problem? You will not sign? This is correct?' I looked at the male and female officer and wondered which one had called him back, and how desperate they were for me to sign on their shift.

I looked into his dark eyes and honestly stated, 'I do not know why I am here - why I was brought here. I had a urine test, and I was honest with the doctor and told him before coming here that I smoked marijuana when I was in the UK. I told him that I had drunk alcohol here and that I had not smoked any marijuana or taken any drugs, whilst I have been here in Dubai. The doctor told me that I would go home, and you also said I would go home. I don't understand why I am even here, why the police came to Abe's apartment and why I was arrested or why he was arrested. They keep asking me to sign this document and I can't even read Arabic. I have asked for a translator, and they have said it will take too long, and if I sign it, I will be home soon. I just don't understand. Where are my rights? A telephone call? Legal representation? What is happening?'

He looked at me perplexed, possibly at the amount of information I had given him and the questions I had asked. He explained, 'You have admitted to drinking alcohol without a license here in Dubai. You have admitted and tested positive for marijuana. You were staying with a man, and you are unmarried. It is prohibited. The laws are different here, and what you can do in your home country you cannot do here.' My heart sank, and he then picked up the document and translated it. 'Your name is Emily.' He continued that I had been arrested for having illegal drugs in my system.

I obviously protested restating, 'But I didn't smoke here. I smoked in the UK. I drank here yes, but it is not illegal to drink in hotels. I have not been drunk and disorderly… I just don't understand.'

'Listen to me. You will go home, but you are now in the Dubai legal system. You cannot argue with our laws. I believe that you did not smoke here, but the Dubai law states that if it is found to be in your system here, then you are guilty until proven innocent.'

I lowered my head and shook it. He then stated, 'You must sign this so that you can be in the legal system and be deported. You will go home soon, I promise.'

With tears starting to stream from my eyes, I answered, 'So, I must sign this document, a document that I do not understand and state I am guilty of smoking marijuana even though I didn't smoke it here, but because it is in my system, I am guilty for smoking it here. That is so wrong. God!'

He gave a half smile before stating, 'Yes,' before walking off and leaving the office.

I fell back in my chair and contemplated how to explain this to my mother and Sah, and how fucked I was. The cell lighting, combined with the sleep deprivation and anxiety I felt, had left me shaking and scared. With the heaviest of hearts, I realised that my signature could condemn me to who knows what and for how long. It was obvious that anyone who commits an illegal act and is condemned legally, after completing the length of their sentence, is left to go home, but the officer had made me feel that I could go home now if I signed it. I knew the law on drugs in the Middle East was far stricter than in the UK, and if I was guilty even though I didn't smoke the marijuana here, but in the UK, I was still guilty because the drug was in my system. I was damned if I did, and truly fucking damned if I didn't. With the greatest of hesitations, I picked up the pen and stared to the place where they had wanted me so badly to sign. And so, I did it. I sank deeper into my chair, shoulders arched as though an angel had lost its wings. I knew I had lost my wings and would not be able to fly away to the direction of my loved ones. I signed it, and with that, my tears started to roll fiercely and uncontrollably. I wiped them away with my sleeve and then tried to compose myself as I didn't want those bastards and that bitch to see me so vulnerable, and furthermore, those tears they may have viewed as being tears of guilt, and I just couldn't have that.

It was some minutes before I had composed my breathing when I turned around to face the officer, or aptly named, 'Bitch,' because that is how she had treated me and asked, 'Excuse me?' to get her attention.

She turned, and her facial expression referenced a 'WHAT?' and this was indeed followed by a verbal one.

I replied empathetically, 'I have signed the document.'

In her harsh tone, she simply said, 'You sign?' to which I nodded.

She got up and walked towards me and looked over my shoulder and a chill ran through me, with a lightbulb moment and flash that I needed to state on the document that I did not understand the document as I do not speak/read Arabic, and that I was told to. I wrote this down in the best writing I could pen together, took a deep breath, and sat back from my upright position when I put my pen down. She grabbed the document and went back to her desk, put it down and then returned to me.

She said, 'Come,' and motioned me to come with her.

I looked up at her and asked, 'Can you please tell me what is happening? I don't understand?'

She looked at me sternly and simply confirmed, 'You arrested. You guilty. You go to court.'

My heart started to pound, and I shockingly asked with my mouth wide open, 'Arrested for what specifically?' needing confirmation that this wasn't a nightmare, and this was indeed my reality for the 20th time.

In her long drawl, she said, 'You guilty of drugs. You go to court and have four years.'

'Have four years of what?' I pleaded.

'Jail.'

I shuddered. I raised my right index finger to my lip, looked up directly into her eyes and aggressively said, 'Four years in jail for doing nothing in Dubai? My guilt was within the UK, as I have stated from the very beginning.'

She nodded her head and shrugged, 'You sign. You guilty'. I could see that this whole exercise was annoying to her, whilst devastating to me. I got up, held onto the desk, breathed, and repeated to myself, 'Four years, four years, four years,' with me simply ending it with, 'Jesus Christ!'

She escorted me back to my cell, and before going in, I asked her for a blanket and for some water. She didn't answer me and locked me up the same as she had previously. I stood there cowering in a fixed fashion. I questioned myself repeating, 'What have I fucking done, Christ?' and I descended into turmoil with flashes of Sah and my mother. My heart pounded with the severity of being locked up for four years for getting high in the UK, and for being in the company of Abe. How could this have possibly happened? Why hadn't I left when Mo told me what was about to happen? Why had I wanted to do it the right way, by communicating with Abe even after what had bloody transpired the night before? I was so angry and disappointed with myself.

I reminisced, and the only thing I wanted to do, whilst I cried, was to hold my daughter tightly, kiss her cheek and gently tell her that everything was going to be alright. My daughter! And my poor mother, a mother whose heart would break even more after the death of my father, her husband. What had I fucking done?

It was a while until the female office returned with a blanket, so she obviously didn't rush. I took it from her and the water she held in her other hand. I thanked her and turned walking to the far left of the cell, crouched down until my arms were cradling my lower legs and fell on to the blanket that I had laid on the cold concrete floor. The blanket was old and worn, but I was in no mood to critique. I shakily opened the water, sipped some to quench my throat, and lay down. Tears wept until I fell asleep, a deep sleep, for some time.

Where I went to, I don't know, but I was to be awoken by the arrival of another cellmate who was accompanied by a new police officer. But what made this new inmate interesting was that she was an Emirati, but a strange-looking white Emirati, who whilst personified the dress and arrogance of a local rich

Emirati, her complexion was a pale grey with the facial features of European descent with a distinguished bone structure and greyish-blue eyes. And when she spoke in Arabic, her tone, the authority she portrayed, and her arrogance personified someone from a high-ranking rich family. She was a young twenty-something Emirati and when she entered the cell and looked around, it was as though she was taking in visually a great Italian masterpiece that adorned every inch and corner of this concrete room. However, when she looked at me, I believe she took in every freckle I had on my face. I looked up at her and then swiftly moved my body up and around to face her, and said a tired, 'Hello.'

For the next 10 minutes we discussed how she had been arrested whilst driving under the influence of coke (the kind you smell and don't drink) and that she had been arrested. She said it so matter of fact as though it was normal, and the officer who had brought her in never left but positioned herself on a chair and was knitting. The officer looked pregnant, but you could never really tell over here as some were just simply overweight. The officer would interrupt and say something back to her making me question that her listening skills and understanding of English were far better than her spoken English. I would ask for a translation and basically, she was the daughter of a rich Emirati man and an American ex-air hostess mother. They were now divorced, she lived with her mother and when her mother would tell her father, by which time she believed he would now know, his lawyers would be trying to get her out. So, she was not worried about her situation, and she thought she deserved to be here as she was guilty. I explained my story and she harshly couldn't understand why I was emotional and crying about possibly being locked up and away from my daughter for four years of her life for something I did in the UK.

She looked at me and said, 'Why are you crying? You are guilty and maybe have six months.' She then said something to the officer, and they conversed, and she then reconfirmed, 'Yes, you will go to court because you have signed and admitted it. You will have to get a lawyer to represent you. Then maybe you will be out in six months and deported back to the UK.'

I just sank even deeper. I was guilty and that was it. It didn't seem to matter that I had done it in the UK, but the drinking without a license and being with Abe was also a no no. Thankfully, that was not written on the document I signed.

I went back to lean against the cold side of the wall and held my old, worn, pale blanket to my shoulders. As I listened to the drool of the Emirati American, it started to grate on me, and her arrogance and falseness of laughter irritated me to the point I started to wish her to shut up, shut up, shut up. When she did, I felt relief, but it wasn't for long before it started again, and I would glance over to her, and it would build and get stronger this urge and need for her to shut up.

It wasn't long until another female officer came and conversed with the pregnant officer who smiled now and again at the other opposite me. It was so transparent how we were both treated differently. It was condemnation for me and admiration for American Coke Emirati. She looked at me with distaste in her mouth, and her eyes narrowed because of it. The Emirati American got up and was all polite to the new officer with nodding and graciousness. She then left the cell. I got up and asked her what was going on and she simply answered that she was being taken to an Emirati jail, with just locals in it, where she would wait for her father's lawyers to get her out. She knew she wouldn't be in for long as it would be of great embarrassment for him to have her locked up, so he would get her out.

I didn't know if this had been her experience of the legal system previously, but she made me feel as though she was going to a jail that was deluxe compared to the other jails that us mere non-rich, non-Arab minions would frequent, inhabit, and live. Further, she illustrated, but not specifically, that her father's wealth would get her out and that possibly one could buy the legal system with the possibility of freedom.

She left without expression and emotion, someone so young who had developed a hard veil of arrogance and superiority. She did comment, 'I hope you go home,' as she walked off with regal elegance.

And I found myself alone again with only the company of the police officer who rested and closed her eyes frequently as the hours passed. I too slipped in and out of consciousness as my exhaustion, irrational and desperate emotions toiled and made me wake up with flowing tears, knowing where I was. I just wanted it all to be alright and for me to be back with Sah, but it wasn't going to be, was it? I could not see her, feel her, or even speak to her, nor my mother.

I couldn't speak to anyone and even when I stirred and asked the officer if I could make a telephone call, I was simply told disapprovingly, 'Not allowed.'

I returned to my hell and waited for it to continue until the end. The hours passed and she had snacks that she nibbled. I had not been given any food whatsoever, not that I was hungry. My adrenaline was fuelling me and building me up for something, but what that something was, I just didn't know or understand. But I still clung and prayed that someone would come and tell me that I was going home, but no one came for me. My time was filled with lying down and trying to get comfy in a foetal position and sleep my time away. I did purposely get up at one stage to go to the toilet to investigate a wet feeling I had below.

I then went and disturbed the officer, asked her for a sanitary towel and explained physically with my hands how I was bleeding with actions of something coming out quickly and violently from my vaginal area. Initially, she looked at me as though I was rather a wee bit crazy, but she soon realised what I was on about, after I then went to the toilet to get some tissue and acted my interpretation of putting the paper in my knickers. She said there were none there and that she would get some for me after her shift and bring them in tomorrow. For the two days that followed, I had menstruated and had had to rely on cheap tissue paper and sodden knickers, stained, dried, stained with remnants of blood, and bits and pieces of tissue. I had asked on numerous occasions for sanitary towels, as I don't use Tampax due to a friend's hygiene in the early 2000s.

We were at the local disco, a rather shit old shed of a building to be honest, where we all thought we were cool in our early twenties and 'It.' I had proceeded to go to the toilets with my friend and for name's sake let us call her Dirty Bitch. Well,

Dirty Bitch educated me within a minute of what an unhygienic bloodied hand and fingers looked like due to menstruating. Whilst we shared the toilet, she literally pulled out a Tampax, flushed it down the toilet and then inserted another Tampax with her finger. And I am not talking posh Tampax with a push lever. Well, she didn't wash her hands, hand or fingers, and they were left blood-stained. All night I watched each sip of her alcopop bottle assisted by a couple of blood-stained fingers. There and then I thought that this method was disgusting, unhygienic and not called for because since nursery we had both been taught how to wash our hands after toileting.

Sadly, the officers here always forgot to lend, well in honesty, to give me what I had always taken for granted, a simple sanitary towel or what I called them, 'ST's.' To no avail, after repeated requests, did I receive one. There were always excuses. I suppose on reflection, to some artists, the stains would have been an expression of something and would have amassed an astronomical cheque to artistic fools. However, to me, I felt ashamed, dirty, and very damp continuously. It was another reminder that I had lost my freedom and rights not even as a person, but as a woman. There is no need in this time for any woman to have to go without sanitary materials. I had always taken STs for granted, and I had never experienced a sanitary towel-less period, to be honest. I firmly believe unless you experience something you have no understanding, but only to show empathy with such statements as, 'I am sorry,' or, 'I feel for you.' You have no emotional pain or distress, but a simple fleeting moment of thought on the matter. Well, this bloody time in history was literally etched onto my very canvas, and it was degrading to me.

I would attempt to wash myself and wipe away the matted toilet paper and blood from my pubic and anal regions. The blood had colourfully slipped down my legs making a rainbow effect of dark plush reds. And by the end of my period, my knickers were literally like cardboard. It was the dirtiest I had ever felt since being a baby with a dirty, wet, and shitty nappy, not that I possibly remember it, but I think you get the meaning.

Another female inmate arrived suddenly, and without notification, on what day and at what time I could not tell you. She was a young, very thin Dutch girl in her late teens or early twenties. She looked like a hippie with her colourful, baggy clothes and her piercings on her ears, nose, and eyebrow and where else I really did not want to imagine. Her hairstyle was interesting in that the sides were shaved and on the top of her head was a bush of thick straight blonde hair that stayed in position when she brushed it back with her fingers. I got to know her well from her short stay with me, which amassed to a couple of hours. Her American English was brilliant. I discovered her story and the circumstances of her arrival with me. She lived with her Dutch family in Dubai and had been driving when she had been pulled over by the police. She was tested for drink driving, for which she was guilty, but they also found marijuana on her. So, they tested her for drugs, and not surprisingly, she was found guilty. She had already served over a year after being moved from Abu Dhabi to Dubai to cells like this and full-blown prisons. She had stated that her family had moved back to Amsterdam, so visits were infrequent. She stated that the court system was a 'Fucking mess,' her words, not mine. She said that she was looking at four years for her case. I questioned why wasn't the Dutch Foreign Embassy helping and she confirmed, 'They have no power. They cannot do anything. However, if my family were important or rich, then possibly it would be a different story.'

She obviously wanted to know about me, and I honestly told her the truth. When I got emotional, she would put her arm around my shoulder and smile saying, 'You have nothing to worry about. You were just unlucky: wrong place, wrong time. You will be fine and home in a couple of months.'

I lowered my head and repeated questioning, 'A couple of months?'

'Yes, a couple of months and you will be home with your daughter. You must push everything you know legally out of the window from your country and realise that this is the Middle fucking East. Their law is foreign fuck.'

We both slouched back against the wall. We exchanged stories of our lives to the time we both got arrested and laughed at each other's experience. Hell, we had to laugh, or we would both wail. But it was a comfort to have her close to me even though it was for a short time, a few hours, and as quickly as she came, she was gone. She also advised me that I would need legal representation to get me out quicker, explained the different processes I would go through from leaving this hellhole to go to another one, a detention centre in Dubai. Here I would be held during my court proceedings until I would either be given four years, six months or released and deported. She had met others during her year in confinement and guessed that I would have six months for a drug offence. This knowledge crushed me more. I don't know whatever happened to her or where she went. I have returned to the Netherlands a few times over the past years, and for all I know I may have walked past her. But wherever she is, I hope that she is happy and healthy, and most importantly, free. That is what I hope for.

She was the last visitor I had in my cell. Police officers would sit at their desk and do their duty of just sitting there. Food would be delivered, but it was basic. Breakfast consisted of a banana and a small yogurt, whilst lunch and dinner consisted of rice that had been cooked with meat. The meat had fallen off the bones and what amount of meat was originally on the bones is very questionable, but the bones were always evident within the stodgy composite. A bottle of water was always given to wash it down, with a gulp, to ensure that the food made contact with the stomach. The cooked food would ensure anyone had their basic rights met, and to ensure survival. I was lucky in a way that I was bleeding, as the blood worked like a constipation gel and allowed me to basically have a shit. Without it, I would undoubtedly have had a very sore bum trying to push my constipated stools out, whether in bullet form or sausage style. It was this drastic change to my new diet that afflicted me with bloating, accompanied by the lack of exercise or ability to walk in my cell that could have possibly otherwise been a good detox and weight loss diet. However, I had to force feed the shit down my gullet, because that is what it was, shit. Shit I wouldn't give to my dog or any dog. This shows how bad it was, because the female officers never had some as a perk of their job, but they would choose to come in with their packed lunches or bags of fries and burgers from fast food houses. That was the only time that a fragrant mouth-watering smell resonated throughout my cell. Other times, I could smell smoke from cigarettes. The smell would travel from the corridor, and I believe it was helped by having a door open that created a suction or funnel. With the hot warm air from outside hitting the air conditioning cold air, I theorised that it helped the smell of the smoke travel, allowed me to smell it and sniff it in the air. Conversation was a no go. I would question numerous times daily, to the officer's dismay, what was happening: could I call someone, when would I be leaving, with such replies as, 'Quiet!' 'Shh!' 'When God wills!' 'I don't know!' followed by silence. I had no answers to any of my questions, or further explanation as to how long this whole sordid affair would last.

The sleep continued, as I was in and out of sleep because there was nothing for me to do. I would have bouts of movement by walking the internal perimeter of the cell and thought of nothing else other than my absolute freedom. I focussed on Sah, and I could see her image so clearly, hear her sweet innocent little girlie voice and remember her beautiful fresh, clean baby lotion smell. How I loved her with all my heart and missed her with each breath. When I curled up on the floor to get comfy, I would imagine her held in my arms and curled up with me, smelling her very being, whilst watching her fall asleep with always a smile. Words alone could not and would not encompass the meaning of what she meant to me. I was no longer whole and ached so badly. I had always known that I loved her from the day that I pushed her out like a mooing cow. And now, I was lost without her. Alone. She had taken my heart, and I would fight for her until my final breath. I knew I had to focus and return from my moments of madness, but it was a vicious circle. No one was telling me anything other than I would be going home. No definite date was given and no information. Hell, I wasn't even allowed to make a phone call which in all television programmes and films was customary, or so I bloody thought.

At moments and believe me, there were way too many to recount, tears would well up and escape freely when I least expected it. I let them roll off my cheeks, down my neck and onto my arms. I wiped them, rubbing them into my skin as I had not bathed or washed properly in what seemed like days. I had not brushed my teeth also, so I used my fingers to scrape the plaque from my teeth and gargled with water. I knew I smelled, as every time my arms opened, or I lifted them, the smell exuded through the pores of my skin, in profuse quantities as a reaction to the heat. I had tried to wash my armpits and under my breasts with water in the small, once white sink, which was now a grey, mildewed dribbling wreck and dry myself on the plain blanket whose invisible bacterial liquid stains I could only just imagine, as I saw some crispy rough patches on the fabric. To say that I felt demoralised and degraded was yet another understatement. In all my years, I had had the facilities for washing and bathing myself with clean water and toiletries, flannels, and towels with the luxury of clean clothing. Hell, even when camping, whether in a tent or a caravan, these facilities were met. But, to have a cardboard G-string, which I couldn't really turn inside out, was simply mentally and physically demoralising. I did think of taking them off and stashing them somewhere, but I couldn't find anywhere to stash them freely. Hell, I was in jail, there was a camera covering the area I was in, and there were alternate female officers observing me. I had nothing but concrete, metal bars and an old manky blanket.

So, I continued waiting and repeatedly asking the same logical questions to whoever was on duty and waited to be served the disgusting garbage that they called edible food. The noise of pure emotion continued from the unknown men in the near cells, but they didn't affect me as much as they had initially. I was shocked at how quickly I had become conditioned to my surroundings. I questioned whether this was the same for all men and women, and animals alike that found themselves encaged, both rightly and wrongly, by the hands of others. I questioned whether poor defenceless animals who are captured, caged, transported to an alien and foreign habitat for conservation or personal ownership whether they experienced the same initial and then continuous moments of loss for the life that was once, hysteria, the uncontrollable physical tears and a force-fed diet which fed the individual purely for survival and existence? Their true nature, freedom, liberty, and choice had and was taken away from them.

I had time to think, reflect and question myself being the highly intelligent creature that I was, or so I thought I was. However, it was the loneliness and loss of control that I found the hardest. The only sincere conversation I had was with my inner self, dialogue spoken privately in my own head and sometimes out aloud, until the odd strange and questionable glare from the officer on duty made me socially aware of my first stages of madness. However, I knew they judged me as I sensed it from my first initial contact with each of them, as I could physically see their disgust and disapproval of me in their eyes, as they looked me up and down. They didn't see me, the young woman in front of them. They saw me as a white European woman who was guilty and jailed for it. I was different to them in everything I was - looks, colour, race, class, dress, and now smell. I could not understand the mentality of the female officers I had met during my time here, and sincerely hoped that I had just been unlucky in meeting a marginal selection of the worst unprofessional female officers working within this section of the Dubai Police Force. Time would tell, I supposed.

But I questioned where the hell the professionalism was. Throughout my life and work history, I knew that a simple smile and call it kindness or politeness went a long way. I didn't judge what someone looked like, where they came from, how they spoke, dressed, and ate. I attributed this to the fact of my upbringing, my education, my travelling, living abroad and my belief that you can never judge a book by its cover. Or was their difference cultural or religious? I did not know the answer, I just knew within me that what I had witnessed from them, so far, was not professional or kind. I just couldn't understand why they couldn't see that I was made of flesh and bones, blood, and breath, with a need for love and friendship. I was just like anyone else, or so I had assumed.

I knew that my mental health had been affected from this bloody ordeal and that my strong inner strength, which I had always known and been a part of me, had started to fade away. When you're in a prison cell nobody speaks to you, nor answers your calls and enquiries. I had never felt like that in my life, it was more than frustration, it was the knowing that I was no-one. No-one with any power to do the simplest things: to leave one room to go to another to get something as simple as a glass of water, to call someone - hell anyone. I was no-one and had nothing here.

Now I am really fucked!

I happened to be sitting upright in my cold, bare cell when the officer sitting at the desk had a telephone call. It was short and sweet, and whilst I didn't understand one word, and I might as well have been listening to a conversation between the Teletubbies, I observed as there was nothing else for me to do quite honestly. The conversation ended just as quickly as it had started, and it was just nice to hear someone talking, even if the conversation had single answers. Then, from nowhere, as I was minding my own business, the officer confirmed, 'You go.'

Now, we were not facing one another as I was sat against a wall looking directly at the opposite wall, so I obviously did not see her facial expression from the words she spoke. I initially questioned if I had indeed heard her correctly, so perplexed I questioned, 'Excuse me, did you say, 'You go?' looking directly at her to ascertain if this was real and happening, finally? She looked up from the desk, put down her pen that made her look busy and looked directly at me dismissively as if to say, 'Really?'

She sighed, shook her head from side to side and opened her arms stating in a lethargic voice, 'You go.'

My mouth opened and after three seconds, I confirmed, 'I am going?' My eyes were like saucers. I jumped up and quickly walked to the cell bars and held on to them, one in each hand. After being caged up I just wanted to be out of this hell, to breathe fresh air, have the sunshine on my face, to feel the hand of God touch me from the top of my head and to feel this warmth slowly infiltrate throughout my body, down to the tips of my fingers and toes. I wanted to run, run like I had never run before to get to the airport and wait hours on end, if need be, to get on a plane out of this hellhole, to get home to the safety of the UK, and the love of my daughter and mother. I had more questions as my forehead wrinkled. 'So, I am going home? To the UK?' I no longer had her gaze as she had returned to look busy in her job by holding her pen.

She didn't even look up when answering me. 'You go. Not to UK. Bur Dubai.'

I scrunched my forehead and questioned 'Bur Dubai?' as I simply had no understanding as to what or where this place was. 'What is Bur Dubai?' She didn't answer. In a higher tone, I repeated, 'Excuse me, what is Bur Dubai?' This sigh was longer as she turned to face me with her eyebrows more arched. I knew that these simple and short questions I was asking her were starting to become taxing for the hard worker who simply sat at her desk. Her tone was deeper and short, 'Police Station!' I gathered she thought I knew exactly the institution she was speaking of. Like hell! How would I? My grip relaxed on the bars I held, and I sighed with relief and despair. I was leaving, this was for sure, and leaving to go to Bur Dubai Police Station, which I kind of guessed was also in Dubai. Was it the main police station in Dubai? Possibly? Or was it the start of my release process? This was also a possibility. Questions started to swirl in all directions. 'Excuse me, when will I be leaving?' There was no response, and this frustrated me so much. She knew I was a foreigner in her country and that my understanding of the legal processes would be zilch. I just couldn't understand her mean, arrogant and superior persona.

In her own time, she did respond. 'You go later. Now ...' and with that, she ushered with her left hand for me to go by waving it in my direction, as though I was an annoying and pestering fly. I sighed, released my grip from the cold iron bars and turned away from her to walk back to the spot I had just stepped away from. I re-sat myself down and bowed my head, holding my hands on my bent knees. I did not know how long I had left here, but I was, to be honest, nervous of what would happen next. Nerves twirled in my stomach and boiled over in moments of excitement at the pure thought of getting the hell out of this shithole, with moments of sheer panic and fear of what the hell would happen next. So, I sat there willing for the time to come when I would leave.

From when I was told to stand and place my arms out straight by the female officer, time flew fast. My hands were cuffed once again, and the uncomfortable, heavy constraint ached on my wrists once more. A male officer stood behind her watching every move, as though he would pounce on me if I became aggressive with contempt. It was he who had swaggered in confidently and suggestively, as he handed her restraints to put on me. He was all in his whites and she was in all her blacks. I chuckled to myself at what a pretty pair they made. I followed them through the doors, the corridors and re-walked my steps. I looked down at the floor as I really didn't want to see what was going on around me or look at the faces I may pass along the way. I had a very good memory, and I didn't want to add unknown faces with unknown stories to my imagination. We got to the reception area after passing security doors, where I had to sign a document for the release of my travel bag and mobile phone, purse, and passport, which was in a plastic see-through jiffy bag. I was then escorted to a car that was parked outside.

As the door to the outside opened, the heat and the sun was a complete shock to my system. The heat went straight to my chest and heated my lungs making them dry, whilst the sun pierced my eyes, making them close to accommodate the light that penetrated them. It took me a second or two to adapt to my surroundings physically and consciously. I slowly got into the waiting car that the female officer stood by with the door ajar. The male officer oversaw my bag, and the female had the jiffy bag with my mobile phone, purse and passport. Whilst he placed the bag in the boot, the female positioned herself in front of me. She turned around to face me and unlocked my handcuffs once I was sat quietly. She then proceeded to give me the contents of the jiffy bag, as I buckled my seatbelt. I grabbed it, knowing that my mobile was in it. After days of wanting and willing so much to send word home of what had happened, where I was and how I needed help, well let's just say that I was desperate, and I had the possible answer in my hands.

The male officer got into the undercover white police car, buckled up before starting the car and driving off into the direction of Bur Dubai. I did not know whether the transfer time to this new destination would be five minutes or longer, so I knew I had to act quickly to get word back home of what the hell was going on. I opened my bag, switched the mobile phone on and proceeded to turn on my mobile phone, waiting patiently for it to load up. I tapped my right knee whilst I held the phone in my left hand. It loaded, and I quickly, without hesitation, dialled the international code, local code, and telephone number of my mother's home address. 'Bleep, bleep, bleep,' it rung, and I waited anxiously while the ring continued. I softly stated, 'Come on, Mammy, answer the bloody phone.'

I willed this desperately, then suddenly a familiar, kind, and loving voice sweetly answered, 'Hello.'

I closed my eyes and quickly thanked God that she had answered as I tried to control my breathing whilst holding the phone tightly to my right hand. High pitched, I squeaked, 'Mammy?' to which a familiar voice answered, 'Emily, how are you? I have been thinking about you.'

My heart jumped a beat with this warmth and love I had always known, but at that exact moment, I felt it and I had a loving warmth feeling flow over me. I knew I had to get as much information over as quickly as possible, as I didn't know when the officers would take my phone from me again for the second time. So, I ensured that the next sentences would be spoken with a clear and precise accent, as I could not allow for any error to be made. I took a deep breath before starting, as I knew the next couple of minutes and sentences spoken could place a shadow on my name in the eyes of those who I loved the most. A shadow of disappointment in the knowledge that I had been arrested and locked up, with the possibility of a six month or four year incarceration.

'Listen, Mammy, listen carefully. I need to speak to Rob now, so please, Mammy, go and get him and bring him to the phone now, Mammy.'

She was puzzled and simply asked, 'What? Your brother? He is in the shower bleaching his hair.'

'Listen, Mammy. Please just get him. I have been locked up for days, I think, and this is the first time I have had my phone. Mammy, please get him. I don't know how long I have.' By now, the pitches of our conversations were rising in tone as they continued. 'What do you mean that you have been locked up for three days?'

'Mammy, get Rob now! Ok?'

Without any hesitation, I heard the echo of the phone being put down and my mother walking towards the stairs, shouting up to my brother. There was no reply, then I heard her steps go all the way up the stairs, then her knock, knock, knock on the door and shout, 'Rob, come now.'

I heard him moan, 'What? I am having a shower.' I am sure the next seconds encompassed him getting out of the shower, putting a towel on, and coming downstairs to the phone. An annoyed brother finally answered roughly, 'What's bloody happened? Mammy said you have been locked up for three days.'

I found myself taking a deep breath as I knew the clock was ticking. 'Rob, listen carefully. I have been arrested for having marijuana in my system, and I have been locked up for three days, I think? I phoned/spoke to you last on the day I was taken. This is the first time that I have been able to phone. They are taking me to Bur Dubai, the main police station, I think. I am not too sure.'

A soft reply stated, 'Jesus, Emily. What the hell happened?'

'Listen, I honestly don't know how much time I have. Police came to Abe's apartment, and we were both taken away and locked up. I don't know what the hell is going on. They have made me sign documents that I didn't understand. They were all in bloody Arabic, but when they tested my urine, it came back positive, Rob.'

His response now was more aggressive, 'Oh, I bloody told you to be careful before you went.'

'I know. I was honest and told them that I smoked it in the UK before coming here, but they say it doesn't matter. I don't understand.'

'Em, their law is so different from what we know and understand.'

'Believe me, I am finding that out, Rob.'

'Are they treating you well, Emily?' he asked.

'It is what it is, Rob.'

'What do you need me to do?'

'Rob, explain to Mammy what has happened and tell her to try and not to worry. I also need you to contact the British Foreign Office and let them know that I am here and going to be in Bur Dubai.'

'Ok, let me make a note of this. I still have bleach in my hair as I haven't washed it out properly.'

'Rob, how is Sah?' This was the first time I had asked about her since phoning, and I didn't feel guilty for it as I knew she was in the best hands, other than mine, and letting my family know where I was, was an immediate necessity before the conversation died at any time.

He pacified me by informing me, 'She is fine. Don't worry about her. She's happy, and I am playing with her.'

I now started to become emotional, and I could feel the tears of my eyes well up, and my throat become lumpy. 'But I do. I do worry for her. They are saying that I could have six months or four years Rob. Six months or four bloody years for doing something in the UK. Hell, I would simply have a warning back home. It's a bloody mess. I have never been without her. I miss her so much. And Mammy? What the hell is this going to do to Mammy? What the hell have I done?'

'Listen, I will contact the British Embassy as soon as I get off the phone from you. What about Abe? Where is he, and can't he help you?"

'If you could let the embassy know, then maybe they can do something this end. In regard to Abe, I think I am here because of him. They came to the apartment to get him. I don't think they expected me there. I just don't know what happened, or what is happening. Nobody explains or tells me anything really. I am scared, Rob; I am really scared.'

I knew this statement would resonate with my brother, as I had never spoken these words before. My brother had never seen me scared or heard the words uttered from my mouth in all the time he had been lucky, or unlucky enough, to be my brother.

'I will do what I can from this end. Just stay strong.'

'I am trying, but it is bloody hard.'

And as I ended that sentence, the woman turned and stated firmly, 'Finish.'

I looked down and a large tear fell. 'Rob, they are saying I have to finish.'

'Well, what's happening?'

'They are driving me to Bur Dubai. I think I was three days in the other place they kept me. I asked them so many times to call someone, but they wouldn't let me, Rob. I did try.'

He interrupted me with, 'Listen, Sah is here now. Do you want to speak to her?'

My body trembled and my voice cracked as I confirmed, 'Of course I want to speak to her.'

'Ok, hold on.' I could hear the receiver move hands and Rob softly say, 'Ok? Good. Now speak to Mammy.'

I heard her sweet breath and I felt close to her.

I started, 'Hello Cariad. How are you, sweetheart? You ok?'

A little giggle followed. 'Mammy. I miss you. When coming home?'

'I am in Dubai, sweetie. And I miss you more than you know. I hope you are being a good girl?'

And with that last question, I said it in a teasing way, a way I spoke to her when I was messing around with her, knowing that I was trying to catch her out innocently.

She answered, 'Yes!' giggling.

Then I proclaimed, 'I love, love, love you.'

And she sweetly replied, 'I love, love you, Mammy.'

Tears of love wept uncontrollably, and as I looked up, the female police officer looked directly into my eyes and firmly stated, 'Finish.'

My eyes lowered, and I softly said, 'Listen, Mammy has to go now. I love, love, love you, and you be a good girl for Mam and Uncle Rob, ok?'

'Ok, Mammy.' With that, she was gone.

My brother returned to the phone and questioned, 'Emily?'

'Ye, I am still here, but I have to go now. The officer has told me to finish.'

'Ok.'

There was silence for two seconds when I knew I had to be strong emotionally, as I didn't want to leave anyone in a panic. 'Right, I will try to call again when I can, and they let me. Put Mammy back on the phone for me to say goodbye.'

'Mammy, Em's here. You take care of yourself. We will get this sorted, don't worry. Bye Emily.'

Rob had gone, and my mother had returned. I knew by her breathing that she was stressed and panicked. 'Emily?'

'Hi, Mammy. I am so sorry, Mammy. I didn't do anything wrong,' I confirmed.

'Shh now. Don't worry. Just look after yourself. Rob will fill me in on things.'

'Mammy, can you please look after Sah for me. I don't know how long this is going to take, but I don't think I will be home on the ticket I booked.'

'Don't you worry about her. She is fine. Just concentrate on trying to get back here.' My heart rate was increasing and my breathing was affected as I tried to say confidently, 'Ok, Mammy.'

She tried to calm me, 'Shh now. Try not to upset yourself. You will be fine. Don't worry. Be strong.'

I whimpered, 'Ok, Mammy. I will try to call you as soon as they let me again, Mammy. I love you.'

'I love you.' Her words were truthful and honest. The conversation ended with a simple and sorrowful 'Bye.'

I tightly closed my eyes to drain the tears before I turned the red button off. The voices of my heart and home were gone. I was alone again. Totally alone. The female officer looked happy as she took the phone from me as it rested in my hand. I sat back, and the weight of my shoulders, back, hips and buttocks sank into the chair. I looked out and gathered, by the sun setting, that it was in the late afternoon or heading into the evening.

Bur F**king Dubai

As I looked out of the car window on my journey to my possible new home, I compared the absurd stark contrast with the surrounding opulence of wealth that I now witnessed after departing my cell. I could see it everywhere from the design and structure of the buildings, roads, decorated pavements and parks with beautiful flowering beds, strong healthy trees and by the expensive cars that passed. Cars I presumed that were worth more than I earned in a couple of years. I also witnessed families as they walked with their maids in tow in their uniforms, happy and so naive just as I had been once, of the true legal nature of Dubai.

As we travelled on the busy road, we suddenly veered off the roundabout and started to follow a road, a road that would eventually take me to the entrance of the police station, Bur Dubai. What I could initially see was that it was a massive compound with surrounding walls that enclosed numerous buildings.

We parked the car in front of the building, and I was released from the back seat by the female. The male proceeded to get my bag from the boot, whilst the female took my jiffy bag from me and inserted my mobile phone back into it. I followed them into the building, and whilst they had a discussion with the males at reception, I stood there, pathetically, shoulders slumped and lower lip protruding as my hands were in handcuffs.

The female then took my bag in such a feminine manner from the officer that I thought to myself, *nothing could possibly make you more attractive, love, and how bloody desperate are you to want something like that?* I was then instructed by her to follow with a 'Come!'

It was like deja vu all over again, walking through corridors that were connected by many doors, doors that looked more like office doors as there were no bars on them. Then, we came to a stair at the end of the corridor, stairs that went up and went down beneath to possibly a cellar. I expected to follow the stairs upwards, but the officer started to descend. I stopped with a puzzled and questioning face before the descent, and this had alerted the female, so she in turn turned around and also reiterated with a puzzled frown, 'Come!' Inside, I felt deep trepidation and such a bad, dark feeling. Even though there were lights that followed the steps down, the stairs seemed to decrease into a path of darkness with a foreboding warning. I knew I had to keep walking ahead of me, as each step closer to the unknown was a step closer to my freedom, but to say I was shitting myself was an understatement.

I followed her down, one step at a time, whilst holding onto the bannister as I still had handcuffs on and really didn't need this holiday from hell facilitated with a trip to an Emirati bloody hospital. We arrived at the bottom and there were two female officers sitting directly opposite the end of the stairs, dressed head to toe in their uniforms. They looked me up and down as I slouched my shoulders, and as they looked at every inch of me, I returned the favour and looked at every inch of them. Nothing positive could be said other than they wore nice coloured lipsticks, the obese one had a nice, luscious brown on her big pouty lips, whilst her amigo and sister bitch had a bright red on her slimline and more western lips. The three of them had a conversation and then my leader down the stairs instructed me to sit. We both pulled out the chairs from the desk and she placed my bag on the floor. She then proceeded to unlock my handcuffs with her key that she had in her pockets and put my bag and its contents on the desk. As I massaged my wrists to relax them, I wanted to get acquainted with my bearings and was I in for a bloody shock.

I turned 90 degrees to my right and viewed a metal cell door with eyes staring back at me. Dark eyes with bright whites pierced from the darkness of what was a cell. Whispers from beyond that I knew were discussing me, looking, watching, and deliberating on what I do not know. I just know I shuddered, and the hairs on the back of my neck, arms and legs went into overdrive and were on their ends pointing outwards, as though to self-protect myself from incoming negative energies. I turned back to face the female piggies who sat opposite me and nodded their heads in respect to what the one sitting next to me was saying.

Then, big pouty lips picked up a pen and turned to a drawer in the desk to get some paperwork. She started with, 'Name.' She wasn't looking directly at me as I was at her, so when I didn't answer her, she looked up at me with her big round dark eyes, and her eyes expressed her annoyance.

I politely stated in my defence, 'Sorry, are you speaking to me?'

'Passport number?'

I gave all the information willingly.

'Offence?'

Now, this is where it was going to get interesting. So, I went into a monologue of everything that had happened, and I spoke to them all so matter-of-factly whilst maintaining eye contact with all of them. I went through each stage with them and by the end of my continuous drawl they had their mouths open, willing me to shut up. They said something between them disapprovingly and then between them they were discussing something when the one next to me said to big lips,

'Offence?' to which she repeated whilst frowning her forehead with concentration. She then looked at me, eyes to eyes, and repeated more confidently with good tone and intonation, 'Offence?'

To which I replied, 'Innocent and arrested illegally without a warrant. And,' I added, 'I have been asked to sign documents that were in Arabic, and I didn't have a clue what I was signing, so I stated on the documents that I did not understand what I was signing.'

Well, with that, they looked bemused and tattled amongst themselves shaking their heads and conversing. I continued to sit analysing the room whilst trying to ignore the eyes to my right that were still watching me. Then yet again, I was asked to sign documents whose wording I didn't have one iota of understanding, so yet again I gave my signature with the addition of, 'I do not understand what I am signing.' I really didn't feel comfortable, and I was right not to. I also had to sign in my jiffy bag with my passport, mobile and purse, which was then placed in a safe. I then had to place my bag in the cell next to the safe, a cell that was packed from floor to ceiling with bags of all sizes, styles, and price tags. How many women were in this bloody cell as there was only one door going into it? I just couldn't imagine how many women belonged to these bags, sure I am a light traveller whilst others pack way too much and can have one suitcase for shoes, one for clothes and one for toiletries and makeup. I always giggled to myself when I witnessed such sights at airport queues, but the baggage cell was wide and long and packed disorganised with bags shoved in wherever they would fit. I assumed that those at the back of the cell may have been in longer than me, and then the question came to me, how long had they been locked up here?

I knew what was coming next and wished there were something I could have done to get out of bloody entering the cell with the beady eyes watching me. There was a heavy, stale, and dry atmosphere, and the lighting which echoed from the cell was a darker misty light that seemed to narrow the further you looked in. Or was it the mass of bodies, dark bodies that littered the floor, whilst sat on mattresses that covered the entire floor from the cell door to the bottom of the cell, and only had a small path of 24cm that allowed you to walk against the wall.

The door was unlocked and I was ushered in until I no longer blocked the closing of the metal door. I heard it close behind me and looked directly in front of a mixture of women, young, old, thin, obese, who were also a mixture of nationalities. There were Indians, Pakistanis, Thais, Filipinos, Kenyans, Nigerians and Arabic women who were a mixture of Emirati, Omani, Persian and North Africa. I didn't know what to do, or where to go. The single mattresses where they sat were pushed together on the concrete floor and were a mix of colours and designs that I am sure in their heyday were very nice as single mattresses, but sadly their day had come and gone, and they would have been more suited in a rubbish dump. To my left, there were tiny rectangular windows that I could see had been pushed open through the metal bars. I couldn't imagine how much air came through those windows, and as the only air conditioning was where the officers sat, I feared that the only view of the outside world and fresh air I would be breathing and seeing would be through the bars of this picture in this basement. To my right, as I turned, there was a cell with three bunk beds, one on each wall. There were two mattresses on the floor and no space to walk on the concrete. There were other cells that continued down the cell on the right, and I was sure I would get acquainted with these during my visit here.

I stood there, not knowing where to go or turn. My legs felt numb with such a heavy weight, as my mind raced to try to understand how I had got myself into such a bloody mess. Then from my right, an Arabic deep voice questioned,

'Are you from Australia?'

I looked to my right and there were many faces yet again looking up at me. There were three on my left sitting on the bottom bunk and one on the bunk bed above, then directly in front of me were two on each bed of the bunk, two above and two below. Then to my right sat another two on each bunk. There were two sat on a mattress on the floor, and whilst they had bedding and pillows, it all looked as though it needed dry cleaning or at the absolute best, burning. The one who had initially asked me the question re-asked. I think she could recognise that I was in shock and still trying to process this God-awful hellhole. She was Arabic with dark features but with more European facial features and had a low masculine voice.

I quietly answered, 'No, I am not. I am British. Welsh British.'

She continued whilst all the others looked at me, 'Why are you here?'

Um! Where did I start with this bloody saga again? 'I was arrested because they came to arrest my fiancé and because I was there with him, they arrested me. And, because I was arrested, they tested my urine and because I smoked in the UK before coming here to Dubai on holiday, I was arrested for having marijuana in my system. So ye, because of that.'

She translated for the others who were Arabic within this little cell. They nodded as if to confirm understanding. 'You are a drug case like her.' She pointed to a small lady with dyed red hair whose withered and tanned skin had aged her beyond her years.

'Yes, um, possibly I believe I am or could be. But I did state this to the police, that I am only guilty of smoking it in the UK and not here in Dubai, or the Middle East. I also wrote on the papers the police wanted me to sign that I didn't understand what I was signing.'

Over the course of that evening I learnt the names of my cellmates. It had been them who had invited me into their cell and encouraged me to sit down on their mattress. And it was strange, being in this cell was more comforting than the cell that was outside, and I wasn't sure if that was to do with the confinement of the previous cell I had been in or because the women here had made me feel invited in when it could have been a very lonely and frightening experience.

They were eager to know what my experience had been from the start with the police. I explained the whole story, then the one opposite me and who had initiated conversation asked me to confirm, 'So you didn't smoke it here in Dubai?'

All the ladies watched for my response, and I clearly and confidently looked at all of them as I confirmed, 'No,' whilst repeatedly telling myself to *keep saying it confidently and look them in the eyes.*

Time went by and I soon learnt their interesting personal stories, trials, and tribulations, and how they found themselves here, with me. The lady who sat next to me on the mattress was named Cynthia, and she was a petite, small and feminine-looking American with short hair and a bounce to her. She explained, amusingly, how she had come to find herself in the situation she was in now.

Cynthia was from New York and had just arrived in the country, as she had had a promotion within telecommunications. She had gone out socialising for a meal and drink with her new colleagues and her manager. In the taxi, returning to the hotel, she had got confused and directed the taxi driver incorrectly. Being new to the country she had got lost, as is commonplace in a new country. The taxi driver believing her to be drunk with alcohol consumption decided to take her to a police station where she was detained and arrested for being drunk. When she left, the girls who witnessed her arrival said that she was indeed very drunk and once locked up and encaged, she loudly slurred whilst holding on to the metal bars and looking at the guards shakenly, 'Do you know who I am? I am an American citizen. You can't do this to me.'

They could indeed, and they did. Whilst her three-day hell was short compared to the majority, Cynthia was lucky that when she was given her telephone call, her employer supported her and arranged her freedom.

Whilst we were very different and possibly would have never met each other on the outside world, we did here, and we shared one common thing that helped us bond, our children. We would speak about them, our lives, Cynthia about her husband's worry and anger at her getting arrested when she had just arrived in Dubai, his fear of moving his family to Dubai and mundane things of likes and dislikes.

I will never forget Cynthia's kindness as she allowed me to share her blanket and some of her mattress on that initial first night. We would share together for the remainder of her time with us. She would have a funny way of making me laugh with her New York comments, and her kindness knew no bounds.

When she had confirmation that she was leaving, she wrote on a piece of paper my brother's name and telephone number, as she wanted to speak with him to tell him how I was doing. I thought that this was exceedingly kind of her, and I ensured that I thanked her. And then she amazed me. The day after she left, she came back to the cell and left some essentials for me.

She had two bags of clothes from H&M with underwear, a bra, knickers, smart trousers, pyjamas, and toiletries. I cried when I received them and read the letter she had written for all the girls to hear.

The items helped so many and whilst to others they may not have seemed like much, they did to me, and to the girls I was with.

This is the letter I received on Saturday, 7th August.

Hello Emily,
I have no idea if this will reach you. I hope you'll be long gone by this time. I spoke to your brother on Thursday. He is still trying to get hold of the embassy. I've been told that asking for your embassy is viewed negatively and encourage you to act accordingly. Rob and I will try to reach the consular for you to see if there's anything to be done. Rob has spoken with you just before he and I talked. I just left a message on your mother's phone line, so nothing new to report.
I'll do what I can to keep tabs on what's happening with you. Unfortunately, I must be in India next Sunday so I won't be able to come by… they only allow drop-offs for women with drug cases on Sunday between 8 and 12. In the meantime, here are some things for you. Please share them with the other women who were so kind to me. I appreciate all their help and support. Be strong. This will not last long.
All my best,
Cynthia

I received my second letter from Cynthia on the 22nd of August, yes, I was still in.

Hello Emily,

I was sad to hear from your mother that you are still here. She said you might be sent home this week. I certainly hope so! If you need a place to stay, come to me at Layia Oak Hotel in Tecom across from the Greens. I'm in suite 1304 under Cynthia. I will make sure the front desk knows to give you a key should I be at work.

In the meantime here are some more clothes, money and a phone card. I hope it's useful to you or one of the other girls who were so generous and kind to me when I was there. My cell number locally is 0*******, though it only seems to work sporadically.

Be strong, my dear. You will be home with your daughter shortly.

Yours Cynthia

Cynthia continued communication with my brother, contacting the embassy and my lawyer once she had returned to her freedom. The kindness she showed was undeniable and unforgettable.

Then, there was the Russian who wasn't Russian, and got annoyed with the others when they called her this. She didn't like Russia, as she came from a country that Russia had occupied. Her name was Anna, and she looked jaundiced, with a small muscular gymnastic frame, whose wiry bleached hair needed a good chop. Now, her story was tragic as during her incarceration of six months here, yes six whole bloody months, her father had passed away from cancer. Even with the support of her lawyer, who she believed to be shit, she could not request permission to leave to attend his funeral.

She was desperate as her father had remarried and she found out that he had not written a will. Her stepmother had taken over the three-storey rustic farmhouse and moved her family in.

Anna was worried that what was left of her mother and father would be lost to her forever, and this is the only thing she ever got passionate about, oh, and how her lawyer was crap, and the legal system is/was in Dubai. Her shouting, whilst standing raising her arms, was sometimes funny as she broke from English into her own language. Some extremities consisted of, 'Fucking idiots, fucking lawyer, fucking fucked up country and fucking bitches.'

Her case was extraordinarily sad, as she had been a successful businesswoman selling apartments and living very well from the commission. Then, when driving home, she was stopped for speeding. An alcohol test was carried out and she admitted to being over the limit, but upon searching her car they also found coke, and yet again, it was not the one you drink.

She had been locked up indefinitely and was waiting to proceed through the legal system. She thought by investing in a lawyer it would speed the process up, but she knew she was possibly looking at up to four years. Due to not being able to work she could not pay her rent and so lost her apartment, income, and life. She knew once her court proceeding started, she would be on her way home by deportation.

She couldn't wait to get out of 'this filthy, stinking, fucking country,' she would say in her passionate voice with an accent of pure contempt for the legal system that now made her a prisoner.

Then, there was my favourite of all, my South African friend. Now Mary was the type of person that when speaking to someone she liked to get up close and personal, and in their faces. You could literally smell her breath as she spoke, but what a lovely, kind, and gracious lady. Her story was a sad one. She had been brought up in South Africa, fell in love, married, and moved to Dubai to start a family. Her husband, when flying internationally for his job, met a colleague, fell in love, and left her. He left her to solely care for her very autistic child. He had been the financial breadwinner in the relationship, and them being in this God-forsaken country where the law was in his masculine favour, well, she was in a right economic mess. She had a poor divorce settlement, which forced her to work.

Her son, who was severely autistic, needed full-time support in the form of a nanny at home and help at school through a teaching assistant who worked solely with her son. The position was financed through Mary at an additional cost to the private international school fees, along with her rent, car, and all other household bills. She had got herself into financial difficulty. She ended up falling behind on payments and one of the many debtors took her to court. She was found guilty and ordered to serve time until the payment was made. She knew this was going to be a vicious circle, but she hoped family would help and her church's prayers would save her. She was always quoting bible verses and then translating them for my understanding. She thought God was punishing me because Abe was a Muslim and I a Christian, and the two were not supposed to be together. I went silent when she started on this conversation, yawned, and made my excuses that I was tired. Mary slept on the mattresses on the floor with Cynthia and me. She had her bible with her all the time, and her faith was inspiring to me. She always smiled and laughed. I liked her; however, I didn't like the way the Muslim ladies in our cell treated her. It was embarrassing the way they spoke to her and mocked her. I could see the hurt deep in her eyes, and her lips curled over as she tried to smile it off. I was not in a position yet to speak my mind, as I had just arrived and needed a bed and some protection, any. I could not afford to be naive here.

Now, let me tell you about the three main Muslim women who were the powerful characters in this cell and in Bur Dubai. The most fiercely terrorising one was the one who had initiated conversation at the very beginning. She was a confident Lebanese woman who demanded respect. She had been held captive here for over nine months and had frequented court on many occasions. Along with three colleagues, she had been found guilty of embezzling thousands and awaited her verdict, so that she may serve her time before deportation.

Then there was a young Moroccan woman who made her living in Dubai from the company of men. She had a boyfriend, but she would also go to private parties of the rich Emiratis and dance for them. She had been 'working' when her boyfriend had picked her up. He had been jealous of something and had beaten her up. When she went to the police to report the incident, she was arrested. You could still visibly see the dark shadows of her bruising on her right cheek. Her boyfriend was Emirati and free. Nothing had happened to him, but when she went to the station, she had forgotten that her visa had expired and that she was, in fact, an illegal alien, which resulted in automatic deportation. She had lost her income, all her belongings and was waiting to be sent home after serving her crime. Her bloody crime? Sure, I did question whether she was a prostitute, but at the end of the day it was none of my business. And boy, could she dance and move her butt and hips. She was very provocative, to say the least, and sometimes she would dance for us and boy, was she bloody good at moving her hips suggestively, whilst her arm movements were mesmerising. The other Arabic girls would sing, and it was a welcomed distraction.

Her boyfriend had got her a lawyer, but there was nothing that could be done. She feared returning to her home country as she would not be able to return to the Emirates after deportation. She had lost a good income, an income that would not be matched elsewhere. She had once run from her place of birth and now she would return there, to an arranged marriage, as she could not be supported by her family. And can you bloody believe it that she bloody cried for the boyfriend that physically hurt and scared her? She loved him and questioned what she would do without him. Bloody bonkers if you ask me.

Then, there was the redhead Emirati woman with weathered skin. She had been arrested in a raid and was waiting for her case to be heard. She was guilty of supplying coke at this party for young Emiratis, and I suppose you could say that this was her kind of work. She made her living from having parties for young, rich Emiratis and supplied them with their every desire. It was her who gave me a lawyer's card and said the lawyer was the best drugs lawyer in Dubai. He was famous for successfully getting victims off drug charges. This was all translated through the medium of her two compatriots, as mentioned above. I also found out that she was divorced from her younger cousin, whom she had sons with. Whilst she was being incarcerated and promised a severe sentence of possibly up to 20 years, her ex-husband would dutifully come, visit her, and bring her clothes and phone cards. Emirati was indeed lucky to still have his support as such a case would ultimately be a great embarrassment to her family.

So, these were the main characters of my cell and the ones I would communicate the most with. Then, there were the three African girls, whose spoken English was very amusing. One was from Kenya and her husband was also incarcerated awaiting court for fraud with an airline. The other two were very dark Africans and friends. I could never understand what the hell they were in for, but it had something to do with theft. They had been in for months, and they would listen attentively to all conversations and then translate, laugh, agree, disagree with large hand gestures and facial expressions. Understanding was always found in the end, although it could take some time with a lot of laughter. But it didn't matter as we weren't going anywhere and had plenty of time available. Their roar of laughter was infectious, and what a pair of entertainers they were.

What I was certain of is that one was heavily pregnant, with the whitest of teeth, and the darkest of skin. She had the bottom bunk on the right of me and her friend was on the bunk above. It was funny because even though she was pregnant, she was still lighter and thinner than her compatriot by miles, and the bedding situation would have been quite different if not for this pregnancy. I would look at her young face and think to myself how awful to be an expectant pregnant mother, stuck in this claustrophobic and heavy atmosphere. It should be a time when mother and baby connect with mother earth and enjoy all she has to offer, not a concrete and metal cell. But, on the plus side, she was the best smuggler in the whole jail. She was a clever bugger using her pregnancy to get things brought into her. For example, nappies were delivered from her sister, and they would have cigarettes packed into them. She was my extortionately priced cigarette lady. They were the most expensive individual cigarettes I have ever bought, but when I did manage to get one and that was not very often, each inhale I took in the toilet through the window was an inhale that also took in the warm air from the outside, and for a second, I felt a little bit of escapism and freedom, which was always short-lived from a bang on the door.

Her friend had the body and muscle of a gorilla, and when she danced her arse moved too. They tried to teach me how to dance, but I was stiff and had laughter from my audience. No matter how much I tried I just could not get down and wiggle it. Their hands would clap, and their vocals were loud and deep. They took us on a journey to the deepest depths of Africa when they sang and danced. It was beautiful.

Then, there was the beautiful, kind, nice Emirati who, like Mary, was in for non-payment of loans. She had a famous surname and had been a presenter on an international famous music show in Dubai. Her father had divorced her mother and married a Russian, and financially they were struggling to pay for her brother's training to be a pilot and it had been left to her to sort everything out, as her mother's health suffered. She was popular and treated differently from all of us, with certain officers inviting her out of the cell when on duty in the evening. She would negotiate phone calls for herself and on my behalf. She was a positive star in the darkness, and I was sad to have met her under such circumstances.

The way the detention centre was set out was that there was a main rectangular room with a width of approximately 25 single mattresses against the right wall. It followed down to the toilet and a shower hole that could also be used as a toilet. There were some steps leading to it, but due to the overcrowding the queue for this was sometimes ridiculous. With only a small gap of about 24cm to walk along the row of mattresses to the left wall meant people lined up with limited or no room. The toilet was next to the shower room and in a sorrowful, disgusting smelly state.

Sometimes the queue was ridiculous, especially if you were unwell or in desperate need. And even if you had queued and wanted to relax on the potty it was rarely possible, as there were others who were standing right outside the door, who also wanted to go. Relaxation was not an option, and it was literally open your legs, push, and let gravity pull your poo out of you, wipe/drip/drip/drip and get the hell out of there, because the stench smelled of fermented piss and shit. A bang on the door was always expected, with utterings of foreign languages being spoken. The smell was grotesque due to housing more than the cell could bloody accommodate. I literally felt sorry for the ladies who were positioned and slept near the toilet and shower room. The poor bastards permanently inhaling stale, fermented, and mixed international piss and shit.

I had my first shower that very evening after a similar meal to what I had previously endured in my other cell, basically food that tasted of shit. The two Muslim women, Lebanese, and Moroccan were called by the officers and left. It was all in Arabic, so I didn't really pay much attention. However, I did pay attention when I was instructed by the others in the cell to line up outside our cell. Within minutes, there was a long line of women standing from the cell door to the toilet. As I looked down the line, I could visibly see that the ladies that were in the small cells that veered off the main rectangular one were in line before all the others. It was like a pecking order of nationalities and the whites from UK, American, and South Africa with the Arabic women, and African ladies, then the other Arabic nationalities, with the Asians, Indians, and Filipinos segregated into their groups.

My turn came to be served and it was interesting to see how we were given the amounts we asked for, and nothing was said of it by the officers, as they just sat there. They had an agreement with these two, and as we finished eating our crap, I could see other women still in the queue. However, what disgusted me was that the ladies who were last had nothing compared to what we did. So, whilst we were full, they stayed hungry. I had only been here a short time and already I had a feeling that things weren't right here. I knew time would tell.

I assumed from what I had experienced so far, was that there must be a unified prison menu that was copied throughout the prison service. The girls had explained to me how the day was run here and that people detained, yes, people detained and imprisoned, got three meals a day - breakfast which was usually bread with either a boiled egg, yogurt, or cheese. Lunch and tea consisted of rice served with vegetables, meat, or bones with a piece of fruit. Food was served in three different compartments on metal trays without or with plastic forks. It all depended on what you were used to.

Further, they explained to me that space was shared, and that it was unlikely that I would have a bed to sleep in, and that detainees in such police stations are held inside a cell 24/7. I was warned that, at times, tension sometimes runs high and that sometimes fights could break out.

Also, every week, the cells would be emptied, and all mattresses and blankets were placed in the officer's reception/office. They seemed to enjoy this, as it was the only time that exercise was attempted by filling buckets with water and throwing them on the floor. If you were lucky, you had a squidgy to push the water down holes, or otherwise your feet. Then, towels would be used on the floor and directed by feet to dry the concrete before the mattresses were carried back manually with all blankets and personal items.

But they left the best for last. Once a week, a shop would come and lay all their products on the floor to sell, with products from chocolates to crisps, papers to pens, sanitary towels to toothpaste. But the best thing about it was the phone cards. We were allowed to use the phone; however, the catch was when the officers willed it. They also dictated how long you could speak. I kept an eye on the toilet/shower queue, and after it had gone down in numbers, I decided to take the leap and scrub myself stupid.

I proceeded to walk the path to the toilet, as it was needed and not only for personal reasons but for those around me. I had to ask permission from the guards to get my toiletry bag, a clean pair of knickers and a more suitable change of clothing, i.e., a baggy t-shirt and comfy trousers.

Now, the change in my personal circumstances with my new lifestyle resulted in my eating habits changing beyond recognition. The simple fact that I was not meeting my dietary requirements by eating enough fruit, vegetables, wholegrain, pulse and other food groups rich in fibre was evident and felt, as I really needed to poop. I was bloated, the stress, anxiety, with my low mood, depression and accumulated with no exercise which would have improved the work of my digestive system, well, let us just say that I needed desperately to clean myself out.

Now, I had got bunged up as a child and told by the doctor that I had a big sausage stuck in my stomach and that I needed medicine to get the sausage out, but for how long I can remember I have always been three times a day, slide them out with ease kind of girl. Thus, constipation has rarely blockaded my poo canal, so I have had extraordinarily little experience of dealing with such a matter. There was simply no action, whilst I definitely had the urge. I could feel the build-up of the boulder wanting to explode from my bottom, but everything I tried – even putting some soap up it (an old wives' tale which my mother had scientifically tested when I was a child) had no effect. I failed utterly to dispose of my poo. It simply would not bloody budge. So, before the shower, I thought I would try and thus, I sat on the toilet. I pushed, squatted on the toilet, and re-pushed waiting, expecting, and wanting to enjoy the sweet exhale of the big, wet, juicy push. And to no bloody avail. So, I wiped any squirts of juice and with my very rosy cheeks on my face and buttocks, my mind went to washing my bits and bobs.

So, I finally got into the shower and knew there were still women waiting in a queue. But, at this stage, I just wanted, needed, to wash away all the negative energy and try to make myself a little bit cleaner. However, this awful negative feeling continued. Possibly it was a fart that had grown in strength. I was old-fashioned and had been brought up to not fart in public as it was not sociable, due to the sound and often smell, so come to think of it, I could not really remember having a good old smelly fart to be proud of since being locked up. But, no, this was more than a fart and it needed to come out. So, I decided to take the matter into my own hands (literally), there and then, and to manually dis-impact myself. This was my only option, and yes, I was going to physically remove a large, impacted stool, as the stool was simply too big and too hard to be flushed out of my now tight bottom hole.

For those of you who are unaware of the term dis-impact, well it is a process that should be completed by a health professional by which they can manually support or aide an exceptionally large and wide stool, which is stuck there stubbornly refusing to come out. Did you indeed know that a faecal impaction is a solid, immobile bulk of human faeces? Well, you know now, and I hope to God you never or will ever have to have this procedure by anyone and certainly not by your own action.

So, I braced myself because I knew this would be no easy job. I stood in a hovering position over the hole which had the same circular diameter of both my thumbs touching and my index fingers, pulled at my left cheek (and no – not the one on my face), pulled at my left arse cheek, and then carefully inserted my right index finger to this Mount Snowdonia's peak, which was the first summit I encountered, and peaked out. I had to penetrate fairly deep to push it forward, and believe me, the process bloody hurt. I was trying very hard not to rip or tear any delicate tissue, but the stretching was very uncomfortable. My poo had formed itself into a series of four large linked hard stools as hard and heavy as granite chunks. After much groaning, pushing, straining, legs shaking with droplets of sweat perspiring down my forehead I could taste the salt from my sweating. Movement could be felt. I heaved and hoed as though a baby was coming, but from the wrong hole.

After all this tedious action, each boulder tumbled out into the water below, and I was finally able to breathe a sigh of relief, with little or no splashback. However, there was a pinkish tinge to the water surrounding the drop zone. As might be imagined, this had been a traumatic and desperate action. As Tesco says, 'Every little helps.' May I speak plainly? This is not a recommended technique to achieve a milestone.

Thankfully, once I had expelled that medical oddity, my system returned to normal, as it or they were out. I had perfected the bloody manual faecal disimpaction technique.

However, my joy was short-lived as there was a gap in the bottom of the wooden door of about 12 cm. As I looked down, I could see the ladies standing and sitting for the queue, and I am sure some, but not all, saw a white British woman shit down the shower hole. There was nothing for it, I shook my head, banished all thoughts of embarrassment, dried myself and departed as quickly as I could. I did feel lighter, though!

Ramadan 2010

Now, I flew from the UK on July 29th, expecting to fly home on the 9th of August. Ramadan, in 2010, started on Wednesday, the 11th of August, so initially, I wouldn't have even been there for the start. Or so I theorized. For those of you who don't know what Ramadan is, it is the ninth month of the Islamic calendar, and is observed by Muslims worldwide as a month of fasting to commemorate the first revelation of the Quran to Muhammad according to Islamic belief. It would continue for 30 days until Thursday, the 9th of September.

Deep inside, I still hoped that I would be flying home on my pre-booked ticket. However, I had now entered the gates of Arabic hell. I didn't know what the hell was happening, and my gut feeling was that I was at the very beginning of this saga. And I knew I was petrified as to how it would end. There was discussion on other people's experiences and personal knowledge of the legal system and laws, but this didn't seem to pacify me.

There was an urn of tea at the cell door, which I was told not to drink too much of, as they said it was drugged with something to pacify the inmates. I ended up drinking a lot of it, as it relaxed me and helped me to sleep throughout the day. Days were long, and along with the overcrowding, it was dismal. I would have tornado moments of anger and violence towards the police officers and their favouritism and treatment of those in the system. Along with the isolation of not speaking Arabic, trying to read, understand the proceedings of your case or even making your way around prison can be incredibly difficult if you cannot communicate. I would go to the cell door and ask whoever was on duty what was happening to no avail. It was so repetitive, and I realised that freedom was priceless.

Depending on who was on duty, and whether they could be bothered to do their duties or give their duties to the Arabic inmates, the phone could be used. Again, being in the first cell, we were given extra time. I can remember the first time I could phone. I bought a card from the officer and was literally shaking with panic and desperation with the need to speak to those I trusted the most, my family. It rang with that strange foreign beep, as I leant my head against the wall and held onto the receiver for dear life willing someone, anyone, to answer it. And then someone picked it up. It was my brother and I simply exhaled, 'Thank God!' My brother explained to me that he had been trying to get in contact with the British Embassy and that they were now aware I was being detained in Bur Dubai, on drugs charges. He informed me that a representative would be coming to see me as soon as it was possible.

I begged him, 'Just get me the hell out of here, Rob, if I have to sell my house, I will do it. Jesus!' He told me he would do everything he could at his end and keep on to the embassy.

He informed me, 'Emily, you are going to have to get a lawyer. I have been given a list, but I think it is best for you to speak with the embassy representative. Don't worry about money. We will sort it out. Try to be strong.'

'Try to be strong? I am Rob, but it is so bloody hard. Do you think I will make my return flight on the 9th?'

Rob has always explained things easily to me. I remember as a teenager of around 12 or 13 years of age, I had returned from school after sitting in a Welsh lesson listening to my friends speak of 69ers. I had simply asked my brother, whilst we both lied on a sofa, what it was. Initially, he wanted to know the girls' names and where they have been doing this. I honestly repeated what they had been discussing and that my friends were members of the Royal Air Force Cadets, and they went away training quite often. They had obviously had experience of it and discussed it freely. I knew it wasn't the chocolate flake on an ice cream because that was called a 99. My brother simply got paper and wrote 69. He then proceeded to show me that one was a woman, and one was a man and that they were kissing each other's privates. I was disgusted, and I was advised by my brother not to hang around these girls.

However, the news I heard from him now was pessimistic. 'Emily, I will be honest with you. I don't think you will be. It is not going to be that simple. I have been reading online and drugs cases are bloody serious, Emily.'

'Ok. Listen, I don't know how long I have left to speak. Is Sah and Mammy there so I can speak to them?'

'Ye, they are here now.'

Sah came on the phone first, and I quickly shook off any negative, emotional weeping and put on a voice that was more suited to a cartoon character with the overly pitched, 'Hi Sah. How are you?' She was shy and giggly, but more concerned when I was coming home. I explained to her, as basic as I could, that Mammy wasn't feeling well and that the doctors were helping me to make me better, so that I could come home. This seemed to pacify her for some time, and I joked with her to be a good girl and that when Mammy came home, she would give her the strongest and longest cwtch.

Mammy came on to the phone and couldn't speak much as she was very emotional and just wanted to ensure that I was eating well (ye right) and that I looked after myself. It was hard to come from the phone without being emotional, and when the time came to an end the conversation, under the authority of the officers and two Arabic detainees, Lebanese and Moroccan, I was compounded with the reality that I didn't know when I would be able to speak to them again or meet this British Embassy representative who I hoped was British.

I returned to the cell and continued to wait. Day and night followed with the continuous monotony of my new life, and those I now lived with. Visitation for drug cases was on a Sunday morning, and it was hard to keep track of what actual day it was. Names would be called infrequently and some would leave for short periods, whilst some were gone for hours, but everyone came back at some point on the same day. I had stopped listening for my name as it never came, and whilst lying on the bed one day, Lebanese said,

'Emily, they are calling you. Go. Maybe you are going to court. This is good.'

I jumped up and sprinted to the cell door and viewed an officer standing there.

She looked at me and questioned, 'Emily Brook?'

I simply said, 'I am Emily Brook,' my palpitations racing with excitement. The door opened and I came out. Then, a woman walked towards me, a petite, feminine and very Arabic lady dressed in a black with a gold trimmed colourful headscarf, smart jacket, and folder.

'Are you Emily Brook?' She questioned in a very feminine voice, with a slight Arabic accent.

I confirmed, 'Yes.'

There was a row of four chairs against the left wall, and she gestured with her right hand for me to sit down on one of them. I followed her instructions and sat down, not knowing who she was, but hoping she was here to help me. She then proceeded to sit next to me.

'Hello, Emily. My name is Hiba, and I am Consular Officer with the British Embassy. Your brother contacted us to let us know the situation you have found yourself in during your stay in Dubai. I have been trying to speak with you, but I have not been able to.' She shook my hand, and I shook her hand back. 'You are here on a drug case?'

I nodded.

'Drug cases are very serious here. You didn't know this? You could have up to 20 years.'

'WHAT?' I gasped with more shock and self-pity. My eyes became like cameras and when each lid closed, they took a true picture of my surroundings, my life. It really wasn't nice. I was heartbroken and in pure dismay at the thought of all the work and experiences I had ever had, and that I had worked for, my daughter, my family and my career could be gone with the possibility of being locked up for years. Hell, if I had twenty years, I wouldn't be out until my bloody 50s.

I hunched over, held my hands to my head and felt as if my head was going to explode. If I could have, I would have banged my head against the wall to try and wake up from this huge, shitty mess.

'Emily, you signed the document. Yes? You signed?'

I looked up to gaze at her eyes, whilst they were sympathetic, I felt as though my judgement had been made. I pleaded with her knowing that we were being watched by them.

'But I didn't know what I was signing. It was in Arabic, and they told me to sign. I asked them to explain, and they laughed. They even joked that they were playing bad/good cop. I wrote on the sheet that I didn't understand what I was signing on a number of documents. And, from the very beginning, I was honest and told the doctor that it would be positive because I smoked it in the UK.'

She concluded, 'Emily, your urine was positive for marijuana. Drugs are a very serious case here. You must be strong. This is not like the UK. The judicial system is very different. You are guilty, as it was in your system, and it doesn't matter if you smoked it in the UK. You are guilty until proven innocent.'

As I shook, she placed her right hand on mine. Tears rolling down my face, every ounce of me shaking internally and uncontrollably with shock. There was no privacy with the bitches watching and listening to every word uttered, every movement made by us. Then, something was said between Hiba and one of the fat bitches, and she looked at me.

'I have to go now. Be strong! I will inform the Ambassador that I have seen you. Do you have legal representation yet?'

'No.'

She handed me an A4 leaflet that had a list of legal companies, their names and telephone numbers. 'Emily, listen carefully now, you need to pick a lawyer to represent you in court. It is very important.'

'What I have to go to court? But my return flight… I am going to miss it, aren't I?'

'Yes, Emily. You must prepare yourself mentally. You are here now.' I knew with her confirmation that I would not be going home anytime soon. I would be going to court as a convicted criminal until I could prove my innocence. What the fuck?

'Do you have access to the phone and money?'

I replied, 'We can use the phone when they tell us and feel like it.' I answered scathingly to those bitches in authority.

'Have you called home?'

'Yes, I have spoken to my brother twice. The first time I asked him to notify you because they would not allow me to call you.'

Then, something else was said by one of the fat bitches and we both looked up from one another to face them. She answered them calmly with understanding, whilst they uttered between themselves, and made facial expressions looking at me as though I was an ugly turd that they wanted flushing down the toilet.

'Under the rules, the embassy representative can only visit on Sundays. I will try to keep updated on your case. You have my card and phone number. Be strong! And finally, what are the conditions like?'

'It is overcrowded here, and I honestly think they are breaching health and safety. I am being treated better because, I think, I am British, but some of the other nationalities are treated very badly. The food - well, my dogs have always eaten better.'

'Ok. I will inform the Ambassador. Goodbye, Emily.'

As soon as she stood up, the bitches got up and approached me and gestured me back to the cell. As I got up from my seat, she then proceeded to push me forcefully, as another opened the cell door. I turned to look at her, to make her know not to do this again. I had utter contempt for her. Upon my return, I entered and looked at the grief-stricken pale faces on the ladies that lay and sat on stained mattresses. This was now my life, and as I looked behind me, the cell door was closed and locked. I returned to my cell where questions abounded. What happened? Who was it? I explained fully that it was a British Embassy official, and they could not believe how lucky I was to have seen someone so quickly.

I looked shocked and repeated the word, 'Quickly? Really? I have been asking for days and I think it is only because of my brother pushing in the UK that I have been seen.' They explained that some embassies don't contact their citizens even after notifying them of their need for help, support, or guidance. Then, you have some who have no money to phone family or friends to let them know where they are, or what has happened to them. And, obviously, if they have no money, how could they even afford legal representation?

After listening, I felt lucky and thankful that I was born and bred in Wales, and that I was British. We discussed the list of lawyers and one of the Arabic ladies asked to look at it. They discussed in Arabic something, and I waited for a translation. They informed me that Emirati was using one of the lawyers, that he was expensive but the best, best, best of them. I was advised by them to go with him. So, my choice had been made, even though the lawyer was unaware. The next trial would be to make contact. So, I went back to the bitches in our reception and asked them.

'Excuse me, can I please make a phone call to a lawyer, as I wish to make him my legal representative for my case?'

I looked through the bars to watch them look at one another. One made a no gesture and the other stated it. I inhaled and exhaled before continuing, 'I have a right to make this phone call. I have my phone card ready and the lawyer's information. I will ask kindly once again; may I please make this phone call as it is my legal right as a British citizen who has been arrested innocently.'

Now by this stage, the cell behind me had become very quiet, and I came to the realisation that possibly I was now the white entertainment who challenged those in authority, when in reality what I asked was logical. I stood there waiting and looking at them. They did not respond and continued to stare at me. I concluded that maybe they were not used to being questioned.

So, I continued. 'I will ask again, please may I have permission to phone a lawyer to discuss my case. If I am not allowed to make contact with him them, the next contact I have with the British Embassy I will inform the Ambassador of Britain here in Dubai, that you are in breach of my human rights as a British Citizen. Can I please have your names, rank and police number?' This was totally made up, and I tried my best to speak confidently and professionally, whilst maintaining eye contact. However, to my surprise, it worked. After something was said between them, the lock of the door was unopened and I could make a telephone call, but may I add, 'Quickly.' I thanked Jesus and I thanked God internally, then proceeded to make I believe one of the most important phone calls of my life, to someone I needed to fight for my innocence. The number was dialled, and I waited for an answer. Then came a deep masculine 'Hello.' I replied quickly but ensured that my pace of speech was slow as I didn't want any misunderstandings.

'Hello. My name is Emily Brook. I am being held at Bur Dubai Police Station. I have met with a representative of the British Embassy, and I wish to employ you as my lawyer to represent me in a drug case.'

'Yes. And what is your charge?'

'I don't really understand. I was on holiday and the police came to my partner's apartment who is Qatari. They came to arrest him, but because I was with him, I was arrested. They tested my urine, and it was positive for marijuana. I informed them that I had smoked it in the UK, but I was told to sign documents under duress and that I would go home. That has not happened and now I am locked up and needing legal representation. Can you please represent me as I have been advised you are the best?'

There was silence then a clear and aggressive, 'Yes, of course I can represent you. I will need a down payment of £10,000 before I will look at your case.'

Now, £10 000 to me was an enormous amount. '£10 000. Right. I will phone my family now to inform them to contact you and make a payment to you.'

'Ok. Thank you. Bye.'

With that the conversation was over and I quickly knew I had to continue using the phone to let my family know the developments in my case. I didn't even look behind me or ask for permission to use the phone. I grabbed the opportunity and dialled the UK, in the hope that my brother would answer.

I tapped my head against the wall in rhyme with the beat of the ring, which seemed to be taking a long time.

'Hello?'

Exasperated I answered, 'Rob. Thank God.'

He seemed shocked that I was on the phone to him. 'Emily, are you ok?'

'Yes, this morning I saw the embassy rep and I have spoken to a lawyer. Rob, on the list you have you need to go with the one called Saeed. Ok? You have to go with him and no one else. He is saying that he needs £10,000 before he will look/take the case. He wants you to contact him, and I suppose he will give you the details.'

'Emily, hold on, I am trying to write this down. We are still in bed here, Emily.'

'Sorry Rob, I had to call now as I don't know when I will be able to speak with you next. But you have to go with him. Promise me, Rob? And any money I will pay you back. If I have to sell everything I have and my house, I will pay you back. I need to get out of here.'

'Ok, Emily. I will look into it. Ok?'

'Yes. Is Sah ok?'

'She is actually on her way down the stairs. We were all in bed. Do you want to speak with here?

I pleaded, 'Of course I want to speak with her.'

'Hang on. Sah, there is someone on the phone for you.'

I heard the phone changing hands and her sweet childish feminine voice questioning, 'Phone me. Who?'

He instructed her to find out, and I waited anxiously to wish her a 'Good morning.'

She came on and I could hear her small inhale and exhale. 'Hello and good morning, sweetheart.'

She exclaimed in a high surprised pitch, 'Mammy. It's Mammy.' She melted my heart and I had to consciously control myself to sound jovial and excited. 'Mammy, when you coming home? Miss you.'

I closed my eyes and took a deep gulp. 'I promise Mammy is trying her best to come home, as I miss you with all my heart. I am trying my best. I love you so much.'

'I love you,' was her answer. I could see her visually speaking with me, no matter how many seas and oceans separated us.

I promised and committed to her that, 'I will do everything in my power to get home to you as soon as possible.' I may have been locked up, but I now knew that I was the author of a new chapter in the destiny of my book. 'I hope you are being a good girl and enjoying being with Mam and Uncle Rob.'

'Yes, Mammy. Uncle Rob has smelly feet.'

'Does he now? Well, have lots of fun and be good and I love, love, love you. Can you help Mammy and put Mam on the phone quickly?'

'Yes, Mammy. Bye, Mammy.'

With that, she was gone, and my mother was now questioning, 'Emily?'

'Mammy, are you ok?'

'Don't you worry about me. How are you?'

'I am ok. I have just spoken to the British Embassy and the lawyer. I have asked Rob to contact him.'

'And how are you, Emily?'

I knew my mother worried, so I pacified her. 'Ye, I am ok. Just waiting to come home.'

Then, as I was speaking, one of the officers came to my right and stood next to me. She had her arms crossed, and I knew my time had come. I looked up to the ceiling, which needed a good bloody paint, and like the rest of this part of the building had been neglected for many years.

'I am sorry, Mammy, but I am going to have to go. Thank Rob, give Sah a kiss from me and I will try to phone when I am allowed.'

We ended the conversation with a love you each, and I placed the receiver back. I stood there for a second to see if the officer would remove herself from my space, but she didn't. Yes, I had taken liberty a wee bit, but honestly, these women.

I returned to my cell, and everyone was in exactly the same place. Again, I was the centre of attention answering the questions that I was bombarded with. I informed them that I had spoken to the lawyer and the price involved to represent me. They tried to work out the exchange rate to understand the value, which meant nothing to me. Some were shocked and horrified, questioning where I would get this money, and the answer was simply from my family.

The monotonous day continued, but at least now I had some peace and understanding that I had possibly acquisitioned the best drugs lawyer in Dubai. A light had been lit and I hoped with time and patience, the flame would increase and grow to the sunlight outside, which would allow me to see and feel my freedom.

That evening, we were instructed we would be allowed to use the phones again, and I thought to myself, *thank you, thank you, thank you,* and that I would be able to speak with my family again. I was greedy and knew that whilst I had already spoken to them, I just didn't care. I had never been selfish, but this situation was different to any other I had been in before. I knew I had to look after number one, at all costs, to get back to Sah and my family. My turn came after the two Arabic cell members called my name. I was the fourth in the cell to be called. Being British made me nearly as high as the Muslims in my cell. However, this time my mother answered initially.

'Hello.' How nice it was to hear her sweet, wise voice. 'Mammy, it is me.'

'Oh, Emily, I didn't expect to hear from you again today. Everything is ok with you, isn't it?

'Yes, it is fine. Well, you know what I mean. We have different officers on, and the Arabic girls in my cell are in charge of the phone calls tonight. Is Sah ok?'

'Yes, she is fine. She isn't here as she has gone for a walk with Rob.' My heart sunk, but at the same time, I was happy to speak with my mother.

'Oh, that's nice. Have they gone over to the river?'

'Yes. They have taken Lucy and Meg over.' (The dogs.)

I needed some normality, so I questioned how my aunties and uncles were. This was always the format our conversation would follow, and as usual, one of them had visited the doctor's or had a hospital appointment in one of the local county hospitals. We hadn't had many phone calls when we could speak so freely, but I knew there were time constraints, so I had to get down to the legal business. 'Mammy, do you know if Rob made contact with the lawyer?' God, I hoped so.

'Yes, he was busy on the phone speaking. I think it is all good.'

'Oh, thank God,' I exclaimed.

'Emily, try not to worry. It will all sort itself out and you will be home soon.' She was always a mantra for the positive, and I loved her innocent soul.

'I bloody hope so, Mammy.'

'Hang on, Em, I think they are back. I can hear the gate and the dogs barking. Oh, they are noisy.'

I could hear my mother yelling for my brother to come quickly to the phone because I was on it, and even though it was only seconds, when you are desperately needing/wanting information, time seemed to take forever.

When he finally came, the poor thing was out of breath through rushing. He was not as fit as I had assumed. 'Hi, Emily. You, ok?'

'Ye, I have been lucky today with two phone calls. Listen Rob, Mammy said that you have made contact with the lawyer – thanks so much. Did you sort out the payment?'

'Emily, I phoned a couple and decided to go with a British one. They only charge £3,000, so they are a lot cheaper than the one you initially wanted. I hope that this is ok?'

I took a big gulp, raised my eyeballs ever so slightly, closed my eyes and scrunched them with my forehead. My throat had become dry instantaneously and I yelped in a high pitch, 'What, Rob? What have you done? God! I told you, Rob, to go with the one I needed.' I cried. 'I told you, Rob! Why? Why did you do that? Oh God!' I broke down whimpering.

He sounded frustrated initially in his response, but he soothed in his extended response. 'Emily, I phoned around and then came across one who is a British trained lawyer and for £3,000. I thought that he was the cheaper option, to be honest. I am trying my best here, Emily.'

I heard it in his voice, the stress, and I had little sympathy as I needed to get my point across without any misunderstanding whatsoever. Hell, I just didn't have the time to waste with any bullshit. However, from my initial feeling of hope with a definite concrete plan ahead of me and us by using the most expensive and best drugs lawyer to defend me would be the best possible choice. No one gets the reputation of being the best drugs lawyer in any country without winning cases, and I was desperate to get back to Sah at all costs.

I had not had time to worry about Abe, he was at the advantage of speaking and understanding the spoken language and culture, he was a low-level Sheik, a businessman and worked and travelled between the Middle East building yachts and renovating them. He would and could sort himself out. And, at the end of the day, he was the very reason the police came to that apartment on that evening and on that day.

'Rob, I know that you are trying your best and I am so so grateful – more than you will ever know. But I told you that you needed to go with the £10,000 one. I told you, Rob. The other girls say he is the best drugs lawyer in Dubai, the best, Rob, and I have a gut feeling that this man can help me get the hell out of here.'

'Emily, you didn't tell me that, that he was the best drugs lawyer in Dubai. Right.' There was a pause and then he continued, 'Right, sorry, Emily. If I had known that I would have gone with him. I will make another transfer tomorrow to pay him, and hopefully, it will all work out. But the other lawyer is paid up, so I assume he will represent you too. Oh, Emily, I don't know.'

'Rob, please just sort the lawyer out and it is a start. He is expecting a call from you to sort out the payment.'

'I will, Emily, don't worry.'

I looked behind me as I heard something, and then I was motioned to finish the phone call with the wave of a right hand, and I had to go back into my cell. The conversation hadn't lasted long, but I felt emotionally drained, exhausted and for the first time, I had no words. I just wanted to lie down, close my eyes, and have blackness. I wanted to feel nothing, see nothing from my past, or future, and to just breathe and feel nothing - not happiness, anxiety, loss, or hope. I needed to be gone from here and to rest, only for a little bit, but with each inhale to rebuild with growth my mental and physical strength, as this conversation had literally killed it.

'Rob, I am going to have to go. They are signalling for me to go back into the cell. Can you put Sah on quickly?'

Rob shouted for her, and I could hear the echoes of a conversation when he returned back to me and confirmed, 'Oh, Mammy just shouted that she is on the toilet having a poo, Emily. Sorry!'

'That's fine, Rob.' I chuckled to myself, thinking of all the times to have a poo, Sah. 'Listen, I have to go. Tell them I love them. Bye.'

The handle was placed back swiftly, and I took a deep breath before turning to the Arabic girls. I thanked them for the phone call because I knew I was taking the piss in the amount of time I had on the phone, and then I proceeded to return to the cell. It was like a conveyor belt of a queue as the ladies stood to speak to their loved ones or friends. I did not have the impetus for positive mental thinking this time, as I had initially, with the knowledge that my brother would go with the lawyer I had prescribed. I sunk into the mattress and with a heavy heart I closed my eyes and put my head under the blanket. I wanted to hide and have some darkness surround me. Darkness that would allow me to drift off to the unknown where I would not feel or think of anything or anyone. I just wanted numbness and peace. I had my seclusion, so that was sorted. However, I would have preferred not to be in jail for the experience. I knew the moments of peace would be sporadic, but I was exhausted, and I fell asleep as soon as my eyes closed, without any discussion.

The days that followed had little disruption with visitors. It was repetitive and easy to learn the routine - breakfast - sleep, lunch - sleep, evening food - sleep, drink the drugged-up tea in between, queue for the toilet and shower for entertainment, and speak shit to each other in the cell when something came up. Sometimes we would be able to make phone calls, but this mainly depended on the officers and their use of the Arabic girls in my cell. I was allowed extra time when they were on, which was one of the main bonuses, along with the extra food we had, and a cell that you had to be invited into, so I was kind of a privileged prisoner really. But I was a prisoner in an unfair justice system that alienated itself from me in every way possible. And the phone calls were just never enough and putting that phone down after speaking to the ones I loved became harder and harder, especially after speaking to Sah and her questions about my return.

I lost track of days, and as there were hardly any visitors or departures to court, nothing bloody happened. Then one day, on which day I still do not know, my name was called. I knew it was morning because we had had breakfast, but not lunch. As usual, I was oblivious and had the girls in my cell telling me that there was someone for me. Now, I had been expecting contact from the lawyer, and if this was it, then this was the start of my journey to freedom. I stood up, pressed my clothes down and prayed that something good and positive was going to happen. I walked out and there was a man standing holding a blue file. He was dressed smartly in a suit and whilst he had Arabic colouring, his features were European, so I kind of guessed that he was possibly Lebanese? Anyway, I approached the locked gates which were then opened for me as I confirmed that I was indeed Emily Brook. I walked out and as there was only the man standing there, I assumed that he was my visitor. I looked up at him, simply smiled and said, 'Hello. I am Emily. Are you here to see me?'

He returned the smile and in his deep, manly and soothing voice he informed me, 'Hello Emily. I am Omar. I am an associate of Saeed, the lawyer that your brother has employed, and I am here today to meet you and ask you a few questions. Shall we sit?'

He was very professional, and my gut feeling told me that there was something nice about him, something I trusted. It was not sexual, in case that's what you are thinking, but I felt as though this man would listen to me, and in his position, be able to help me.

We both sat and I thanked him for coming to see me. 'Thank you so much for coming to see me. I have been waiting and didn't really know what was happening to be honest. Nobody tells me anything.'

We sat under the watchful eyes of the officers before he proceeded to ask me legal questions concerning my case. 'Let me begin by asking you questions.' He went through my name, age, home address and then the difficult questions started.

'So, Emily, you are a drugs case, and let me be honest with you, this is very serious. In your words, can you tell me what happened?'

So, the saga continued again. 'I work and live in Qatar and returned to the UK to visit my family at the beginning of July. We lost my father at Christmas, he died, and it was really hard. The house is a small three bedroom and with me, my daughter, my brother and his family and my mother, I just couldn't cope. Abe, my partner/fiancé was doing work here, so I thought I would visit him to get away, and just be myself for a bit. I am a single mother and hadn't really mourned my father's death yet, I mean properly. I couldn't cope with the noise and my father wasn't there. I just couldn't cope. It was my home, has always been my family home, and I couldn't relax or settle. I asked if it was ok if I could leave my daughter with my family, so I could go to Dubai with Abe and just sort myself out really.'

I maintained eye contact throughout and did not allow the officers to distract me, as I needed to get everything out as honestly and factually correct as possible. I continued, 'So, I flew to Dubai and was here a couple of days when the police came and took us to a police station. I was taken to a doctor and I gave a urine sample, but I was honest and told him that I had smoked marijuana in the UK at my mother's, so I would test positive. I was honest, and then I got locked up. I was interrogated every couple of hours, I believe, and I kept telling them that I didn't understand what they wanted me to sign. They even joked that one was a good cop and the other a bad cop. I asked for a translator and was told firmly that it would take too long, and the quicker I signed the documents, the quicker I would go home. I signed the documents but also wrote on them that I didn't understand what I was signing. I believe I was locked up for three days without any contact with the outside world before I was transported to Bur Dubai and given my mobile back to allow me to phone home, and I did. I let my family know and asked them to help me. I have been here since.'

'Emily, a drugs case is very serious. You have admitted to having drugs in your system, and you are guilty.'

'The British Embassy representative told me that, and I am sorry, but the only thing I am guilty of is smoking marijuana in the UK, and then coming here for a holiday. I was arrested for not doing anything illegally. I have never ever been in trouble with the police and have always been good, or as good as I can be.'

He looked down at his file as he scribbled notes. 'Emily, I am going to be very honest with you. This case is serious, and you are looking at a sentence from six months to four years.'

'Yes, I have been told that by others and that is why I want you to represent me because you are supposed to be one of the best, BEST drugs lawyers in Dubai.'

Something was said arrogantly by one of the female officers and he immediately took a deep breath and, in a stern, louder voice he retorted. I did not understand what was going on, but whatever he said had a direct effect on them, as they looked at one another as though they were taken aback. I wished I had known what he had said as it had clearly shut them up without any response, and he gave them a somewhat look of disgust.

I wanted to laugh out loud with a big smirk and grin but knew that if I did, the consequences could be great, as he was getting out of here whilst I was stuck. I really didn't need it and knew I was not mentally prepared for any retribution. I had lost all my power. However, I had witnessed a weakness of theirs, and that was having someone fiercely question their authority or dictate something to them. They did not have the confidence or mental ability to answer, I theorised. This was something that I could use to my advantage, and I clearly looked at each one of them to acknowledge who was present and how this could be used to my advantage in the future. The conversation continued, and he continued to make notes.

'Listen to me carefully now, Emily,' his voice lowered, and he spoke closer to my ear. 'Say nothing. If you are asked a question, any questions, you say nothing. You have said too much already as you have admitted that you willingly smoked. It doesn't matter where, whether here or in the UK, under the law here, you are guilty as the evidence is in your body. Emily, you are guilty, and it is important to know that you will be here for some time. You will go home, but when is questionable. These cases are very difficult.'

I looked down at my lap. 'But I am a single mother. My daughter is three years old and in the UK with my family. We have never been apart since the day she was born. My mother is disabled, and even though she manages, she is not well. And then there is my job in Qatar - I have to be back in the first week of September.'

'What is your job in Qatar?'

I half-smiled and answered, 'I am a teacher. I teach English to speakers of other languages and sometimes with learning difficulties. I love my job and my life. My daughter has learning needs, and my job is important as I want her to have the best education possible, and I believe this school is the best for her needs. It is also a good job financially and is the best-paid one I have ever had. We have really struggled the last few years, and this was the chance for a new beginning.'

He, in turn, looked down and then returned his gaze sympathetically to me.

'What about your daughter's father? Where is he and can he help your mother in the UK?'

I looked up at the ceiling, rolled my eyes and then returned to direct my eyes at his. 'Her father does love her in his own way, but he has never cared for her and sadly doesn't know her. I don't think he could be trusted to put her needs first, and if Social Services get involved, she could be taken away as my mother is disabled. They may question whether physically she can care for her.'

'And your brother?'

'My brother returns to Africa in August with his family. He lives and works as a teacher out there.'

'I see. Well, going forward, the payment was made by your brother, a... Rob Brook, and we will be representing you. But you must understand this will not be an easy case, Emily. We will do our best though, Emily. I believe you.'

I had no understanding of what would happen next and eagerly asked, 'So what happens next?'

'Now we wait for a court date to start your trial. But you must be aware of Ramadan, and this will affect the timing of court cases here. Your case started on the 5th of August.'

He could see my dismay and loss of hope. Sah was on my mind as always, and what the fuck was going to happen to her?

'This is my business card, Emily, and I want you to contact me if anything happens. How are they treating you here?'

I took the card and scanned it. 'I suppose, in reality, I am lucky here as I'm British. Some of the other nationalities here are treated badly, but since coming here I have been invited to stay in the first cell with some others who have been here long term and they have been advising me. In fact, one Emirati woman here advised me to go with you as you are the best and you are representing her.'

He had no interest in the Emirati woman, but he was interested in my treatment, and I thought to myself *at least he is professional in keeping legal professional privilege*. It was reassuring to know that every word I spoke was confidential.

'What do you mean the other nationalities are treated badly?'

'It is the way they are spoken to, made fun of. They do not have the same amount of food as us or telephone allowance.'

As I said this statement, I consciously glared at the four officers who sat at the desk like pigs resting after a big feed. My distaste for them grew stronger each day to the point where my facial expressions towards them all, and individually, illustrated my contempt for their very being, as though I had eaten a rotten egg that stank.

He continued, 'Emily, you have my card now, so please phone if anything changes. I will be in contact with you to notify you when I have news. I also have your brother's information, and as the full payment has been made, we will now progress. Do you have any questions for me before I leave?'

'No. Just please help me to get out of here. I have never been so desperate in all my life.'

He kindly smiled at me and then said something to the officers. He stood up and I followed his move. 'Thank you for coming to see me today,' and with that statement, I shook his hand and turned to face the cell door. It was opened by one of them and I entered.

I turned around and smiled at him as he left before returning to my cell where they were all sitting facing me. I knew I would be bombarded with questions, so I answered each one. Who had come to see me? Why? What was said? So, I willingly answered. However, Emirati woman asked questions through Lebanese and her facial expression was serious.

'Emily, she wants to know if he asked to speak with her?'

'No, I am sorry. He didn't ask me.'

The conversation continued between them before she came back to me.

'She is not happy and doesn't understand why he did not speak to her when he was here. She has been here many months.'

I shrugged my shoulders and said, 'I am sorry.'

Then, she continued, 'He gave you something?'

I nodded my head and answered, 'Yes, he gave me his business card.'

Emirati put her hand out, so her understanding of the English language was stronger than her very basic singular words that were spoken. I lived amongst these women and knew I had to comply to ensure my stay continued with them. I handed it over and she pursed her lips together before stating, 'I have.' She handed it back to me before I sat down. I sat and contemplated believing that now things would start, and I looked forward to speaking with Mammy to tell her. It was a start and I had to remind myself continually that, 'It is now starting - my fight for freedom.'

I did indeed call my family to inform them that I had had a visit from the legal representation, and they wanted to know every single detail. It was always difficult to speak honestly on the phone, as there were always listeners. If I was speaking to my mother, sometimes I would break into Welsh at moments when I wanted privacy. My Welsh wasn't brilliant, but over the years my lack of use of it had caused me to lose my confidence in the spoken word, but I could, when need be, use my singing Welsh lilt. There was no point with my brother or Sah, as they would not have had an iota as to what was being said. But, when my mother asked me, 'What had the legal representative told me?' I could not lie and endeavoured to repeat the conversation as confidently as possible.

'The man was really nice, Mammy, and gave me his understanding of such cases and he was honest, very bloody honest.'

'Emily, can you tell me what he said?'

I sighed. A deep sigh that started from the bottom of my belly, rose past my mouth and to the beginning of my nostrils, and I exhaled deeply. 'He said that I was looking from six months to four years for a case like mine.'

'Oh Emily…' I could hear her break down uncontrollably.

'Mammy… don't upset yourself now. Come on. I honestly don't think it will come to that amount of time because I have been honest from the start and did not do it here.'

The silence continued.

'Why did you have to smoke that…? Emily in the garden? And what about Sah? Rob will be going back to Africa soon. What am I going to do?'

'I am sorry, Mammy. You will be ok. Try not to worry, and I know that is hard, but I have faith that I will be home definitely before six months, Mammy. And you need to be strong for Sah. She is a good girl, Mammy and just look after her as best that you can.'

'But Emily, I can't walk far. I can't take her out.'

'Mammy, you are the best grandmother that she could ask for. Don't worry about walking and going out with her. She has lots of things there that will entertain her. And remember Rob is a telephone call away.'

'Ok. Try not to worry. We will manage. We always have.'

'And if it comes to it, phone Sperm to have her for a couple of hours. Tell him that I am stuck in Dubai and unwell in hospital.'

'NO! I am not saying that. What if he gets Social Services involved? They could take her as I am disabled. He wouldn't have her, would he? That would be too much bloody work?'

'Oh God, Mammy, be careful. If he phones to see her then let him, but otherwise leave it.'

'He hasn't really bothered with her since being back, Emily.'

'I know, Mammy. I know.'

Trying to be upbeat was so exhausting, as I knew the legal truth of my situation and the predicted lock-up of times. But I admittedly believed that I did not deserve to be here, locked up in such awful conditions, with no rights whatsoever, because of a legal system that deemed all guilty instantaneously, with laws that did not match the country's cultural development. However, innocence had to be proven after being pushed continuously to sign documents of guilt without even knowing it. How could I have been so ignorant? I had lived in the Middle East, but I had never contemplated what the bloody legal system was like or heard of such cases. Hell, I always watched BBC World for news, and I never came across such stories. I didn't read local papers because for one, I didn't read Arabic, and secondly, the ex-pat world didn't discuss such things. We worked, socialised, and lived together in an unrealistic and unnatural utopia. And, most importantly, the longer this went on, the harder it would be for Sah.

I mean, how could I explain to a three-year-old that I was being held in a jail in Dubai, a country she loved to holiday in, swim, play and eat, the most important things to a child, that I was now incarcerated for smoking weed in Mam's garden, bathroom, my bedroom, over by the river and in the living room when everyone was asleep. And the reason for smoking it was to escape the pain of losing my father, my daddy, to try and cope with it and with not having him here with us. She had and would have no understanding, so the medical situation of illness in hospital was used throughout to pacify her. Whether this was right or wrong, I had no comprehension. I just tried, the best way I could, to manage the situation.

The conversation continued, 'But how is she, Mammy? Is she ok?'

'She misses you. We got a taxi back from Ammanford yesterday, and the first thing she told the driver was, 'My Mammy is in hospital in Dubai.'

'What? Who was this driver?'

'Oh, I don't know, but he told her that he hoped that Mammy would be better soon and home.'

'Oh.'

'But what really upset me, Emily, was something that happened the other day. I can't remember when, but we were outside, and I think Rob was doing something in the garden. Sah looked up at the sky Emily, and was shouting, 'Mammy I am here. Come back! Mammy I am here,' as an aeroplane flew past. She was waving her hands up like an S.O.S. Emily, it was heart-breaking.'

She sniffled her way through that sentence, and I simply said, 'I am so sorry, Mammy. I promise I will do everything I can do to get home to you.' My heart was breaking literally, and I felt the ache. I gulped, trying to breathe, whilst wiping the tears and snot from my nose and eyes. It was then that I saw the nod to get off the phone. 'Listen, I am going to have to go. Tell Sah I love her to infinity and beyond 100 million billion times. Bye, Mammy.' The line went dead, and my heart broke into little pieces at the thought of my beautiful girl fiercely calling for my return, as she thought I was on a plane.

It was so cruel. I knew that the guilt I would feel for everyone concerned in this sordid mess was something that would live within myself forever. It was something that I accepted, and the guilt was heavy, crushing, and unbearable.

Days followed with little amusement. The drugged tea helped to pacify and control my mood swings, anger and contempt for everything and everyone that was connected to the legal system, except for my legal representation, who I willed with everything to get me out. The saying, 'No news is good news,' fell flat, as everyone here was desperate for some news, well, hell, any news and for the most important thing, our freedom. A freedom that would allow us to leave.

However, one positive is that I got to know a couple of the other ladies, namely, the Filipino gang. Mary was friendly with them because of their strong belief and commitment to prayer, and I got to know them in the toilet queue. They wanted to know why I was here, and I explained the whole sordid story. I also got to know theirs as I started to have invites to their cell, which was nice escapism from mine, and it was only a few steps away. The majority were maids for rich Emirati families, and I could not believe some of their unacceptable stories.

One of the many stories consisted of a woman's employer not renewing her work visa, and this made her an illegal worker. She had been illegal for two years and had been unable to return home due to not having the funds to buy a plane ticket.

She had been arrested, then entered the Dubai legal system, had been here for nine months with no legal representation, no visit from her embassy and a family who depended on her financially in her home country. Another maid was not being fed by her Emirati family, so she went into a rubbish bin on the property and ate some pizza slices that had not been eaten by the family in the pizza box. She started to eat it and was caught by the family, who reported her to the police for stealing. I could not fathom the mentality of these people.

Then, there were other cases of accusations of adultery and prostitution, alcohol intake with and without a license, theft, having parties that had been reported, and the list went on. But what made my anger boil was how these ladies had been locked up, sometimes through no fault of their own, for long periods of time unnecessarily, without legal representation or support from their embassies. They had nobody and no hope. They were in such a desperate situation.

Deep down, we were all dealing with the situations as best that we could. But each second, each minute and hour of every day was difficult.

I became close with one of them. Her name was Clara, and one day she handed me papers with prayers on them. She had seen that I was struggling, and in her own words, she had told me, 'I see you, Emily. You are a good person, and you must remember that God has not forsaken you. Read these, Emily, and may they give you strength in difficult times.'

I hugged her, thanking her for her kindness. I went back to my cell to read them.

To Emily 31/8/2010

Psalm 27.1
The Lord is the light of my salvation whom shall I fear
The Lords the stronghold of my life whom shall I be afraid

Jeremiah 29:11
For I know the plans I have for you
Plans to prosper you and not to harm you, plans to give you hope and good future

Joshua 1:9
Do not be terrified, do not be discouraged, For I am with you wherever you are.

Our friendship had started with a smile in the toilet queue, and sadly, her story was another reflection of the reality of the fucked-up Dubai legal system. Clara had been imprisoned for overstaying her visa on her passport. Her previous Emirati sponsor had kept her passport and did not return it to her, so she had been working illegally with no funds or passport to leave. She was stuck in Dubai and awaiting deportation. However, with no funds for legal representation, and an absent embassy, she was stuck in the system.

Over the weeks, we had had many conversations on my way to the toilet. I held on to those papers in desperate times, and do you know what, they did give me strength in times where I felt so alone. There were too many times to count when I referenced the words, repeating them like a chant. Those papers are still with me today and are kept safely in a box. I know I will always have them with me for the remainder of my life. And I sincerely hope that I will not have a need to reference them at any time in the future, but I know they are there and always will be if needed.

I had to read them initially a couple of times to make sense of them, as my mind was foggy and my concentration skills had become limited mainly to the stress of the situation, I believe. But the message was clear that I was not alone. He, God, was with me all the way and that there was a reason for this. What that reason was I had no idea and I couldn't comprehend, but what meant so much to me was the kindness this woman had shown me when she didn't have to. Again, I was shown such kindness in an awful, depressing situation.

Then, one morning, I had a new visitor, and this new visitor had some news for me from Abe. Ye, bloody Abe. It was a normal, mundane, boring beyond belief morning, when this time, I actually heard my name being called. Immediately, I felt a spring in my step, and I bounced to the cell door to view an Arab man in a dish dash.

I approached him once the door was opened and I viewed a thin and small framed Emirati who had a rather high pitched, feminine voice who questioned, 'Emily?' as he grabbed my right hand to shake it.

'Hello,' I naturally answered, perplexed and questioning who the hell is this guy and if he is the lawyer that I paid 10K for … well, really? I lacked immediate confidence as he did not have an awe-inspiring formidable presence and I simply thought to myself, *I am fucked.* I am not sure if my facial expression and deep, sad oval eyes showed my exasperation, but he was so animated and excitable he seemed to be bouncing up and down on his seat like hot water in a saucepan whose heat got turned on and off continuously.

'My name is Ali, and I am representing you and Abe. I am here to meet you and to make sure you are happy?'

'Happy - are you being serious?' He could see and hear that his 'happy' statement possibly gave a reaction that wasn't expected.

'No, no, no. Happy wrong. Are you ok?' he questioned sympathetically.

'Well, to be honest, no, I am not alright. I have been arrested, locked up and been treated… well, pretty bloody awful really, and it has everything to do with Abe. His friend did warn me that the police were coming and to leave, but I still haven't got the foggiest bloody idea of what he has done. So, if you ask me am I ok, then the bloody answer is a big fat no.'

He looked unsure of whether to turn right or left in his bobbling movement and looked anxiously at me.

'I am sorry. I am here as I am Abe and your lawyer. I will represent you on this drugs case.'

'So, Abe is also a drugs case? Is this what it is about - drugs?'

'Emily, try not to worry about Abe. His friend reported him to the police because he was jealous of him. He wanted money and Abe would not give him.'

'Really?! You are telling me that I am here because one of Abe's friends, or workers or whatever he bloody is, reported him to the police because he was jealous and wanted more money?' I just didn't buy it, but then again, his friend did warn me that the police were coming. My introduction and meeting with this lawyer just made the whole experience more fucked up in my assessment.

'Yes, Emily. I tell you the truth. We will go to the prosecution this week, and I will represent you. Do you have any questions?'

'Yes, I bloody do. I am being locked up because of something that happened in the UK. I was arrested and made to sign documents that state I am guilty. I am not guilty of smoking in Dubai but was made to sign documents with the promise of release and that I will go home only then to be told that I face six months to four years. So, tell me, how you are going to get me out of this mess and home to my daughter in Wales?'

He smiled and tilted his head down and to the right to look at me closely. 'You are sad, Emily. I see this. But do not worry, you will go home.'

'Oh, my word! Seriously?! Really?! The number of times I have been told that… Of course, I will eventually go home, but the bloody question is when? Everybody has the freedom to bloody go home after serving their sentences. My word!'

However, my words did not faze him, and he sympathetically looked at me. He then changed the conversation by asking, 'You like Dubai?'

I laughed out loud, and the officers just looked at me, as though I had disturbed the peace. 'Like? I did once as I lived and worked here, and I had some pretty amazing experiences here. That is why I have always returned, but now what I have seen and experienced … well, I would have to say a big fat NO. I no longer LIKE!'

'Do not worry. We will meet soon.'

'Hang on. Before you go, you should know that I already have a lawyer.'

He was shocked, 'Really? Who?'

'I have paid Saeed to represent me as he has an incredibly good reputation as a drugs lawyer in Dubai. He is supposedly the best."

'Yes, yes, I know him.'

'Also, I have a British lawyer representing me, but that was my brother's choice because he was British and cheaper. I can't remember his name sadly."

'Oh, I think you have three of the best drugs lawyers in Dubai representing you,' he jovially answered.

'We will see how good you are with how quickly you get me out of here.'

He went into his pocket and handed me his business card. 'This is for you. If you have any questions, then please call. Before I go, tell me, do you have any friends here in Dubai that you could stay with?'

'I know an Emirati family in Al Ain. I have spoken to them over the years, as I taught their son and became close with him.'

'I live in Al Ain.'

'I used to live there and have some good memories.'

'If they lived in Dubai then this would help, but no, it doesn't matter.'

It was strange as the officers had not been as aggressive and negative with this lawyer as they had been with the previous one, or I hadn't noticed them as I had been animated myself in my retorts. He left after holding my hands in his, smiling and politely bowing his way out, as I remained perplexed about the meeting I had just had. I returned to the cell where the ladies waited for news, hell, any bloody news. I stood at the doorway and looked at the pale bodies and sad white faces and commented whilst I scratched my head, 'Well, that was funny. I have another lawyer.'

Lebanese sat up and deeply replied, 'What, you have another lawyer?'

I stood there with my right hand resting on one of the bars. 'Ye, it seems Abe has got a lawyer for me who is from Al Ain.'

Anna joined in the conversation, 'So, now you have the best lawyer who cost £10,000, a lawyer that your brother chose and one from Abe. I don't think I ever heard of someone having three lawyers here. Who is he?'

'To be honest, I am not impressed. I am sure he is very nice and qualified, but he was just... I don't know. I don't think I have confidence in him.' I looked back and analysed my meeting with him through flashbacks, then confirmed, 'Ye, the whole experience was just odd. And do you know what? He didn't even ask me any questions really concerning my case. Bonkers.' I passed the card, and they had never heard of him. I sat back and just thought to myself literally, *what the fuck?*

Days continued, then one morning my name was called, and I was informed that I was going to the Dubai Public Prosecution Service to meet my prosecutor. Now, it is very funny to me personally when you read the Dubai Public Prosecution website. It personifies how the service 'strives to create a more secure community by protecting the legal rights and freedom of the community, using justice, independence, and cooperation with its partners to ensure a fair and secure society. It believes in transparency and accuracy of investigations and uses modern techniques to create an efficient public prosecution for Dubai. Justice is achieved by protecting the rights of all parties involved in court cases, irrespective of gender, origin, religion, or social status, on the principle that the accused is presumed innocent until proven guilty. It conducts all investigations independently and imposes charges based on clear and precise evidence.'

If I had known the above upon my first meeting with the prosecutor, I am sure I would have been more articulate and professional, legally, in my presentation. However, I did not. Now, the transparency and accuracy of my investigation was nil, as I had been a tourist and was in accommodation that was visited by the police and arrested automatically. So, what modern techniques were they using to create this efficient public prosecution? And the principle of the accused is presumed innocent until proven guilty, well, that was a laugh in itself. Why the hell did I sign Arabic documents that I didn't understand under duress, which admitted my guilt if this was the case? And where was the clear and precise evidence?

Dubai is ruled by Sharia Law, the legal system derived from the Koran and seen as the 'Word of God.' Whilst they may wish to personify their country's values, identity, and rules of being more western in this multicultural world of ours we now live in, I was no longer fooled, and my eyes had been opened wide, with my ignorance no longer acceptable. Hell existed, and it was here; I was in it.

I was notified with a 30-minute warning that I was to go to the prosecutor. When I went back into the cell and the girls educated me that the prosecutor would question me to find out the facts of my case and listen to my pleas. I knew I had to compose myself, dress smartly, present a confident, articulate, and professional manner to ensure that my story was heard my way. I was allowed to go into my bag to get a change of clothes, put some makeup on and spray some perfume. I only really had my nice, dirty bloodied Monsoon maxi dress, but knew that with the addition of my black Mark's and Spencer's cardigan it would make me very presentable. I hoped the Prosecutor's first initial judgement on meeting me would be positive. Thank God my maxi dress was black and floral, as I really don't think I would have got away with wearing a lighter colour than black. But it would have been interesting to see the facial expressions of the Emirati's pure disgust at the bloody evidence and stains left, that had a worse effect on my pubic hair, vaginal and anal area and don't let me get started on the streams down my legs.

Handcuffed, I left by myself and under the care of a female officer. We left the station and I felt it immediately, the sun burning my eyes and forcing them to close, whilst the dry heat filled my lungs and made my whole body heavy and weak at the same time. I sat with my head rested on my right arm against the window, closed my eyes, allowing the bright shine of the heat from the sun to show me the shadows of the objects and things we passed in the police car I now found myself in. Even though the air conditioning was on I could smell and taste the staleness of the air.

The male driver and female officer didn't speak in front of me for the whole journey. I was such an open and friendly personality, well, I used to be, that I found it hard not to be polite and just naturally speak. However, since becoming incarcerated, I had been judged and condemned by them, and now this is how things were. But this journey was different as I only felt peace and an ambience of tranquillity and strength, as though the hand of God was shining down on me, and his light surrounded me on this journey. I felt no sadness, anxiety, or darkness, but with each inhale and exhale of the warm, heavy air, I felt the circular movements of my breathing with the pure heat that shone around me, that it fuelled me, made my soul and my very being calm, relaxed, and prepared me for what would come next. I felt as though I was breathing for the first time, that what had been had passed and that I was so much lighter. Or was I being delusional that with the loss of my father and with everything else I had dealt with on this holiday that all this personal turmoil with the realisation that this next meeting I had reached an ultimatum and possibly the most critical point in my life, that I was having a breakdown?

We arrived and I was escorted from the car through entrance doors, corridors which passed offices with chairs lined up outside of them, and several staff and visitors like me in handcuffs and officers in different coloured uniforms. I was so embarrassed to walk past these people wearing these handcuffs, so I held my head and shoulders arched and lowered. For one they were uncomfortable, and two, only criminals wore handcuffs. I mean, what did those people think I could have possibly done here - prostitution (God no), murder (as if, I mean, I may think about getting away with it with certain people, but hell no. I wouldn't be able to sleep at night), theft (I only buy what I can afford, and if I can't afford it then I won't have it - simple as that), and then there were drugs, and they would be right in this judicial system, except that it was not bloody experienced in Dubai.

There were others there in the same gang as me, the handcuff gang. Men in lines of handcuffs, who were mostly Asian and in their own jail jumpsuits, stood emotionless and full of self-pity. They looked broken, weathered, and lost. I felt for them. I peeped up from time just to slightly view them. I mean, I couldn't walk with my head high with confidence as though I was walking into a disco, this place and situation was serious, and my future could depend on this very meeting.

The female officer obviously knew where we were going, so I followed. We seemed to walk for a couple of minutes, as the building was noticeably big with many floors. I was told to sit down outside of an office, whilst she knocked on a door, opened it, and what followed was a conversation between herself and something masculine in voice. This ended with her closing the door, and then sitting herself two seats away from me. I remained calm as I sat there, and I looked up and down the corridor. Some workers walked past with files, and then I had to do a double-take. I blinked my eyes to make sure that I was not seeing things, and then it hit me, 'Fuck! It is Abe.' My heart immediately beat quicker, and my breaths became deeper, and I felt the anger rise from the bottom of my spine and rise sharply to my neck. My head tilted forwards, my lips pursed, jaws clenched, and an invisible dark veil engulfed me.

He walked coolly as though he didn't have handcuffs on, but as though he was happily walking the corridors of a nightclub. With his swagger, his dish dash followed, and then he had the biggest smile on his face as he approached me.

He joyfully commented, 'Immi!'

I quickly turned to the officer and said, 'That's Abe! What do I do?' She looked at me and showed no emotion or interest. I shook my head as my eyes focused right to left, left to right. I could feel my cheeks burning darkly and felt my nervous red blotches growing on my chest and neck. I looked up at him as he stood in front of me, not saying a word. His officer had sat down on the left and Abe softly said,

'Hi Immi. Are you ok?'

I looked down at my hands that were in handcuffs, and then I looked up at him and deep into his eyes whilst shaking them. 'Am I ok?' Really, Abe? Am I ok? No! I am not ok!'

He sat down next to me, and I couldn't distinguish whether he had a look of anger or anguish, then he held my hands, and I suppose, in a funny way, our handcuffs met and touched. I couldn't look or face him, as I was just so angry.

'Immi, is this how it is now? Why are you like this?'

He removed his hands and sat upright in his chair, and I honestly believed that he was shocked by my reaction. I mean, what did he bloody expect from me, a warm embrace where I grabbed him and kissed him on his lips and face. Hell, that would get me arrested for public indecency or something ludicrous, which could mean a longer sentence. This was all so messed up.

We both sat back in our chairs deflated, I turned to look at him and watched his eyes and facial expressions when I questioned, 'Abe, why were you arrested? What the hell have you done?'

I could see that he did not like my questioning, but at this point I didn't care a flying fuck, to be honest. He pursed his lips and then smirked wryly, with big wide eyes, before abruptly turning to face me.

'Immi, I do not understand why you are like this?' he answered with indignation.

I immediately shook my head, then looked at him deeply highlighting, 'Abe, think of Sahara. She is at home, and she does not deserve this. And I still don't know why I was initially arrested with you? What the hell have you done? And was it worth it, because look at us, Abe, bloody look at us.' I held my handcuffs in the air to highlight the 'Look at us,' but he had no answer for me. We sat there like two strangers with no words. I felt so numb inside that even my conscience had stopped working, and I felt nothing. I could feel Abe moving in his seat, and then he started speaking Arabic. I turned to my right to see who he was talking to, and to my surprise, it was Abe's lawyer who was also representing me. He was as animated as ever, and whilst I watched him, he reminded me of a nodding chihuahua dog head, like the ones you see in cars.

He smiled at me once he had finished yapping to Abe and joyfully said, 'Hello Immi, and how you are today?'

This guy I thought… This guy… How does he bloody think I feel? I am here in Dubai charged on a drug conviction for my first meeting with the prosecutor, and now I have been joined by Abe who, I believed, was responsible for me being in the situation I now found myself in.

I knew I had to answer politely, so I smirked and answered, 'Hello. I am well.'

He returned the smile and then continued to chat with Abe. It seemed to be getting heated as Abe was raising his arms and the tone, pitch and speed of his voice changed. I looked to my right, and to my surprise the officers were not interested in the conversation, and they continued to look at their mobile phones. How odd was this situation?

Then, the door opened in front of us, and a man called us in, firstly, by questioning our names to which we both confirmed and then we entered. It was a large white square room with chairs placed in front of a desk, his desk, and it was a room with no warmth but very sterile. However, the fragrance that the prosecutor was wearing was very welcoming and had been delicious in smell and to my very taste with the fragrances I had experienced of late. The atmosphere that enveloped us was cold and he looked at us with questioning eyes, big dark brown eyes. The lawyer sat in between Abe and I, but he need not worry as I wasn't going to jump up and punch the living daylights out of the turd that got me into this mess, as I knew it would only add on a couple of years to my sentence. I wasn't that stupid. I mean, come on?

The conversation turned into Arabic, and I did not have the foggiest as to what was going on. I looked around to witness my officer behind me, looking as vacant as ever. I questioned her suitability to this job and came to the quick decision that neither she nor her comrades were suited to this profession and what was going on employing such beauties?

Before I had a chance to delve into this realisation, I was brought back to my reality as Abe informed me, 'Immi, please, he speak to you.'

I turned to Abe and then looked at the other Arab faces looking at me and smiled with a simple, 'Sorry. I didn't understand what you were saying in Arabic.'

The prosecutor had my attention as his eye contact was piercing. He was a young man in his early thirties, and there was something about him. So, I waited to see where the hell this conversation would lead.

'Emily, I am the prosecutor. Have you been treated well?'

I wanted to laugh out loud, but I knew this would serve no purpose whatsoever. So, I refrained from laughing and in all seriousness answered accordingly, as to the facts that I knew.

'Have I been treated well? Well, I was arrested, and I still do not know why, locked up for three days in between being interrogated by a good cop/bad cop and forced to sign a document, or more aptly documents, to say I was guilty on a drugs charge for smoking marijuana in the United Kingdom and not here. And I did write on the documents that I did not understand what I was signing as I was not even told initially what the charges were for. So, after being locked up for three days, I believe initially without a telephone call to my embassy or family, and more importantly, bleeding without sanitary towels for my whole period after asking continuously for some. And don't get me started on Bur Dubai. What I am witnessing there is a human rights abomination. And the topping on the cake is that I could be locked up for years for something I did not do in the United Arab Emirates. And the most important point of all is that while I am here for reasons that I still cannot fathom, my daughter, my four-year-old daughter, is waiting for me in the UK not knowing or understanding why you have kept me here and will continue to do so for however long you deem fit for this travesty.'

I had tried to my best ability to convey what I was thinking and feeling to three perplexed faces, so I continued.

'And, I will be very honest with you when I question how this lawyer can represent me and Abe together? It is questionable. I already have lawyers, to be honest, as my brother in the UK organised it. And, if he is here for Abe then where are mine?''

He interrupted me, 'You have lawyers? What are their names?'

'I have their names here. Please wait a minute whilst I find them.' I wasn't daft, yes, I didn't have much common sense, but I knew I might need such evidence.

He chuckled to himself, which I found offensive if I was being honest. 'Emily, you have the best drug lawyers in Dubai representing you.'

I affirmed, 'Yes, I have been told that, and at an extortionate price as well may I add. I will have to sell my house to pay for the legal bills, and then there's my job in Qatar. I need to get back to it by September, or I will lose it and all our belongings there. It is all such a mess.'

The prosecutor looked at me questionably and then asked, 'What is your job in Qatar?'

'I work as a teacher and teach English to learners whose first language is not English. I also teach Special Needs. That is why we moved to Qatar because my daughter has difficulties, and I wanted to provide the best education and life for her.'

'Your daughter has special needs, yes?'

'Yes, she has dyspraxia tendencies. It is a disorder affecting fine and/or gross motor coordination, planning, organising, and carrying out movements in the right order in everyday situations. It also affects her articulation and speech, perception and thought. She is a beautiful little girl who deserves the absolute best from life, as it will be challenging and harder for her than others.'

I looked back down to my lap and awaited the stream to flow uncontrollably.

When Abe interjected, 'Immi has done nothing wrong. Can you please let her go? This is nothing to do with her. I mean why? Why this?'

He sat back in his chair and sighed, 'She is in the system. There is nothing I can do.'

Abe lifted his right hand and repeated, 'But she did nothing!'

'It is out of my control. If she wasn't in the system, then she could go now, but that is not the case.'

There was then a knock on the door and words spoken between the prosecutor and our joint lawyer. The person knocking on the door then opened it. I turned to see what the hell was going on and another dish dash man walked in. He had a large black case in his right arm and was rather large and round in size, but he was not overweight as his frame suited his build. He was not out of breath or sweating but had a cool demeanour as though he was in control as he walked into the room. He reminded me of a rugby player, if I was honest, and he had the attention of everyone.

He stood still at my side, and I looked up to him, as he looked down at me, whilst continuing to command the room with whatever he was saying. It was so frustrating not knowing what was being said. Then, he stopped, and the prosecutor replied. This continued like tennis from right to left when the conversation came to me.

He looked down at me and said in a deep but friendly voice, 'Emily, I am your lawyer.'

I questioned, 'Which one are you?'

'Your brother employed me to represent you. You met my colleague at Bur Dubai, and he questioned you.'

'Oh yes, so you're the best drugs lawyer in Dubai, aren't you?'

When I said it, I realised that this could have been rather offensive to the lawyer to my right that was also representing me through Abe, but my lawyer started to chuckle and so did the prosecutor.

Then, the prosecutor continued with, 'And she also has this gentleman representing her and...' The conversation then continued in Arabic.

He yelped, 'What? You have three lawyers? Are you crazy?'

Now, the others laughed as they thought this was very funny, and I felt the strong need to clear up the reasons why I had three lawyers.

'Yes, I have employed two lawyers who are supposedly the best in drug case law. Where the other one is, I do not know, as I haven't met him yet, but I initially wanted you, and my brother went for the cheaper offer, but we sorted that out and I have you representing me finally. You,' and I referenced to the lawyer sat to my right, 'well, Abe employed you to represent us and is that even ethical here in Dubai? Is it ethical to have the same lawyer?' They concurred with nodding to confirm that indeed it was legal. I shook my head whilst they still seemed to be amused by the number of lawyers I had.

Then Abe leant forward in my direction, whispering unsuccessfully, 'Immi, it is good that we have other lawyers,' looking at our joint lawyer in the middle with some distaste. I didn't know what was going on there, but if he thought I was going to pay extortionate prices for the lawyers for him too, then he was in for a shock. I needed to get home to Sah, and that was my only obsession and priority here and now.

I looked up to catch his gaze and simply said, 'I am sorry, Abe, but I am losing my house to pay the price for these men to get me back home to Sah. I will lose my job and everything I own in Qatar. My return flight date has gone as I have been locked up and could be for months or years. You have your lawyer, and he will represent you only as I have my legal representation. I wish you all the best, Abe, I really do, but I still don't know who you really are if I am honest and why you were arrested.'

He pursed his lips and retorted, 'So it is like this? Once I loved you, but not now. No more. Halas, Halas, Halas.'

'Did you ever love me, Abe, or was it all lies? And don't get me on the bloody engagement. Was that just a control thing?' I pleaded to know.

He did not respond and looked straight ahead. *What a bastard,* I thought. The lawyer in the middle raised his eyebrows. He had observed our conversation with swift births of head movement from right to left with each response. I could see he did not know where to look.

I sat back and looked up to watch the prosecutor and my lawyer laughing and chatting like old friends. I could clearly view that they had an incredibly good relationship and hoped this could possibly be an advantage for me personally. But as I looked at Abe, I shook my head in disbelief with the realisation he had never loved me truly. Had he used me? I lowered my head, closed my eyes with a *not again* realisation and a simple why?

I was interrupted by Abe's lawyer who asked me, 'Immi, where is your other lawyer?'

'I have no idea as I have never spoken to him or even met him.'

'Oh, I see.' I then pointed to my lawyer and the prosecutor who were happily speaking about what only the Arabs in the room would know and affirmed, 'They seem very friendly, don't they?'

'Yes, yes, yes. They are. They are family. So, of course.'

'What? They are family?'

'Yes. Cousins, I think.'

'Is that even ethical for my case, I mean, having him as my lawyer and prosecutor? I mean, isn't there a conflict of interest or something legal like that?'

'No, no. It is fine. You are fine.'

'I don't know what to say.' I was in disbelief at the legal system here, but then the intelligent slow-witted brain of mine started to realise that there could also be benefits to this family relationship. It could possibly help get me out of here quicker. I sat upright and more poised. Abe looked at me smiling. He was no idiot, so I assumed he had come to the same realisation, otherwise, it meant that he was a complete bastard and he was rubbing salt in the wound of my heart. I needed to know what the next stages in this case were, so I knew I had to raise the point with the men in this room, so I politely asked, 'So, excuse me?' I waited before proceeding, as I needed their full and not partial attention. I had all the attention as I observed the faces in the room in a semicircle. 'What is going to happen now to me? When can I go home, please?'

My lawyer said something to the prosecutor and after a short discussion, he turned and walked towards me, bending down to be at my eye level. He smiled and softly spoken answered, 'Emily, I will be honest with you, this is a serious case. You should have said nothing as you admitted the drugs. You signed. Now we go to court. You will go home Emily, but I cannot say when. You will see your daughter.'

I just couldn't believe the seriousness of the situation. 'Thank you for being honest with me. I just need to get home to my daughter. She has just turned four and it has always been us two. My mother is elderly and if I am here for years there is a possibility that she could go into care, and I will lose her. She doesn't deserve this! What I have experienced since being arrested has been punishment. I have learned my lesson.'

I didn't realise it until I looked up, but all eyes were on me in a conversation I believed was private. I don't know if my words would have any bearing and help my case, but my desperation and need to hold my baby girl was so great that I had no control over this permanent internal ache.

The prosecutor said something and then everyone except myself stood to their feet, then I followed instinctively. They continued to speak, and by this time, Abe's lawyer had joined the two legal relatives in their conversation. There was laughter amongst them, whilst Abe and I stood uncomfortably and closer than I would have liked to be. I had nothing to say, not one single word, then he said my name.

'Immi?' I looked up at him with pursed lips and handcuffed arms. I felt as though I was dealing with a naughty student who had really done something unforgivable, and I had no understanding why they had done what they had. Any empathy had gone.

With a curt voice I answered, 'What Abe?'

'It is good that we have all these lawyers. I believe, yes, I think it will help us.'

'Abe, let me get this point clear to you. I am locked up facing a six-month to four-year jail sentence. My daughter, you do remember her, don't you? Well, she is back in the UK without her mother. I have lost my job, most probably in Qatar, and all my possessions and all Sah's possessions since birth - our home. And you tell me you don't love me anymore after telling me to sleep with Mo?' I got closer to him clenching my fists with a need to hit out and scream at him for all this bloody mess. I couldn't, but I had so much venomous anger towards him. It worked because my voice became darkly evil, deep, and gruff. 'What do you expect, Abe? Seriously?'

His face became a shadow of doubt and he answered, 'Immi, I am sorry. I did not want you to go through this. I do love you, but I am very angry. What did you tell the police?'

His words were said sweetly to no avail of affection from me.

To the point and with a matter of fact, I answered, 'I told them the truth Abe, that I had smoked marijuana in the UK because of the stress of my father's death as a coping mechanism. And, that I came out here to run away and make sense of the loss, by myself, and to be close to you, my fiancé.' I looked directly at his eyes with my final sentence, 'And I believe this is and will forever be the biggest mistake of my life.'

He stepped close to me until his mouth was a few centimetres from my right ear. 'Immi, let us work together to get us both out of here and home. Then, we can be back together, all of us.'

If he thought using my daughter would pull on my heartstrings, he was bloody mistaken.

'Abe, I thought I was clear that you have your lawyer and I have my two. I do not need your help and I will fight this with everything I have. I still don't know why you were arrested, for God's sake.' I paused and then I went close to his left ear before continuing, 'And after you tried to prostitute me out to your friend and God knows what else has been going on, well, let's just say we are fucking finished. Done! Dead!'

I turned around to face my female police officer and questioned, 'Can we leave now?'

She shrugged her shoulders and had little understanding herself. I mean, though I didn't want to return to the hellhole of Bur Dubai, I thought the sooner we are all out of this office, the sooner my lawyer can start on this case, whether making court dates or whatever he did in the capacity of his position, legal and illegal.

Then, my lawyer left his little hareem of legal workers and approached me. I stood back from Abe and he informed me, 'Emily, next time we will meet, it will be in court. Do you have any questions for me before we leave?'

I gave a small smile and said, 'No, I don't really, as you have been open and honest. Just ... how long will the process take? I just need to get home to my daughter.'

He could see tears rising and he instructed me to, 'Walk with me, Emily.'

He said his farewell to the others, and I smiled and said a simple but clear, 'Goodbye and thank you.' I thought it would be a nice touch to shake their hands and did so. I knew a positive presentation from me could only help to make them remember me when they read my name on forms, make me personable and real to them as a human being and not a convicted drug user. Or so I assumed.

I could not ignore Abe as this would be childish, and I knew I still had to show some respect to this prick in the male-dominated society we found ourselves. So, I walked up to him and kissed his right cheek and then his left, before standing back from him and looking up into his eyes. I could smell stale smoke, cigarette smoke, I believe, or it was teeth that hadn't been brushed in a while. With my right hand, I raised it and touched the long curls that circled his head and softly said, 'Goodbye and good luck, Abe.'

I walked and followed my lawyer until we were both out of the door, with the female officer behind us. He raised his right hand as we continued walking and in an amused loud voice he chuckled, 'Look, here is your other lawyer. Ha, ha ha, ha.'

I looked upright to view this other lawyer who was also wearing his whites which were grey with age. They spoke and looked at me as they discussed what I still don't know, and I assumed it was all about me.

'Hello, Emily. I am your lawyer. I am sorry I am late, but I was in court on another case.'

He had a posh British accent, but that meant nothing as he could have been sent to a private school in the UK or USA, been anglicised with western culture, history, language, art, as realistically, money is no object to the wealthy. However, what I found from my experiences in the Middle East is that their indoctrinated faith expelled their experiences that expanded their senses, knowledge and understanding, and one returned to the womb of their faith once they returned, reverting to their old ways once they returned home to their Arabic country.

I confirmed, 'Yes, I am Emily.'

'Well, it seems that you have the best drugs lawyers in Dubai representing you.' They both laughed and touched one another's arms.

I quickly answered, 'It seems so, and if you are the best, I expect you to do all you can to get me out of this hell and back home to my daughter.'

They both looked at each other and then returned to my gaze. I was sure they were not used to being spoken to like this, and

I must be honest, it was a rare occurrence for me to be so direct and to the point. I could switch off to a lot and roll my eyes, but if I was narked or extremely pissed off, it could emerge, but very rarely.

He retorted, 'Well, I can see you are in good hands, so I will say goodbye.'

'Firstly, my brother paid you to represent me. And this is the first time we have met.'

I could see he did not know where I was going with this, but I was obviously questioning his professionalism and that of his law firm. I had no faith in him, and I was correct in my initial gut instinct to go with my initial choice, and to push my brother. My mother was and had always been correct in her estimation that it is better to pay a bit extra for better quality. £3,000 down the pan, thank you very much, brawd. I looked at him in dismay and whether he realised it, I will never know. And as soon as he arrived for his late meeting, he was gone. What was the point of it?

My lawyer was still walking with me when he suddenly stopped and said, 'I must go now. Now, listen to me carefully, say nothing if you are asked. Say nothing. Already you have said too much.'

'What?' I was really perplexed as I had always assumed it was in the interests of the individual to cooperate with the legal system.

'Emily, they should never have arrested you. You should not have given them any samples. You should have said nothing until you were given legal representation. You should not have admitted your guilt even if it was in the UK.'

'But they would not give me legal representation when I asked, no phone calls, nothing. They told me to sign the documents, and I stated on them I did not know what I was signing. I am and was damned if I did, damned if I didn't.'

He looked sympathetically, 'I will fight for you, Emily, and I give you my word. Be strong, and now wait. Next, I will see you in court, but if you have any questions, then contact my secretary who gave his card to you in Bur Dubai, Omar.'

I nodded and with that, we said our goodbyes. He left in one direction, and the female officer then instructed me to our departure point. To say I was conscious of the stares as we walked past departments, officers, and office workers was an understatement. I also felt drained mentally and physically. I had no idea what had happened to Abe, and if I was honest, I didn't care or have the energy to give to the man I now knew he was, and possibly had been from the very beginning.

We made our way out to the car park where the car was awaiting with a male driver, and it was a different one. The heat was dry and the sun not as bright as it had been when it first glared at my poor sensitive eyes upon our meeting. Handcuffs on, I managed to connect my seat belt and open the window six centimetres to allow the heat and air to purify my being, to take me to a higher level and feel the warmth upon my soul, letting me know that He hadn't forgotten His child, who was indeed in need of His strength. Then, it occurred to me, 'Oh my word, now I sound deeply religious. What the f…?'

I dreaded the thought of going back to the cell and that atmosphere of loss of life and hope, and the bombardment of questions that would follow. Whilst simultaneously, I also looked forward to the opportunity of letting my mother and brother know of the new developments if I was allowed to make a phone call. I am sure I had missed my usual daily lunch, but to my surprise the girls had kept me some fruit to eat which was exceedingly kind of them.

Lebanese and Emirati, as usual, were extremely interested in my case and my meeting with the lawyer that we shared. I explained that Abe was there and the bloody shock of seeing him.

'What? You saw him?' Anna questioned.

'Yes, he walked up to me as though everything was ok. I couldn't believe it as he was so cool, as though nothing had happened.'

Anna was sat on the bunk bed and said in her Russian accent, 'Bastard. Men are bastards.' The others muttered in agreement possibly reminiscing and reflecting on previous relationships. I thought it wouldn't be hard, as I was sure we had all encountered one or more during each of our lifetimes.

'And do you know what pissed me the most was the fact that I had the best drug lawyers in Dubai. They thought it was amusing. And did you know that our lawyer is the cousin of the prosecutor? My God, how corrupt could that be? Bloody bonkers.'

Lebanese bitch asked, 'What will happen next Emily?'

'Well, my lawyer said that he will see me in court next.'

Lebanese commented, 'Then you will go to court soon.'

'Oh, I bloody hope so if it starts the process of getting me out of this fucking place.'

They laughed in response to understanding how I felt.

'Oh, and you know that lawyer Abe had for me? Well, I kind of said Abe can have him and I will have my two. But my second lawyer didn't turn up until we were leaving and said that I was fine as I had the best drugs lawyer. So, I don't know if he is representing me anymore and whether I only have one lawyer now. What a waste of money.'

'At least you have lawyer, Emily,' Lebanese retorted.

'Oh, you misunderstand. Yes, I am bloody lucky to have legal representation, but the money I spent on that lawyer, well, any lawyer, I just don't have, and I don't know how or how long it will take me to pay it off.'

I sat back and munched the banana the girls had kept for me. I also ensured I had a couple of cups of the drugged tea and lay back to close my eyes, and with the noise of chatter around me, tried to the best of my ability to re-analyse the events of my day. I came to the swift conclusion that the whole experience was bloody mad and slept quietly until the routine buzz of our evening meal awakened all the souls I now lived with.

The long days and nights continued. We had the weekly cleaning and shopping day, and sporadic phone calls, but with

Ramadan everything seemed to change and slow down. Now, this didn't affect me personally, as I am not Muslim, so we had our daily food, but for the practising Muslims it was hard and long for them to fast all day. There were moments where you knew they found it difficult, as if they were trying to rest and if there was any noise from outside of our cell they would shout, 'Be quiet,' and I assumed the equivalent in Arabic. Sometimes this would be done from the comfort of their own mattress and sometimes with a sprint to make their annoyance visible.

Then there were times when we would sit for moments and have a funny five-minute episode where silly shit was spoken. On one occasion, and to this day I do not know where the conversation started on this topic, but sex with different nationalities came up. And the Arabic ladies asked plainly what sex was like with Abe.

I replied honestly and answered, 'Well, he wasn't the best, to be honest. His willy was small, thin and brown. It was like a quick wham bang. But, he had big droopy heavy balls which banged against my arse as he went up and down, up and bloody down.'

'So, no good?' asked Emirati in her broken English.

'Well, he was ok, but as I said, not the best. And the funny thing is he didn't do oral sex.'

Something was said between them and the translation in Arabic given when Emirati returned to me and said a long 'Ah', and started to stick her tongue in and out, illustrating the method used for cunnilingus. I furrowed my eyebrows as she seemed to enjoy herself, and I then looked around the cell to see amused, shocked and confused faces. I wanted to laugh out loud. She then sat forward with her elbows on her knees in anticipation that this conversation would continue.

'Ye, he would not do oral sex with me because he said he needed a special and very expensive scent to massage me first.'

Lebanese immediately questioned, 'WHAT?'

'I know right? That is what I thought.'

'Emily, I am Arabic, and I have never heard of this scent before. I know many men do not like to give it but receive it, but with no scent?'

She then continued to speak Arabic to the others there and then Emirati stated, 'No true,' before continuing, 'Gay!'

'Oh, I hope bloody not. One thing is for sure though, I will be going to an STD clinic for tests as soon as I get home. God knows what I could have picked up if what I have been told is true.' I could see that they had no idea what on earth I had said, so I expanded, 'Sexually Transmitted Disease Clinic to make sure I have no sexually transmitted diseases from Abe'.

Whether they understood I do not know but Emirati in her broken English asked me, 'What British men… like?'

Anna shouted out, 'British men small. No good. Russian men good, big and hard.'

We all laughed at her as she acted out the small, a smile with the good, a horse-sized penis with the big and hard.

'You can't say that for all British men, Anna. I have had some very big, thick willies and on the other hand I have had sex where I didn't know they were even in me. Anyway, they say it is not the size of it, it is what you do with it that counts.'

The conversation continued, 'So Abe no good?' Emirati continued.

'No, I am not saying that. What I am saying is that he wasn't the best and I have had a lot better.'

Moroccan joined in, 'Arabs not big like white men.'

Then, pregnant African shouted, 'No, you not say that. I have some big and good. Some so big they make we walk funny.' She got off the bunk and walked across the mattresses doing a cowboy walk. However, I thought she looked as though she had done her back in.

Mary whispered to me in her ever so feminine South African voice, 'Emily, I feel really uncomfortable discussing such private things. I am going to go and pray before they ask me such questions.'

I understood clearly where she was coming from, as I was not one to discuss such private matters as my mother always told me growing up, 'I don't want to know things like that - it is private, Emily. Your father would kill me if I discussed it with anyone.'

Lebanese waited for Mary to leave before asking, 'Where she go now?'

'Oh, Mary is going to pray with the Filipinos I think.'

'Yes, she goes to pray for our souls - for forgiveness, as we speak of fucking.' she stated, with laughter from the others. I didn't find it funny and looked down at my hands before the conversation continued.

'My husband,' and she laughed as though she remembered something, 'No, my ex-husband,' followed by more laughter, which stopped dramatically, 'He good you know. I … children.' She illustrated seven fingers, so she had been one busy rabbit.

I simply smiled and said, 'That's nice.'

Pregnant African on her bed with her legs separated at 8 months, 'Well, mine do something right,' laughing as she rubbed her belly.

'Emily, who best?' Emirati asked with concentration. What was it with this woman about sex and a penis - any penis?

'Oh, well this is my opinion which others may disagree with, but the best I have had, and may I add that I haven't had many, well, not as much as my old friends, I would have to say that the best I had are English, Danish and Welsh. The English because I am sure he had Viking DNA and boy was he big, the Danish boy was and by God he was beautiful. He definitely had Viking in him, and do you know those two were both blonde? I have to say Sah's father, it was his size and not what he did with it because he was so lazy, or drunk or stoned that he couldn't do much. It is strange but when I was younger, I was a lot thinner because of all the riding I did.'

I sat back and daydreamed for the two previous, one who I

had loved many years ago whilst young and foolish at university, and one that I lusted for, my Viking, from the time I lived and worked voluntarily in Israel. Ye, going there when I did, I mean Israel, was not my best decision. But what an experience.

'Ah, look Emily smiles,' Emirati stated.

'Oh, can we change this bloody conversation as it is getting me going,' as I crossed my legs.

'What?' was the question from the puzzled faces. Lebanese interrupted to translate, and they chuckled.

Then, the Africans started in their deep African accents, and non-pregnant one concluded, 'You know Emily, what they say about black men it is true. I have had many, many men and yes, some I swear as long and... thick, yes, thick as a horse. They hurt me you know, and I scream, scream, scream, oh but I like. I like a lot. Mmm.'

Pregnant one looked right to her and said, 'Where you have like horse? Me I have like elephant and I not walk after. Very very sore.'

She got up and walked holding the bottom of her skirt as to show she was in pain.

Lebanese was to conclude, 'No more sex talk please. Look, we have no men here, only women. No good.'

Anna jokingly said, 'If you want you can. We have lesbians here?'

I immediately questioned, 'What? Who?'

Lebanese replied, 'You not see them here, Emily. They are the manly ones and ones who will do anything for money.'

'You have to be joking, who the hell is going to have sex here? There is no privacy and well, to be honest, it isn't the most romantic of places, is it?'

Lebanese explained, 'They have sex in the shower, the toilet and the cell. Remember the Indian woman who was here, well, she used to leave and go upstairs with a police officer. It helped her to leave quickly. And you have the female officers here. Some are lesbians.'

I had a distasteful expression and just said, 'Well, nobody better try it on with me here. Be warned. I have no issues whatsoever with people's sexuality, but I am a no-go area here.' I got up to get a cup of my herbal drugged tea.

The cell went quiet as we all got back on to our mattresses and slept or daydreamed for a short space of time. I just looked around and hoped that no funny business would go on near me in this cell, as I wouldn't know how to react or where to look. It wasn't as though I could leave. I concluded this place was bloody bonkers and the sooner I got out of here the bloody better for my own sanity.

Endless days followed and there was some respite as depending on who was on those who could afford it were allowed to order a takeaway. It was only allowed because of Ramadan and the police officers were too lazy themselves to order the food. We were also allowed more time for telephone calls, well, those with phone cards and who could afford them. This meant calls back home, and voices I yearned for were daily, but with no updates from my legal team.

After a few days, another conversation erupted, and Lebanese asked me whether I would get back with Abe upon my freedom.

'Like bloody hell I will. No way! No fucking way.' The conversation continued and I stated, 'I have had so much time to contemplate things here and I now believe he saw me as an object and I suppose he wanted to control me through getting engaged, wearing fancy dress and there are other things too. I remember he woke me up one night gone 3am and I was going to be up at 5 to drive to work. I had been sleeping for hours whilst he had been drinking and smoking downstairs with his friends. I felt him get in to bed and then he got up close to me and whispered in my left ear, 'Immi, I am horny, horny, horny.'

Lebanese retorted, 'He said that?'

'Yes, he always told me he was horny, horny, horny before we got down and dirty. But this night, well, I was sleeping, and he continued to whisper, 'I am horny, horny, horny.' I hoped by ignoring him he would have the decency to turn around and go to sleep. But he didn't give up and by now I was getting pissed off. He shook me by holding on to my left hip, so I calmly stirred and turned to him firmly stating in my sleeping voice, 'Abe, I am sleeping. Go wank yourself off.' Well, if I did. He jumped out of bed and shouted, 'Immi, I am the man, and you cannot speak to me in that way. You understand! I am horny, horny, horny! You must do as I say. This is the way. Now, I am horny, horny, horny.'

I replied, 'Yes Abe. I hear that you are horny, horny, horny. But you must remember that I am British and if I do not want sex, then I will not have it. Because you are a man, it does not mean you can or will ever dictate to me what I can, can't or should do. Now, either go and wank yourself off, or just shut up and please go to sleep. I am trying to sleep Abe and have work in a couple of hours.'

He shouted something in Arabic whilst looking at me and then calmed down and got into bed. We slept cheek to cheek that night and it was never discussed again.

The Arabic girls translated for Emirati and then they all laughed amongst themselves.

Anna commented, 'Good for you, Emily. If you not want sex, not have sex. Who he think he is? Fucking men.'

Then Anna questioned, 'Did he wank?'

'Did he hell. He went to sleep the lazy bastard.'

The weekly cell wash and shopping day continued, but then out of the blue I had a telephone call in the days that followed. What day and when exactly I do not know, but my name was called, and I was let out of the cell to answer it.

'Hello?' I said, and this was followed by a happy,

'Hello. Is this Emily?'

'Yes, who is this?'

'Oh, Emily, this is Hiba from the British Embassy. I have been trying to come to see you, but they will not give me access.'

'I can well believe that. The sad thing is they don't really do anything, so there is no excuse, and I am always here, so they can't really use that.' I looked behind me and smirked at them.

'I see. So, you have not been to court yet?'

'No, I had a meeting with the prosecutor and my lawyers, but like you they keep saying this is a serious case.'

'Are you being treated well?'

'I suppose I am a lucky one. I have lawyers, my family and I am treated better than other nationalities. But the conditions are not good. If ever there is a fire here, then I know I am dead. And the food – Jesus - rice and bones. Well, I should be losing weight.'

'But is there any way I can help you, Emily?'

'Yes, if my brother sent you a photo of my daughter, could you bring it to me please? He could send it to you through email, in an attachment, and then could you print it out for me please? It is just that… I am finding it difficult, this experience, and sometimes I can't see here clearly as my mind is foggy.'

'Yes, Emily, I can do that for you. When you speak with him tell him to forward it on and I will bring it with me when I next see you.'

'When will you come to visit me next?'

'I will come when I can. But please phone me if you need to speak with me. If I do not answer immediately, I will call you back.'

I thought to myself good luck with that one then. I understood that there was little power she had, hell, she couldn't even speak to me when she wanted to as the bitches were in control. I guess I was lucky she got through to me today.

'Emily, have you been given a court date yet?'

'No, sadly I haven't. I do call the lawyer's secretary, but he has no news for me.'

'Well, hopefully you will hear something soon.'

'Insha'Allah,' I answered.

'Yes, insha'Allah', she replied. When God wills was such a popular saying over here, but I needed him to will it soon, now, immediately.

The telephone call ended, and I returned to my cell. The others commented again that I was lucky that my embassy contacted me at all, as some of them had never heard from them after being in the legal system. I knew I was lucky on the face of it, even though they really couldn't do much legally.

But I questioned myself, 'If David Beckham, his wife, or any other rich celebrity had been stopped for any reason, such as speeding, then would he/she have been taken to the cell that I had been in, interrogated, made to sign documents and held in God-awful bloody conditions like I and many others found ourselves? Or would they get away with such things as the negative publicity could affect the tourism of the country?'

I think you can make your own mind up about that one.

One day, out of the many, no police officer was on duty. Whilst we did receive our breakfast and ate it, there was no officer on duty and the lovely Indian man had to deal with Lebanese and Moroccan. We ran out of water and a group of us started to shout from the cell entrance to attract attention, which did come in the form of a male officer in his whites. He too was shocked that no one was on duty and stated he would investigate it. My argument to him was that there was a serious breach of health and safety.

'This really isn't on, is it?' I questioned him. He looked confused, so I expanded, 'What I mean is... well... if there was an emergency, then the delay in getting help could really affect the situation. I mean we have elderly women here, a pregnant woman, and a cell without water for hours with nothing to drink in this heat in this place. Well, anything could happen. And you wait till I tell the British Embassy!'

Anna continued, 'Even a fire.'

I looked to my left to look at Anna to see if she was indeed serious, 'What? A fire?'

In her Russian drool, she said, 'Of course a fire is possible. There been a fire here before and women died.'

'WHAT?' This was the first I had heard of a fire down here, where I now live, which had taken lives.

Anna continued whilst this officer looked on confused, 'Isn't it true that fire killed people here?'

Lebanese confirmed, 'Yes, there has been fire. And yes, some dies. You know if the Egyptian officer was here this would not happen. Since she went on leave, not organised here, list of people to go to court, officers do what they want. Bad, very bad.'

I returned my gaze at the officer and stated, 'There are definitely health and safety issues here now. You get someone so we are supervised as is your responsibility to place us in a safe environment.'

He breathed heavily and said something quietly before responding, 'First I get water to you. Then, I find someone to come here. Ok?'

We all looked at one another and confirmed in our own way without saying anything that this pleased us. We waited and water did arrive, but not quickly and the poor Indian man with no teeth handed bottles individually to each of us through the bars. An officer did arrive, but later than anticipated. He played on his phone, made phone calls and did pretty much nothing. However, my Arabic friends used their feminine seductive techniques to warrant telephone calls, and whilst the day had been testing with the news of a fire and the deaths, the long telephone call that I had with Mammy and Sah was wonderful. The officer was useless, like the females, in his capacity of an officer, but he was not full of bitchy and condescending looks and comments like the women.

And as for this Egyptian officer, this was totally new to me, so I couldn't wait to find out more about this woman. After quizzing the ladies, I learned that the head of the female officers, the captain, was Egyptian and organised in her position. She had been on leave back in Egypt, but they were expecting her to return soon. They informed me that when she was on duty the officers were organised, professional and things ran in an orderly fashion. Well, that's how I interpreted their information. They all stated that as she was Egyptian, the highest officer, the other Emirati officers didn't like this fact, as Egyptians were seen as a lower class of nationality. I made a connection here with science and Darwin. Now Darwin and his 'Evolution Theory' conceded that the fashion for wealthy families to marry within themselves had a detrimental impact on human health. I had made my observations on the female officers and concurred that there was a need for foreign blood to assume more responsibility in the hierarchy of all their organisations, which also contributed to the entire growth of the region. The scientific advancement of study and data on interbreeding has come a long way with eliminating genetic, physical, intellectual, sexual, and emotional problems. I had lots of free time to analyse such points and concluded that the female police officers, bar the Egyptian who I had not met yet, could possibly be suffering from intellectual issues as their English was non-existent, they didn't know anything and had vacant stares for the majority of the time when not on their mobile phones. I wish I could have carried my own experiment out with them by clicking my fingers in front of their faces to see if there was a reaction, any, but sadly I could not.

I further concluded that they were just inept in their profession. They did not seem to have a work ethic, if at all, or emotional barriers, as the anger and resentment they felt towards the individuals in their care was apparent and visible to see by all. They were really screwed up. I concluded that I should not have contempt for them, but compassion for the poorly affected officers, as we did not have the medical advancements and technology to help such individuals I believed. The clear answer for them was to stop whatever they were doing and to become more selective in their breeding. I also made a correlation in my own development, to practice what I now preached going forward in future relationships and to be more selective as Darwin theorised.

The conversation did come up with me questioning the girls one long boring afternoon. 'How the hell did those bitches get jobs as police officers as I know in the UK and other police forces that you indeed need qualifications, and to be over 18? Specifically, English and Mathematics at GCSE level and for higher positions a degree.' However, it was all to be explained to me.

Lebanese, who was in more control than the officers, explained, 'It is called Emiratisation and it…' she paused, 'it is government policy to increase Emiratis in jobs. I think to stop other nationalities taking all jobs and make Emirati's work in jobs, private and public. It will help the economy as they work for their money and not given it freely by the government.'

In theory it made sense, both economically and politically, to employ the local nationals of a country such as the Emiratis, rather than to employ other nationalities with the same qualifications, skills and experiences. I experienced something similar in Australia and New Zealand when I lived and worked there, and agreed with such policies, on the condition that local nationals were medically, and intellectually qualified and in a realistic position for such jobs.

Pregnant African started laughing, 'They want to give the women jobs to stop them have babies. It is contraception no, less of them for the country?' This was followed by a huge laugh by her. It was a funny statement and a few of us quietly laughed with her.

Lebanese continued, 'Come on, some are good, come on.'

Pregnant African questioned, 'Who? Name?'

This was followed my more laughter as Lebanese could not give a name.

Anna then awoke and from her bed stated, 'They are shit, shit, shit, shit. Not human. Very bad.'

'I concur with you, Anna, and possibly the government does because let's be honest, this is the best place to hide the shit, isn't it?' I continued, 'And do you know if this is the government policy then why not encourage less sex with relatives to ensure a more intelligent and prettier workforce. All the plastic and brain surgery or therapy in the world cannot help these… women.'

Anna was more motivated. 'This country is fucked. Dubai is fucked. Bur Dubai is fucked. We are fucked. Who puts women to work here who only speak Arabic? I mean … intelligent to put women who speak English as we all speak English here.'

We all looked at one another, I suppose in agreement.

Pregnant African was rubbing her tummy and looked at me and said, 'You teacher Emily, teach them.'

I chuckled to myself, 'If they haven't learned English yet and basic humanity, then there is no hope for them. If this was a farm back home and we had animals born that behaved like them they would have been shot by now.'

Lebanese asked, 'And you eat them?'

Pregnant African started laughing, 'Emily wants to eat them? Ha, Ha, Ha.'

'Fuck off. If I was going to eat a human then yes, I agree they have the size and weight of an animal they don't like, but I can't imagine them doing much exercise, so I would imagine the meat would be tough. Oh, there's a bloody thought.'

Pregnant African added, 'I know. The government can use their women to feed us. Think how much meat we have to eat with our rice, instead of bones. Ye, make government policy.'

Anna ended this conversation clearly. 'I will not eat any fucking bitch. Disgusting.'

'Ladies, can we stop talking about this? Maybe they would be better off in a zoo, but then again, the animals are innocent, and do they deserve such abuse?'

Whilst most of us were in agreement that the officers were not best placed in their forced positions as officers, I hope we were all in agreement for not eating them. Personally, I hoped that the officers' empathy, understanding and kindness would grow, but I held little hope of it ever actually happening.

Visitation came and went, and I had nobody as usual. However, we were all compatriots, and I understood their feelings. The day arrived when I was called and informed that I would be going to court. I asked to call my lawyer to confirm this, but they would not allow me. I had little time to change and put my blood-stained dress on. Of course, the blood could not be seen due to the blackness of my dress, but it added a firmness. Whilst getting my dress out of my bag I also got my lipstick and mascara out, brushed my hair and tried to make myself presentable. The girls also enjoyed the lippy and mascara and even though it wasn't much, it did make them seem happier and prettier. I went when I was called after putting my stuff back in my bag, and I allowed them graciously to put on the handcuffs. I had a black cardigan to cover my shoulders, so I hoped as I walked the corridors I would not be judged as a prostitute. But, to say I was scared, nervous or worried was an understatement. My heart thumped so fast, and I knew I was perspiring, because I could feel and smell it.

The sunlight, as usual, blinded my eyes initially and the dry heat burned my lungs. We meandered through the city in a van that clearly belonged to the police as the metal bars on it literally advertised it so. The female officer sat in the front with the driver, and it was so silent. After parking, I was ushered out to a large opening in the building where lots of male prisoners stood handcuffed and legs chained in a line. They were mixed in age, but looked so defeated, traumatised, and weak. I did not form opinions as to why they were there as I was ushered by the police officer quickly through stairways, corridors until a doorway opened into a large room. I assumed that they could be innocent until proven guilty in a fair legal system.

There in front of us was a huge room with stairs proceeding to higher levels. It was bustling with people, some in their traditional outfits and others not. Some had files, mobile phones, and paperwork. It initially made me slightly dizzy, as it was alive with a heartbeat, with real soul. The air was fresh and cool and as I watched those around me, my police officer reminded me with a jerk to keep moving. I was jolted back to my reality, having had my feathers ruffled, to continue my journey onwards and upwards.

We finally approached a rather large room that was packed with stalls of wooden seating and people seated on them in rows. There was a male seating section and female, and in front of me sat, I believe, the judge and his minions on a wooden mantel, raised above to look down. It reminded me of portraits of Jesus raised above all others, looking down with judgment. The judge was round with little hair and kind of reminded me of an old Arabic *Spitting Image* character as he sat there. I was instructed to sit down, and the officer sat next to me. I quickly glanced around to see if I could see my lawyer, well any lawyer, who was or had been asked to represent me, but to no avail.

We sat there and I was like a child in a sweet store, looking everywhere, watching individuals as they proceeded to stand in front of the judge and watched facial expressions and body language. I noticed that the Indians that were in front of the judge stood small, with hunched shoulders and concerned eyes. I quickly believed that standing tall, shoulders back and tits out, with direct eye contact would be the best way to initially greet these legal men, if they actually were qualified and legal, immediately. Time went slowly and I had no way to understand the other cases in front me, or even to ascertain if this was the drugs court. The bustling sound of voices and movement made my head hurt and I felt as though a headache was at its embryonic development.

Then, my name was called by a deep, throaty, gruff voice. I immediately looked at the officer hoping that she would give me some instructions as to the procedures. Surprisingly, she had no words to tell me, but with her hand she instructed me to get up and go. So, I apprehensively got up, looked at her and then at the judge, around me and shat myself. With each step I took I had to remind myself to stand tall, tits out and be proud. I finally walked up to the great wooden mantel, whose creation I am sure was due to the skills of Indian carpenters, and looked up at the old judge.

Now, I had been informed by my compatriots that at court you should have a translator and if not, the case would be adjourned. I understood that all conversations would take place in Arabic, so my understanding would be nil. However, the translator would not, I repeat, would not give a word-for-word account, but a summarised account and would quite often miss out specific points. Now, I could easily believe this due to my experiences so far with the Emiratis that have to work due to government policy. Anna had stated from her experiences with her lawyer that they don't care. What I understood from group discussions was that if you had a lawyer then he would say everything to the judge and ignore me, that I would probably say nothing only to confirm my name. Judges don't like anything other than Arabic spoken in the courtroom. How nice and international for such a cosmopolitan country, I concluded.

There were three people on the bench, the judge was in the centre, his male secretary I was told would be on his left, and the public prosecutor would sit on his right. Now, whether this was true or the three people had the professional capability of knowing these facts and adhering to them would be surprising to me in my current mental state. Not surprisingly, most defendants were found guilty in this fair legal process. Ye right! Not!

Knowing these facts from my ladies made me desperately search/look in the hope and anticipation that my lawyer or lawyers would appear miraculously to represent me. But they didn't. I was on my own. I returned my gaze and watched the judge's every movement. He was reading something and then looked up at me and then returned his gaze to his paperwork. He had a pen, it was expensive and didn't look like the Bic pens I used, but it was silver in colour.

He questioned, 'Emily?'

'Yes, I am Emily.'

The two men watched my every move, and I knew I had to contain eye contact without blinking and looking away. I had previously read something that liars cannot maintain eye contact and often look away when speaking, so I focused on keeping eye contact with all of them continuously.

In his deep and controlled voice, he said 'Guilty!'

Now, I didn't know whether he was questioning me whether I was guilty, or in fact he was confirming my guilt and sentence.

I immediately and sympathetically replied, 'Excuse me?' whilst maintaining the gaze and eye contact of the three of them.

The man to the judge's right smiled and stated, 'Are you guilty?' It was a man that really didn't look like my prosecutor. *Did I have a new one that I had not been introduced to,* I questioned?

I took a deep breath knowing that what I said next could make a difference to whether I had a short- or long-term spell in jail. I knew I would have to speak slowly with my accent and control my nervousness, as we Welsh are known for speaking quickly when nervous.

So, I started, 'My name is Emily, and I am guilty, only for smoking marijuana in the UK and not in Dubai.' I simultaneously thought, *where the hell was the translator and why was this court appearance continuing without my bloody lawyer?*

The judge looked at me and then proceeded, 'Guilty drug smuggling and use drug in Dubai?'

This immediately threw me. Inside I was questioning, *'What the fuck? What the fucking fuck is this? I mean, I knew they were right to lock me up if I was a drug smuggler. That I understood, but seriously. Jesus!*

I could feel my eyes tearing and had to stop them with all my might. So, I positioned my hands against the mantle of the desk. I wanted to scratch it but calmly I rested my palms on it before proceeding, 'I am not guilty of drug smuggling or taking drugs in Dubai. I have been honest since being taken from an apartment. I was not told once why I was being arrested. But I was arrested and before giving a urine sample. I honestly told the doctor that I had smoked marijuana in the UK. I respect the law and culture of the Middle East and have worked in Dubai and Qatar. I was forced to sign documents that I did not understand and told that it would help me return to the UK quicker and my four-year-old daughter, who waits for me with my mother. If you read these documents, you will see that I wrote on the documents that I did not understand what I was signing. I speak the truth and the only thing I am guilty of is smoking marijuana in the UK.'

I maintained eye contact with them throughout and modelled my puppy eyes. However, the demeanour I showed had been consistent and I believe I had eloquently told my story, well, as best as I could anyway. He wrote something down and then when finished, placed his pen on his papers and told me to, 'Go.'

I repeated, 'Go? We are finished? But my lawyers are not here yet?'

The one on the left them questioned, 'Lawyers?'

I gave the names of the lawyers who had been employed to represent me.

The judge re-held his pen and made some further notes. As soon as he had finished, the left one said, 'Finished. Go!'

'Then I thank you. Goodbye.'

I turned round to see the officer standing near the entrance door of this large room, and with each step I took I had to concentrate and hold on to my strength, as I just wanted to fall to the ground and scream. I honestly felt faint and touched the surfaces of the benches, and then any walls I could touch as we walked. The journey through the building to the outside was horrendous as my mind raced to and from the possibility of now being charged with drug smuggling. What the hell had I signed and committed myself to? It was surreal as the faces I passed I no longer cared what they thought of me and of what I had committed, but I had continual flashbacks of Sah, Mammy and a cell room I would be locked up in wearing a jail uniform.

With each blink of the eyes, and each inhale and exhale, I was clinging to the fact that we would near the car. We continued to walk, me behind the female officer until she came to a standstill. The driver opened the doors from within the car and we got in. My hope had gone. Any strength I had, and it had waned over my weeks of incarceration, was also depleted. I had nothing left to fight this system, an alien system that made no sense.

And what the hell was I going to tell my mother? 'Hi Mammy, I went to court today and my charge is smuggling drugs into Dubai now. My lawyer didn't turn up, well, actually the two lawyers that Rob paid for didn't turn up, but I tried my best to defend myself. But if I am honest, I think they said I was guilty, so the next court case I believe I will be sentenced. They were saying before that my case was serious, but I had no idea that they had added smuggling to it as well as taking drugs in Dubai. So, at the best I could be looking at 20 years which will mean I will be 53 coming home. YAY!' I mean what the hell was going on here?

As we drove back to Bur Dubai I could feel the anger building from the bottom of my gut, and in no way was I ready for a bombardment of questions by the girls. I had to get my head down and wait to phone my lawyer and his assistant to see what the hell they had to say. To say I was pissed was an understatement. Most of the journey was a haze of emotions. There were moments where I cried uncontrollably, moments where I would wipe my tears away and try to focus, but I was an emotional wreck.

We got back to Bur Dubai, and after walking down the steps to the pit below, my handcuffs were taken off and the door was opened for my return.

Immediately as I walked in Anna questioned, 'Emily, how was it?'

I looked up from the floor to meet her gaze and Anna with a concerned face repeated, 'Emily, how was it? What happened?'

My voice was broken and answered, 'Listen, it wasn't good. They have added smuggling to my case?' All the girls looked at each other with faces of trepidation, which translated to me as, 'She is fucked!'

'The fucking bastards!' Anna replied. 'How can they do this? Drug smuggling?'

I looked up at them holding on to the right bar of the metal frame of the bunk bed. 'Listen I can't talk about it now, but as you can imagine I have had a hell of a shock. My lawyers weren't there to represent me and I didn't have a translator, so I had to protest my innocence.'

The African ladies questioned, 'What protest?'

Lebanese translated for Emirati and Anna tried to for the African ladies. 'You know I am not guilty. I am innocent?'

Pregnant African then responded with, 'So you shout this at court? You crazy white woman?'

Now, under different circumstances I would have laughed at the interpretation that they had given me of protesting my innocence by shouting in the court. Yes, a white woman on a drug smuggling case jumping up and down whilst ensuring all could hear my bloody innocence. Honestly!

I shook my head, my shoulders slumped, and I felt weak. I asked Moroccan if I could lie down on her bed to rest, as sometimes when she was in a good mood, she would let me, even though in Arabic she would complain that I was too big to share her bed. She agreed, I believe out of sympathy, and let me scoot in as close to the wall as I could and then sat back on the mattress facing others.

I placed my left hand over my mouth. I hushed my uncontrollable sobbing, and it didn't matter how tightly I closed my eyes as the tears ran down like a continuous, wet, and overflowing stream. I tried my very best to do this privately, but there was no privacy. I visually revisited the proceedings of the court, 'Guilty and drug smuggling', pictorial images of my Sah and mother were continuous and unrelenting. I tried to control my breathing, which jerked my whole being, and Moroccan could obviously feel my jerks. She placed her hand on my shoulder and whispered, 'Emily, stop this it does not help you. Believe you will be good.'

I had no words to reply and waited to enter a stasis of blackness. There was no light left and as my eyes blinked the darkness became permanent, as exhaustion had taken me whole, and for a little while I slept.

I was awoken by Anna. 'Emily, wake up it is food time. You need wake up.' She gently nudged me from my darkness to the horror that surrounded me.

I turned to view her peering at me, whilst the others lined up.

'Emily, are you ok? I am worried.' Her facial expression made this clear.

'Thanks, Anna. I am ok. How long have I slept?'

'Not long Emily. You, ok?'

'I just umm…,' my eyes looked at her, but I had nothing that I could say. So, I got out of the bed and Anna put her arm around my shoulders and softly spoke,

'Emily, they are fucking idiots here and maybe they make mistake you know. Your lawyers said nothing on drug trafficking?'

'No. It was the first I heard of it. I mean they all said it was a serious case, but fuck me, Anna, I could be in here for years and years.'

Anna was calm and insisted, 'Emily, you need to phone your lawyers and embassy. Tell them what happened and ask lawyer why he not there. Crazy you pay money and not there. Should have been there.'

'Anna, I totally agree with you. But what scares me is that the judge said 'guilty'. I really think that the next time I go to court that I will be sentenced. I have honestly never experienced anything like this, Anna. I am fucked.'

'This is a fucked up country. Feel sorry for them, Emily. We will leave one day and say fuck Dubai, fuck Bur Dubai, fuck you, bitches. They unlucky. You will go back to your daughter. I believe this in my heart. Now come eat.'

Anna was a lovely girl who swore a lot. Most sentences had the word 'fuck' in them and I thought to myself if she ever visited us in Wales, I would have to speak with her about her language as my mother would not be impressed. Hell, I didn't swear at home and in other places very seldom. This was a bad habit I was developing consciously, in my spoken language and my internal thoughts, and had become a necessity for me now to use when I really wanted to personify my anger.

As we lined up in front of the line, I questioned one of the officers, 'Excuse me?' I managed to get her attention after repeatedly asking her, 'Excuse me?' And, I could not have been more polite in my questioning.

Her eye roll said it all while she sat there with her phone on the desk. The bitch was busy with boredom. I imagined that their work would be quite boring and repetitive if their work consisted of not actually doing anything mentally or physically. Or maybe that was expected of them, but I looked forward to the arrival of the Egyptian boss to observe whether her presence embellished them into a frenzy of activity.

I did get my telephone call that evening and boy, I had venom boiling within me waiting to vent all my court ills at my legal firms. I dialled the number from the business card and phoned Omar. It rang and I tapped my left hand's index finger impatiently with each beat of the ring, then a deep and tired man answered. It was him with a 'Hello.'

'Hello,' I answered as sarcastically as I could. 'It is Emily, you remember the drugs case in Bur Dubai?' I waited, and with the second in the delay to the response he must have had one hell of a day, but not working on my case, thank you very much.

'Yes Emily. How can I help you?'

I immediately responded, 'Well, you can first tell me why I had no representation at court today? Then, you can inform me why I now have a drug smuggling charge added to my case? I mean come on.'

'Emily, I, sorry, we did not know you were in court today. Listen to me, I am very sorry. And the drug smuggling charge, well, that is a mistake.'

'It does not help me, does it? A payment has been made to represent me and when you are not there, I have no translator, I mean, what the hell am I supposed to do?'

He obviously heard the panic, and God-damn right frustrated emotion in my voice as he calmed. 'Emily, calm down. Now listen to me. The same has happened at court. We have been there to represent you and you have not been there. As for the drug smuggling it is a simple mistake.'

'A simple mistake? A simple mistake? This is my life we are talking about here. Seriously, a silly mistake? Tell my blood pressure that. Well, if you could please correct your legal system and ask them not to add on fabricated and absurd new bloody convictions, then I would appreciate it. And, as for me missing court then you need to take that up with Bur Dubai Police Station, as I can't freely leave and they should be running a professional, I don't know what, but a legal policing system that actually does its bloody job. My word!'

'Emily, I hear that you are angry, but this will not help you. Did you say anything in court?'

'I told them the truth that I was not guilty of drug smuggling and not guilty of smoking in Dubai, but the UK as I have protested throughout this whole bloody experience.'

'Ok. I will try to find out what is happening and try to come and see you. It is very difficult to see you, Emily, as they do not give permission.'

'Nor take prisoners to their court cases when they should it seems. But that is out of my control, and you need to make a complaint as you know it is wrong.'

'We will try to speak on your behalf, Emily. I promise.'

'And believe you me I will be telling my embassy whenever I next speak or hear from them. They too have said it is difficult to get a hold of me and it's rather ironic when you think because being locked up makes it so easy to find me.'

'Is there anything else I can help you with, Emily?'

'No.' (Pause.) 'Just please speak with my lawyer and ask him to just represent me and be there when needed. And to sort this drug smuggling case too!'

'I will, Emily. I give you my word.'

'Thank you. Goodbye.'

''Goodbye, Emily.'

Throughout our conversation I could hear sound in the background. The sweet sound of life, in a home I imagined where his family lived. It was Ramadan and the sun had set, so I imagined the noise to be that from enjoyment and feasting. I managed one deep breath and then focused on calling my mother's number and my family. I got through quickly with her beautiful, sweet voice saying, 'Hello?'

'Mammy, how are you and Sah?'

'Emily, it is so good to hear from you.'

'I only spoke to you yesterday, Mammy.'

'I know, but it is good to hear you. Are you ok?'

'Ye, I am fine. How is Sah?'

'Sah is fine. She is here. Hang on.'

I heard the phone fumble and them a little voice say, 'Hello.'

'Hi. How are you sweetheart? Are you ok?'

'Mammy.' This was followed by the sweetest giggles which made a few teardrops fall. 'Where you Mammy?'

'Sah. I am still here in Dubai.'

'Better?'

'Hearing your voice makes me feel better and as soon as I am told I can leave I am coming straight home to you, and I am going to cuddle and kiss you all over.'

'All over?'

She chuckled as I confirmed, 'All over.'

'I love you, Mammy.'

'I love you so much... to infinity and... what is it?'

'To infinity and beyond 15 million billion times.'

'Good girl. Is Mam being a good girl?'

'Yes, Mam is a good girl.'

'Is she giving you lots of kisses and cwtches?'

'Yes.'

'You can never ever have enough kisses and cwtches.'

With that she said, 'Bye, Mammy.'

I heard the phone fumble again and my mother's return.

'What happened there, Mammy?'

'She has gone back to watch the television. Oh, she is funny.'

'I know. Listen, I went to court today and it wasn't good, but I spoke with Omar, the guy who works for the lawyer and he said he would sort it out.'

'Sort what out?'

Now, I knew I had to be careful with my wording here, as not to make my mother worry any more than she already had to.

'Listen, at court today the lawyer wasn't there, and the judge accused me of drug smuggling.'

'WHAT?'

I could hear the panic in her voice, and I sincerely hoped she knew that this wasn't me trying to gently let her know that this was indeed my offence. 'I know, Mammy. But listen, I just spoke with Omar, and he insisted that it was a mistake. It will be sorted.'

'What the hell is going on there?'

'Ye, I know. He said that there have been a couple of court dates that I had missed and that it was difficult to get hold of me. And the embassy said that too. It is just bonkers, Mammy, and how they get away with it, I honestly don't know.'

'Jesus, Emily. What a bloody place.'

'I know. You should try being here. No, on that thought, I would not want you here. Listen, I am going to have to go soon as I am getting that look off the beauties.'

'The beauties!'

'I will tell you all when I get home, Mammy.'

'Ok. Well, look after yourself and call when you can. Ok?'

'Will do. Love you, Mammy, and kiss Sah from me.'

'Love you too, Emily. Bye. Bye.'

The phone call ended, and I held it in my hand and paused only for a short time before placing the receiver back on the handset. I thanked the officer for allowing me to use the phone and Lebanese and Moroccan. I hated that there was no privacy here and that those two knew everything that was going on.

I returned to the cell and as usual Anna was the first one to ask, 'What happened Emily?'

'You were right, Anna, the drug smuggling thing is a mistake.'

'What? A fucking mistake! Are they crazy?'

Anna was so dramatic, and her Russian accent enhanced it. The others muttered amongst themselves, then I added, 'He also stated I have missed court dates and getting hold of me has been an issue/problem.'

'What, you have missed court dates? Those stupid fucking bitches. They can't even organise a driver and officer to take us to court. Fucking stupid bitches. This country is fucked. How we go home if they not take us?' This statement from Anna was a daily occurrence, and each time she made it we all agreed with her.

By the time I had queued to brush my teeth and toileted it was nearly time for bed. I know when I closed my eyes, it wouldn't be long until I felt at peace in my own blackness. But, before my consciousness entered my realm of peace and nothing, I made a mental note that my next step in these endless winding stairs was to contact the British Embassy, let them know the shambles and neglect of the legal system which they resided in, and to remind them of their duty of care to support British nationals caught up in such situations.

Days followed and Anna like me had been called to court unexpectedly, along with a couple of Filipinos. She returned with the convoy of other ladies, and their faces said it all. Anna looked broken and the Filipinos had no visible facial expressions, except for their shoulders which seemed to carry invisible weights. Anna walked in, and the tears immediately started to roll. She was extremely passionate as she told us how her lawyer was shit, again, and she was looking at up to six months imprisonment on top of the nine months she had already served. She could not understand why she would not be released, as she had served her time already. She blamed her cheap lawyer for not fighting for her. She knew that when she was deported, she would lose her career, apartment, possessions, and future memories to be made in the country she had called home for some time. She had lost her father to cancer whilst inside, and had not been allowed to return home for his funeral to say goodbye because of her situation. There was no feeling, and my heart went out to her. She would have to live with all this, the not being there when she needed to be in one of the most traumatic times of her life.

I had been with Daddy and living with that experience, whilst still raw, I knew that I had not dealt with its full impact yet and how it would affect the rest of my life. How I would deal with it, still frightened me. The loss was unknown, traumatic and life-changing, and Anna had only had her father since her mother had passed when she was a young girl. When I looked at her, I felt sadness and loss, and there was nothing I could do to take her pain away, make her smile and her bleached blond wavy hair shine.

And, then there was the poor Filipinos who got it the worst. They had no legal representation, little or no contact with the outside world and were lost in a legal system that at its absolute best failed and was failing all who were in it. The police officers were not qualified/trained and had no understanding of how to do their basic job, and there were individuals locked up in its system where freedom was a word with no meaning. It was what it was.

The days obviously continued and one morning three Emirati men came to the cells. We heard the gate open and deep voices speak with the female police officer. Heads turned to see the excitement of what was going on as nothing happened here. The routine and timeline continued daily, weekly, and monthly, so anything of interest woke the cells up and everyone in them. I was near the cell door, sitting on a mattress, and I had a clear view of the three men. The one to the left was tall, thin and a religious-looking man in his 30s. He had the Bin Laden whiskers, whilst the man in the middle looked like an obese tallish dwarf who could be used as a tenpin bowling ball. His head was so round and shiny. The man to the right was of normal build and a bit of an Arab hottie. I quickly thought that they were brave men coming here to a feast of women who were hungry and possibly sexually deprived as they scanned us and we scanned them.

The female officer looked nervous and followed their conversation intently and nodded robotically. I don't know if they rocked her world in some peculiar and twisted way, and the thought of any of the men with this beauty provoked a facial expression and reflux in my throat that could have been the start of projectile vomiting. She opened the cell door for them and they slowly, but steadily, with short steps proceeded to enter with jerky head and neck movements that looked similar to a trio of chicks with Mad Cow Disease. Possibly, they were nervous as I know I would be in their situation walking into a cell full of women who shared one toilet and shower. Then I questioned did we smell or were we used to it? My shoulders shuddered and awoke me to the action in front of me.

They continued to walk in single file with their small steps talking, laughing, and looking around them. I looked around and behind me to see what I could make of the ladies' reactions: pure bemusement as to what these men were doing here. Their adventure into the wild cells did not last long as then they stopped and started to retreat from the start of the mattresses'.

I wanted to know what they were doing here, so I asked Anna, 'Why are they here?'

Anna shrugged her shoulders, then pregnant African piped up,

'Hey you. Why you here? What you want?'

In her pregnant state I didn't imagine that there would be any retribution for speaking up and questioning these dudes. The men looked at each other and two returned to continue to walk towards the cell door.

I could see that as Bin Laden stood there, he was trying to think for the language to respond, 'To look. To see.'

The others turned around and bowling ball said something in Arabic which made the others laugh like little girls. I asked Lebanese, who sat opposite me what they were saying, and she replied,

'They laugh because they come to see how nice it is down here.'

This rattled me, so like a spitting Cobra I replied, 'They laugh because they want to see how nice it is down here. What the…? Seriously. Turn around and walk to the bottom. See the toilet and shower that is shared. Smell the aroma that surrounds it and see the age of colours and fungus/bacterial growth. Stand by the window and feel the air and sky that surrounds us here. Count the women in here, where they sleep and how many mattresses we must share. Ask the female officers how many court dates we have missed, how embassies and lawyers cannot contact us and get to see us? Ask the police officers, male police officers, upstairs how there was no staff here for a full day and we ran out of water here? And please join us for lunch. It is free and you really should see what we eat daily. Oh sorry, it is Ramadan. Come down this evening and please eat with us.'

As I stopped speaking, I took my eye contact away from his gaze and that of the others, pursed my lips and shook my head in disgust. The silence was deafening, so I looked up and the three amigos were no longer laughing. Then, I thought to myself, *I shouldn't have said those things possibly? I have been told not to say anything, and who the fuck are they? Oh, shit! Oh, shitty, shitty, shit.*' It wasn't as though they knew my name and case, but they could easily find out from the officer. It was a double *oh, shitty, shitty, shit, shitty, shitty, shit.*

They left and Anna started, 'What they want to look down here? To see how bad it is? Will they change it? No. They very bad as they see with their own eyes what it like. I hate them. I really hate them. This is bullshit.'

I always agreed with what Anna had to say, but I didn't agree with the tone and language often used. 'I agree with you, Anna.'

Lebanese then interjected, 'I have not seen that before. Since I came here, they have not been down this place. Maybe complaints said.'

'Well, I know the British Embassy representative who came to see me said she was going to report to the commissioner what I had said about this place. And I am going to be telling them about the bloody farce of not going to court on court dates and missing them, and the difficulties in communication with legal representatives and seeing them.'

'Maybe, Emily? But it will not change. They say they build a new one like the men. They can go outside, and it is better they say.' Lebanese had mentioned something on the lines of this before.

'Oh, to go outside and feel the sun and breeze on my skin - that would be so nice,' I imagined.

'Yes, and to smoke cigarette and say fuck you to them, that would be good too. Ha ha.' Anna always made me laugh with her comments and hand gestures, as she stuck her middle finger up.

Life returned to normal within five minutes of our visitors' departure. Later that day, I asked the officer if I could make an important phone call to my embassy and was told a firm 'no'.

That phone call came a few days later when we were next allowed to phone. I rang the number and waited patiently not expecting an answer, as it was late in the evening. A voice did not answer, and I listened patiently. Then the answer phone message started in Arabic and then English.

'Oh, hi. This is Emily from Bur Dubai. I was wondering when I will see the photo of my daughter that I asked for? Also, I would like to tell you that I have missed court appointments, as I was not taken to them. My lawyer also has difficulty communicating with me and cannot get hold of me.' I could have added so much more but thought that is enough for now. 'I hope to see you soon. Thank you. Emily.'

I would now wait and see how long a response would take, if indeed I would get any. But, fortunately in my current situation, I had all the time in the world to wait. I was going nowhere.

A few days later there was a change in the atmosphere and when I arose from the bunk I now shared with Anna, there was a buzz. Anna had left the bunk and disturbed my sleep facing the wall.

I turned around to hear and see chatter.

'Good morning, everyone,' I said.

Anna was speaking with the Africans when she said, 'Emily she is here. They now say things will be better. We will go to court appointments and speak with lawyers.'

It was like an overload of information. I focused my eyes to see the girls and said, 'What?'

'Egyptian here. The big boss woohoo.' She clapped her hands, and they went up in the air before she started to do an African dance which consisted of her twerking her arse and waving her hands oddly in the air.

I just looked at them and commented, 'The boss being the head of the female officers? God help and we will see.'

I turned around and shortly rose once breakfast was being served. When lining up, I observed the four female officers looking busy at their desk with pens in their hands, and files and papers in front of them. Then, there was a new lady as I had been informed. You could tell she was Arabic; however, her features and colouring were more Mediterranean. She instructed and they listened to her. She had authority over them, and what a joy it was to watch.

In the days that followed, if the telephone rang for one of us during the day shift, which was when she worked, then we were called and could answer it with no time limit. On the notice board, future court dates were scheduled for all to see and read, if you could, in Arabic. Luckily, Lebanese and Moroccan would translate for those it concerned, but my name never came up.

But how the arrival of this Egyptian transformed the cell. She may have been ignorant to the fact that this gave us hope and that we would not be forgotten in this crazy system. She was not afraid to use her voice and at moments her voice would get higher and louder.

The bitches did not answer her back and were obedient, and there were no facial expressions made at her like the others used to give to us.

Whilst my personal waiting game continued, I was called to answer the telephone one morning. I asked, 'Who is it?' to which I was given no answer.

'Hello?'

It was the British Embassy woman who I had previously called. 'Oh hello, Emily. I am sorry it has taken me some time to get back to you, but I have been on leave. How are you?'

'I am ok thanks. I hope you enjoyed your leave,' I said rather sarcastically, but she didn't know my personality, so I knew I could get away with it.

'Yes, I did Emily. Thank you.'

'So, do you have a photo of my daughter for me?'

'Yes, Emily. I will bring it in on Sunday to you.'

'Oh, thank you so much. I can't wait to see her.'

A lump quickly grew in my throat, and I gulped it away quickly. Whilst tears started to fall, I controlled them. These were happy tears.

She continued, 'You said in your message that you had missed court dates, Emily?'

'Yes, I went to court and my lawyer was not there. When I spoke to him, he said I had not been turning up to court on court dates, and it had been impossible to speak/contact me.'

'Emily, I gave your previous feedback to the high commissioner, and I know he was going to discuss it with the commissioner of police. He said he would investigate your claims. I will look into it and report this. You must remember that you are not in the UK, and it is very different here.'

'I know this is not the UK, as in the UK this would not happen.' With that comment, I looked behind me to the female officers who I knew were listening intently, but I purposely did not make eye contact with the Egyptian, as it didn't happen on her watch.

'I have to go now. Is there anything else, Emily?'

'Yes, the court added drug smuggling to my case, but my lawyer said that this is a mistake.'

'A mistake, I hope so, as otherwise it is a very, very, very serious case. I will question this to make sure it is an error.'

'Thank you for your help.'

'It is no problem. Goodbye.'

'Goodbye.'

I returned to the cell and informed them that to my delight I would soon have a photo of my daughter being brought in by the embassy representative. But, for the first time during my time there I noticed that some were not genuinely happy for me. Their smiles were false.

Anna was happy in saying her, 'Good, good, good.' But the three Arabic women were different, and I felt that they had a hidden triangular unified understanding, but it was not positive. I sat down and then reflected. They had been here months and months. They were going through the court process like me with little success from their lawyers. They faced deportation and possibly jail too and the loss of everything they had. Then, this white European comes in and has her embassy contact her, they help her get a photo of her daughter, they report back to the ambassador, she had initially three lawyers to start with and one of them was the best drugs lawyer in Dubai, and she phoned home when permitted to a family who were doing everything they could to help her. I was not a jealous person by nature, but I knew jealousy existed in many forms. I had also noticed that when speaking with Omar, or my lawyer, Emirati always asked if they had mentioned or asked for her, and I always noticed bewilderment and frustration in her eyes. But there was nothing I could do, except possibly keep more to myself. It was something I would now try to do going forward, and not to be so forthcoming with my personal information.

That Sunday, the British Embassy representative was true to form. My name was called but the cell door was not opened. We had a meeting in between the metal bars where she gave me an envelope which contained a beautiful portrait photo of my baby. I opened the envelope as she spoke informing me that the commissioner had spoken to the chief of police who said he would investigate the concerns. He had reported back that he had found no concerns, but the only thing I could focus on was my girl. I did comment that it was a pile of rubbish, and it was then that I reassessed that we were just prisoners. Why would or should the conditions be like a hotel? I got that, but it could have and should have been better.

Her visit was short and sweet. She informed me that they would be following my case and to be strong. I returned to the cell clutching the photo and like déjà vu the questions started. I simply replied to each one as they came. Yes, it was the embassy woman. Yes, she had a photo of my daughter which I then showed to each of them, as I held it and illustrated it in a semi-circle movement around the cell. There had been an investigation into our conditions by the head of police and no concerns were found. Between us we questioned if the three amigos had indeed been the investigators, with 50/50 agreeing yes/no.

I wanted to, no, I needed to lie down, so I asked Anna if I could squeeze behind her to face the wall and look at my beautiful daughter. I did and automatically the tears rolled, my body started to shake, and boy did I cry. I cried harder and longer than I had ever before and it flew uncontrollably down my cheeks, to my neck and on my hands as I tried to wipe them away. My skin tickled slightly as the streams dried on my skin slowly, as it was never cold down here in the cell.

She turned to me and placed her left hand on my left shoulder and whispered, 'Emily this is no good for you. Please try stop now.'

I softly turned to face her and admitted, 'I just miss her so much.' I turned my head back to face the wall and pulled my knees up into a foetal position. I held myself and her image until I had no emotion or energy left.

In my weakness, I slept once again in blackness and emptiness. But at least I could hold Sah now, and I could hold her near my heart, seeing her image in front of me. I just had to get home.

Days followed with little excitement for me. I would call my mother when I could, and Omar to update me and to ensure I was kept in this non-existent loop of information. But there was never any news really. I would be informed that my lawyer had spoken to someone whose position or rank meant nothing to me, and was always told this is good.

I stopped telling the girls if I spoke to anyone legal or my embassy, as I wanted and needed them to feel that I was in the same boat as them. Deep down I knew I wasn't, but I had to ensure that if I did go down for time in a big prison, I didn't need any negativity or stories of how I was running to my embassy and lawyers all the time. It certainly wouldn't help my case and could make me a lamb to the slaughter.

One morning, I had gone for a shower to wake me up and on returning and sorting my stuff in the opening under the metal bunk bed, I quickly looked under my pillow to have a quick peek at my girl and her smile. But it was gone. It wasn't there anymore, and I knew, I knew it in my heart and mind that I had placed it between the mattress and pillow.

I physically jumped back and addressed the cell, 'My photo of Sah - it's gone!'

Anna looked at me from where she was sitting and said, 'What you mean it gone?'

'It's gone, Anna.'

She jumped down and had a look herself. We then looked under the bed. The others protested that they had not seen it, but it was gone. Throughout the day I would have moments of looking for it just in case, but it wasn't anywhere. I could not comprehend why someone would do this and what satisfaction it would give them, but they did. No one owned up and that was the end of that. But whilst I didn't have the actual photo, I could see her clearly, so they did not win. Sah would always be with me, and sadly, this was a stark reminder that I really didn't know anyone in here or what they were capable of.

Two days later, in the early afternoon, the Egyptian called a list of names that would be going to court the next morning. My name was one of them and the excitement I felt was rewarding, as it filled me up all day and night with hope.

The morning came and I followed the same routine with the same dirty dress. The walk to the outside with handcuffs was still a shaming experience, along with the drive, and the humiliation continued once we arrived and walked through the building, stairs, and corridors of the court. The female officer and I positioned ourselves on the last row of seating on the right. I scanned the room hoping that my lawyer was here, or within the vicinity of the courtroom. We sat there for what seemed ages as court cases were presented, I believe. I wasn't even sure what the cases were about, but one thing was for sure and that was I felt sorry for some of the men before me.

They were Indian, I believe, and looked so poor with ragged clothes and dishevelled hair. They looked as confused as I felt.

It was one after the other, then my name was called. The officer looked at me and told me, 'Go!'

So, I got up and turned to walk down to where I had viewed all the others stood. As I walked, I saw him – my lawyer was here with a file of papers and nodded his head at me as we made eye contact. He stood to my right and we both waited. I looked up to the bigwigs who were the same ones who were there previously. You know the ones who added drug smuggling?

A conversation ensued and then I heard my name loudly. I looked at all concerned, and my lawyer instructed me, 'Is your name Emily?'

To which I replied, 'Yes.'

I did not say anything more and after a conversation of what seemed to be as little as two minutes, at best, my lawyer then nodded and smiled at them, turned to me and said, 'We are finished. You can now go.'

'What?' was my reply and he walked towards me and grabbed my arm as we walked.

'It is good, Emily. Believe me. But say nothing to no one. You hear me?'

'Yes!?!'

'Ok, Emily. Go to your prison officer. Goodbye.'

With that my officer came towards me and he was gone. Again, I was confused. As we walked back to the exit my mind replayed his comment, "It is good, Emily. Believe me.'

I started to smile to myself and felt lifted. As my feet continued to follow the officer, I concluded that this was the Middle East and good to him may have meant a different good to me. But wasn't good universal in all languages and cultures. And the 'Say nothing?' Why? Whatever his reasoning I had to trust him.

The return journey in the car calmed me as the sun shone on my face and it warmed quickly. It felt as though my soul rose at times with each inhale and exhale within the warm, strong glare from the sun that followed me on my journey. I questioned whether this was the hand of God letting me know that He is and always has been with me, and that everything would be ok. But then I frowned and questioned am I losing it? Am I imagining the 'good,' because I was so desperate in my need to get home? I looked up, closed my eyes, and then turned my face to face the sun once more. Whatever this was I was going to soak up as much of it as I could, because I didn't know when I would feel like this again. I felt full with hope or peace, and on a higher plain that lifted me up, and I was thankful for this experience or whatever mental state I was in as it was comforting.

When I got in the girls were all up and eager to ask me how things went. I needed to cut them all off and simply stated the truth in that I went to court, agreed that I was Emily and then came back. Emirati looked directly at me and asked in her drool, 'You speak lawyer?'

'He was there, but no, there was no conversation. He spoke in Arabic which you know I don't understand.'

Lebanese then questioned, 'What happen, Emily?'

'I waited for ages, then my name was called, I said I was Emily. I stood there and then the officer came and we left. Very confused to be honest.'

'But… lawyer not tell you anything?' Lebanese questioned.

'No. But at least he was there which I am grateful for.'

I went to the toilet and returned to sit with Anna. We quietly chatted on the top bunk whilst playing a game of cards. Someone had invested in a pack of cards and Anna didn't know how to play SNAP. So, I taught her.

'Emily, you quiet today. You ok?'

'Ye, I am just tired to be honest, and I have been advised not to say anything to anyone here.'

She nodded and came closer to me, 'I think that good advice. People jealous here. They see you come here, you go to court when they here months and long. You have lawyer, sorry lawyers.' She laughed as did I and she continued, 'You have family that love you and help. Most not have that. You are lucky, Emily. It is good advice. Say nothing and smile.'

Anna was a quick learner and she smashed me at SNAP. We continued to play other games and I taught her Patience. She would sit there for hours and get lost in the cards. She tried to teach me a Russian game, but it made no sense to me, and we laughed over it as she thrashed me continuously.

I obviously told my mother what I had been told by the lawyer, meaning 'the good' and the 'not to speak to anyone.' I followed his instruction instinctively; I would do anything and everything to get the hell out of here. But the days passed with the repetition of breakfast, lunchtime, cleaning once a week, shopping once a week with little movement and visitors. Phone calls were sporadic, and I continued to use my poor health as a reason to my delayed return and that whilst I was better the doctors would not allow me to fly just now, but we hoped it would be soon. Or so Sah thought.

Part 4

The Good?

It was late morning when the phone rang. It often rang but not often enough for any of us lot as it was the office phone and not the pay phone. The calling of the names of the ladies was very infrequent, however, surprisingly one day my name was called, and I was allowed out to answer it. It was an old-fashioned phone that could do with a clean and as one of the officers handed it to me my nose pinched slightly. If I had had a wet wipe, I would have given it a quick clean, but I didn't so I couldn't.

There was a seat available, so I sat next to one of them and said 'Hello,' whilst questioning who the fuck this was.

'Hello, Emily. I have good news.'

This good news made me sigh. 'Oh hi, Omar. What news do you have? Do we have a court date for my sentence?'

This was not good news for me personally, but it meant that I knew how long I would have to live here, and then organise things for Sah. It was both practical and logical, or so I assumed.

'Emily, I have good, very good news for you. You have been found innocent. You are going to go home.'

'WHAT?'

'Yes, there are some papers to sign but you are going home. You are innocent.'

I screamed, 'Oh my God! Oh my God! Jesus! Thank you, thank you, thank you so much. I can't bloody believe this. What the…?'

My throat went dry quickly and my heart felt as if it jumped in shock with my breathing short and shallow with shock.

'Yes, we worked very hard. Now listen to me, you must wait patiently. It will take time but know this, you are going home. You will soon be with your daughter.'

'Jesus, you all said that this was serious. And then with the drug smuggling - well, I thought that was it to be honest. They believe me?'

'Yes, they believe you. You were very honest throughout. You are free!'

'Well, not just yet.'

'No, but do not worry it will be soon, Emily. Insha'Allah.'

'Yes, hopefully. I need to be with my daughter.'

'You will be soon and then you can forget this.'

In a high-pitched voice my reaction was immediate, 'Forget this? I will never forget this experience. It nearly… nearly cost me my life with my daughter. My God!'

'Yes, it is a big surprise/shock to us believe me. This is not common, Emily. You are very lucky.'

'Lucky? Yes, I am. My God. I am sorry, but I am in shock.'

'Believe me. You are innocent and going home Emily.'

'Right!' I started to laugh and cry simultaneously. I quickly pulled myself together, 'So, what will happen now, Omar? I am sorry, but I think I am in shock a little.'

'Paperwork will be signed for your deportation. I will come to see you soon for your signature. Then it will be processed. Do you have money for a flight?'

'Yes. I do have money in my account to pay for my flight.'

'Good. Then you will buy a flight home to the UK, and you will be deported. Do you understand what I am saying to you, Emily?'

'Yes. I think so.'

'When the paperwork is ready, I will come to see you. Ok?'

'Yes. Thank you so much for everything you have done.'

'You are a client, Emily. It is our job, but I am happy for you. That is the truth. Now, I must go, you have the good news, so I will leave you now.'

'Yes, I have the news. Thank you. Can I phone my family and tell them?'

'Yes, of course.'

'And what about the girls at Bur Dubai, my cell mates?'

'Yes. Just say that you have confirmation that you will be deported shortly and that you know nothing else.'

'Ok. Say I am to be deported shortly? I can do that. Wow! This is real.'

'Ha ha ha. Yes, it is real. Now goodbye, Emily and I will see you soon.'

'Yes, goodbye and thank you.'

Now, I knew when an Arab says shortly, it could be whenever it happens or when God wills it. I hoped God would will my deportation quickly, but realistically I knew this could take some time. I put the phone down and thanked the ladies. Then I questioned, 'Can I please phone home to tell my family that I will be deported shortly once paperwork is completed?'

I had a quick reply of 'No!' followed by a look of disapproval from the clown next door to me who wore bright purple eyeshadow with dark brown lipstick, which when surrounded by her thick curly hair and obese body - well, where the hell was her mother or maid letting her out of the house like that I questioned?

So, I pleaded once again, but this time I looked to the Egyptian. 'Please may I phone my mother and daughter to let them know that my lawyer has said I have been found innocent and I will be deported?'

She simply nodded and said, 'Ok. Hurry.'

I ran back into my cell to get my phone card, cutting the ladies off and letting the others know before their questioned started, 'I have to phone home quickly. I am sorry. I will speak with you soon.' It had been the quickest I had moved in weeks and possibly months. I grabbed the phone card from where it was kept and ran back to the phone. I followed the instructions and waited anxiously for the ringing tone. 'Please answer, please answer, Mammy.' It rang and rang and my heartbeat in unison with the ringtone. Then it clipped and, 'Hello?'

'Mammy, it is me.'

'Oh, Emily are you alright? You never phone this early.'

'Ye, I know. The Egyptian police officer kindly allowed me when I asked her.' I looked behind me to ensure she had heard this compliment. I hadn't given one personally before, but given the situation and my news, knowing very well that she did not have to allow me this right to phone, her common decency and kindness had prevailed. Was there hope for the others under her authority? Like hell! But it was just and warranted.

'Mammy, you are never going to guess what just happened - the lawyer's secretary called me.'

'Oh, Em, what has happened now?' I could hear the trepidation in her voice.

'Mammy, it is good news. I have been found innocent and I will be deported soon.'

'WHAT? Oh Emily, that is good news. How? When will you be home?'

'I know, Mammy. It's bloody brilliant and the best news ever. I thought I was going to be sentenced, but now this. I am coming home!'

'This isn't a sick joke now, Emily, or a mistake by them?'

'No, Mammy. He phoned to say that they had worked very hard and now papers would be signed, I will have to buy a plane ticket, and then I will be home. He told me to forget about it all when I am home.'

'Forget about it - how the hell are you supposed to forget about it, Emily?'

'I know, Mammy. But at least I know I am coming home.'

'Oh, Em. I can't wait to have you back here.' She started to cry.

'Don't cry, Mammy. It will be ok. I will be home fucking soon, and I am not going anywhere.'

'Emily, don't swear now.'

'Ok, Mammy. Sorry. Is Sah there?'

'I will call her now. Sah? Sah come quickly as Mammy wants to speak to you. She is watching *Teletubbies*. To be honest with you it is driving me crazy. I don't understand it.'

'I tried getting into it too, Mammy, when she was young, but I couldn't. I used to watch and watch it and be so confused.'

With a little fumbling I heard the receiver of the phone be given to Sah.

'Mammy?'

God, I loved this little girl and my heart filled with the fact that I would be home with her soon.

'Sah! How are you, Cariad?'

'Mammy.'

Then, as usual, 'When home?'

'Sah, the doctor just said that I can come home soon. I don't know exactly when, but I will be home as soon as I can. I love you so much.'

'I love you, Mammy.'

'So, I need you to be a good girl a little bit longer for Mam, ok?'

'Yes. Presents?'

'Oh, presents? Well, you will just have to wait and see. But I promise you will have something nice and the biggest kiss from me.'

'Wet kiss?'

'Oh, I don't know about that. Wet kisses!'

'Noooooooooo!'

I laughed and then I could hear behind me, 'Finish.'

'Listen I have to go now sweetheart. I love you.'

'Love you, Mammy.'

'Can you put Mam back on?'

'Yes. Ok bye, Mammy.'

She was gone and my mother was back.

'Emily?'

'Ye, listen I have to go. I will phone you again when I can.'

'Ok. Love you, Emily, and good news. I am going to phone Rob now.'

'Ok. Love you, Mammy. Bye.'

The conversation was over and now I had to go back into the cell. I placed the receiver back onto the handle, and quickly lay my head on it and took a deep inhale and exhale to calm myself in the frenzy I found myself. I was still in shock.

I willed myself to walk back into the cell knowing the truth that I would not be here much longer. Well, I bloody hoped so.

I turned and thanked Egyptian before walking slowly back in. I held onto the metal bars of our cell and the girls knew something was up, as they all looked at me.

Anna had a frown and then sympathetically said, 'Emily, what is wrong? Are you ok?'

I looked directly at her and simply said, 'Yes, I am fine. The phone call was the secretary of my lawyer.'

Lebanese asked, 'And is everything ok?'

'Yes, everything is wonderful. I am to be deported once the paperwork is completed.' The shocked facial expressions surrounded me.

Anna was the first to jump down from the bunk bed and hug me. She kissed me strongly on both cheeks like a proper Russian kiss and said, 'Good news Emily. You should not have been here.'

Then slowly the smiles appeared.

Moroccan held my arm and said, 'Very good news Emily. I am happy that you will be home with your daughter soon.'

The Africans did a ceremonial dance of some sort whilst clapping their hands and making pretty good music whilst moving around.

Moroccan then shouted out of the cell for everyone to hear, 'Emily is innocent. She will go home.'

I cringed inside and said, 'Sh.'

She turned to me and said, 'Emily, we all need hope. This is good news. Be happy.'

'I am.'

Then, Lebanese and Emirati started conversing and I knew this was a conversation I did not want to have.

Lebanese asked, 'Emily, she ask what the lawyer say?'

'What I just said.'

'But why you are innocent?'

'They found me innocent, and now I will be deported after papers are signed.'

They conversed again.

'Was she spoken of?'

'No. I am sorry.'

'She does not understand Emily how you have the same lawyer and you have contact with yours and he does not contact her. You understand.'

'Yes, I understand. If I were you, I would be pissed off, believe me. But we have very different cases. I am/was marijuana in the UK and you were coke in the United Arab Emirates.'

Anna had listened patiently before interjecting, 'What you are not happy Emily go home? Really? That not good. Be happy for her. She is innocent and she go home.'

Then, the big muscular African stated in her deep African voice, 'Yes, we should be happy for Emily. Not nice and very bad.'

'No, no. You misunderstand. She doesn't understand how you have serious case and now you go home. She been here months and she not understand.' Lebanese pacified.

'I can fully understand, but she needs to phone and chase them. That's all I can say.'

Lebanese translated and then Emirati smiled at me and said, 'Ok, ok.'

I sat down on a mattress near Anna and she quizzed, 'Emily, you are happy?'

'Oh God, Anna, of course I am happy. I am just in shock. They all said I had a serious case, and it was doom and gloom. I just can't believe it.'

She held my hands and said, 'This is good news. It give hope to all of us… here … now.'

'Anna, I don't think it gives hope to everyone. Look at the women in here, look, some have been locked up for months with no visit from their embassy and no money for a lawyer. They have families and children too.'

'Emily it is life. You not worry about that. You are free. Go home to your daughter and forget all this shit in this shit country.'

It wasn't long until I went to the toilet. I had waited for the queue to die down before sitting on the toilet. I just needed some time where I could sit by myself. As I did, I could see my mother and Sah smiling in the background, and I smiled too.

I spoke to my mother a few days later with no updates. Then, on the Sunday, during visiting, my name was called. When my name was called out, I looked at all the girls as to say,

'Who the fuck is here to see me? Could it be the lawyer asking for my signature?'

When I approached and the door was opened, I saw who it was I was shocked and internally I spoke to myself, *oh, it is the British Embassy representative.*

She sat there patiently, however, this time when she saw me approach her, she was full of smiles.

'Hello, Emily. How are you?'

'Hi, yes I am fine - still here.'

'Sit please,' and after I sat down next to her with my knees facing hers, she continued, 'Good news, Emily. You are innocent. We are so happy that you will go home soon.'

'Thank you, but I have always told you that I was.'

I really didn't know what to say to her.

'Yes, it is very good news.'

'We have been following your case, Emily. The ambassador wants you to know that we have fully supported you and done everything that we could do to support you.'

'Yes, I am incredibly grateful for your help in getting me a photo of my daughter.'

'Yes, yes. And the ambassador also brought up your concerns with the commissioner of police.'

'Yes, and nothing has changed for these ladies. The conditions are the same, as you can see. And you know the truth.' I held out my right hand and pointed in the direction of the cells where the bodies of ladies lay and sat.

'I have some information here for you when you return home. Read and maybe they will be of some assistance to you when you return to the UK.'

I took them and thought to myself that at least I had something to read for the rest of my stay here.

'Is there anything else I can do for you?'

'No, I don't think so. I am just waiting for the paperwork to be signed and then to be deported.'

'Well, have a safe journey home and take care, Emily. You are very lucky as in such cases before the individuals have been found guilty and served a prison sentence. Yes, you are very lucky.'

'Yes, I know. Thank you and please thank the ambassador for all his help.'

As I made that statement I thought, *God, the British are always so polite and even when I don't mean it - seriously?* I questioned why I couldn't be honest and inform the British representative that whilst I would always be grateful for her communication with my brother and for bringing me Sah's photo, I honestly did not see the value to British taxpayers of paying for international grand embassies. Yes, they had specific functions such as if you had a spouse who wanted to apply for a British Spouse Visa, British Tourist Visa, renewing a British passport or obtaining a British passport, if you were in an accident, or registering your marriage or children. But surely the costs involved did not warrant such glorious embassy buildings, the amount and cost of the employees whose employment packages would include housing, medical insurance, flights, security, drivers, private education for staff/children etc.

I wondered if the nations of the world could unify and share a building, which would in return decrease costs, staffing, and the bloody pomp of it all. My viewpoint at the time, and to this day, is to still question their current function in the world and the cost to hard-working British nationals whose tax contributes to an imperial idealism, which is defunct in this ever-changing world. This was my ideology and whether it was right or wrong I did not know, but it was the way I felt.

I knew I would never see or speak to this woman again. I questioned if I had been biased or negative towards her because she was a woman, like the police officers, and was a Muslim as her head scarf personified her faith. Would I have been happier with a non-Muslim representative, and the answer was yes.

After the behaviour I had experienced with most of the bitches of Bur Dubai, I can still remember my initial spasm, jolting body movements and sheer panic of experiencing further wrong in this fucked up story of mine.

I returned to the cell with the leaflets and sat down initially to scan over them before being interrupted. Lebanese questioned, 'Who was that Emily and what are you reading?'

Now, I had never ever been so nosy as to ask such questions, but it was to be expected now. It was a trait I didn't like, however, in my current housing situation and incarceration, well, I couldn't really complain. I looked up quickly before returning my gaze to the documents as I/we spoke.

'Oh, it was the British Ambassador's representative. She came here to congratulate me I suppose,' I commented questionably before continuing. 'And she gave me these documents to read.'

'Can I see them?' Now this was very cheeky in my eyes and my eyebrows arched in agreement. I looked up at her to see her lying on her bed and leaning against the wall. 'Yes, sure you can read them, but not now. I have just got them and will need to read them a couple of times before I take it in, as they are formal documents. Ye, sure, once I finish with them, and then I will want them back.'

'Of course, Emily.'

I did a double grunted cough before returning my gaze to my documents that consisted of information from Prisoners Abroad, a charity whose help I may need once back home. The documents were handed around the cell that day. How much of the information that was understood by the ladies was questionable, but they were all in agreement that my government was a good government, and that I was lucky to have such a government. In comparison to all of them I had been lucky, as no one else from any national governmental embassy had visited and there were lots of nationalities to pick from. Also, they had come once they knew I was in the system to see if I was ok, needed anything, and they had responded in kind to my needs and concerns. They had also been honest and told me what I faced, given me a list of lawyers, communicated with my family and me when they were allowed, and their final gesture of coming to see me, happily, giving me more information and encouragement, well, yes, I was lucky. I smiled upon this realisation and had hope that whatever had happened during this whole bloody experience I still held the capacity to see the negative and positive. However, my hope of having the same resolution about the bitches of Bur Dubai was frugal.

A knot developed in my core at their mere thought or mention. The utter contempt and hatred I had for them grew in strength, and so did my judgement of anyone who looked, sounded, or had their facial expressions or mannerisms. Even the bloody colours of their eyeshadow and lipstick turned my stomach. And their smell of overpowering musky strong scent that you could taste made me very alert. It was a further trigger to behaviour I was not accustomed to.

I reread those documents daily as I waited for confirmation of my departure date. Daily I would ask the Egyptian when she was in, and there was no news. So, I had had enough of waiting for my freedom to return home and to breathe fresh air in an open space. Every day I had my things ready under the bed in case I was called to go, and every day I waited and waited. There was nothing. It was soul destroying and the anxiety of waiting grew.

So, after lunch I asked the Egyptian, as I held on to the bars, 'Excuse me, I would like to speak with my lawyer as days and weeks are now passing. I have been told I have been found innocent from my lawyer and the British Embassy. I need to speak with him as this is just cruel now. I am waiting each day and there is nothing.'

The Egyptian looked at me and for a moment I saw pity in her oval eyes. She simply nodded and without smiling said, 'Quickly. OK?'

'Thank you.' I looked at her directly saying this while my heart sank against the strength of the cold metal bars. I had my phone card on me in hope and I was quickly allowed to call. I could see the disapproval of the others and I clenched my jaw as I stared at them whilst waiting for the phone to be answered as it rang. Then it did.

His deep voice simply said, 'Hello?'

'Hi, Omar. It is Emily. How are you?'

'Yes, Emily I am fine. Are you home?'

I shook my head from left to right. 'Um no. I am still in Bur Dubai. I am still waiting. I just want to go home.'

'Emily, I am sorry I thought you had returned to the UK. Why are you still there? I do not understand?'

'You don't understand? Jesus… I have been waiting every day... waiting with nothing happening. Even the British Embassy has been here to sort of congratulate me. Can you please let me know what it happening as I really don't know how much longer I can do this here? Firstly, I was told I would be locked up for six months to four years and that it was a serious case. Then, I am told that I am innocent and will go home. Why are they keeping me here because—?' I was speechless. I just couldn't take it anymore. I wanted/needed Sah and to go home. 'And you never came here for me to sign the papers.'

'Emily, I swear to you I will look into this. You should not be here. I am sorry but I thought you were with your daughter and family.'

'Please, please, please help me. Find out what the delay is as I really don't know how much more I can take here.'

'Call me tomorrow evening and I hope I will have some news.'

'Ok, and thank you.'

'Don't worry you will be home soon.'

I rolled my eyes and thought to myself, *not fucking again*. I rested my right elbow on the wall and had the telephone in my left hand. With a 'Thank you and goodbye,' the conversation was over, and I thanked Egyptian. I explained that I needed to speak with my lawyer tomorrow evening and asked if it would be ok, and she nodded yes. I said 'Thank you' again and returned to my cell where I lay down and placed a blanket over my head. The long wait had started, and I couldn't wait to speak with him. My sanity now needed this to be over and my shakes in the neck and lower head were starting to mimic a tick or reaction to stress.

I lay there with the weight of the world pushing down on me from above, and I cradled myself whimpering with complete exhaustion. My battery had been pushed to the limit with the ups and downs of the previous weeks. I knew I was going to break soon. I was crumbling from the days of waiting, hoping, waiting, nothing and I was so empty inside. As my eyes swiftly moved from right to left processing everything; images of Sah, my mother, Abe, my house, work, colleagues, students, Sperm Donor, the bitches of Bur Dubai, well, everything was like a merry-go-round. It was exhausting and I moved my right hand in a fist and held it to my mouth and bit on my index finger. My breath was dry, stale, and hot as it bit my finger and I sobbed as quietly as I could, so not to be heard under this dull, dirty and old worn blanket. *What the fuck is going on?* I repeated this so many times in my head that it was like a record player on repeat. I lay there jolting, ignoring everything and everyone around me. They must have respected my need for privacy, or I scared them, but I woke up hours later. I woke up like a great weight was still pushing against me and everything seemed heavy within me, and dark, so dark. I was there in body and spoke when spoken to, but for the time that followed until my next conversation with Omar, I became like a minion, following the routine of it all. I needed to conserve my energy for the next fight that lay ahead of me of actually bloody getting out of this hellhole. I had been found not guilty, and I still did not have my freedom to leave this place.

I waited anxiously but patiently all day wondering what was happening with my case, where was Omar and who was he contacting to get this bloody thing sorted. I tried to sleep at intervals, but I was just in mental overdrive and my body was raring to go, but with the metal bars I was limited. The evening had finally arrived, and it was the approximate time to make a call. I left the girls without saying anything and approached the cell door. However, when I asked politely, I was told a firm, 'No!'

My hold on the metal bars intensified to the extent that the coldness from them made my fingers cold. 'Excuse me…. No?'

'Yes. Go back. No.'

Now, I had politely asked to use the phone and informed her that Egyptian had said that I could do so yesterday. I had also stated the background to my case and that I had been found innocent and was now awaiting deportation. Well, she had the bloody audacity to say, 'No!?!' I was dumbfounded once again.

I shook my head from left to right and then clicked my neck and manoeuvred my head in a circular direction. I positioned my eyes in direct eye contact with hers. I started with, 'Let's try this again. What is your name?'

She looked at me puzzlingly and her right lip raised a little as she sat on her chair doing nothing. 'Why?'

'Why? Because your captain gave me permission yesterday after I spoke with my lawyer regarding finding out what the delay is in holding me here, and not deporting me back to the good old United Kingdom. We agreed that we would speak this time tonight. If you do not allow me to call him now well, I want you to call whoever is in charge up there on your phone or I am going to start calling and believe me I will get attention. You can even call Egyptian if you want confirmation, but I tell you one thing, I am going to speak with my lawyer tonight. Hell, you can stand with me and listen if you want to. But if you do not let me do this, I will be contacting the British Embassy tomorrow and my lawyer and I will be reporting you. You! Do you understand? So, you have 3 choices. 1. Let me make a phone call out of good faith. 2. Speak with the Egyptian to confirm and then let me make the call. 3. Not let me phone and then face being reported and believe me I will, with or without your name, as I can just report the woman who was on duty at the time. So, do you want to be reported? Do you? Because as you can most probably tell, I am in no mood to play around.'

She kept eye contact with me and whilst I am not too sure if she understood everything, I believe she got the gist of it. She took a long deep breath in between her bright purple lips and then slowly grabbed the keys and got off her rather large lazy bottom and approached the cell and opened it.

As I walked through, she stood looking me up and down, then emotionlessly stated, 'Quickly.'

I wanted to smirk a wicked grin of successful negotiation but thought against this and said a confident, 'Thank you,' before I proceeded to the telephone and grabbed my phone card from my pocket. I inputted the numbers slowly and patiently as I wanted to make sure time was not wasted. I knew I would not have long.

It rang for what seemed like long seconds before he answered.

'Hello, Omar, it is Emily.'

'Hello, Emily. I have been expecting you. We are chasing one signature. We will get it tomorrow and then I will come to see you, get a signature, and then take it to the office to be processed. I will not leave until it is. You will then be processed and deported in say two to three days at the latest.'

'Oh my God. Are you for real now? Honestly?'

'Yes. You have my word. But we had to work very hard, Emily, and I will need payment?'

I sank my forehead into the wall. 'Thank you for your work and how much?' My eyes were closed and the sheer dread of the amount I would next hear frightened me.

'It will be 3,000 English Sterling Pounds. Can you pay this, Emily?'

'Um… Ye, but I don't think I have the funds in my bank account. I would need to go home and pay you from there?'

'Ah, I see. Could your brother pay it for you?'

'My brother has returned to Africa, and I can't contact him.'

'What about your mother? Could she help you?'

'No. My mother is a widow, and she does not have that kind of money. I am sorry, but I will have to sort this out when I am home. I know I have enough for a flight ticket home but not this extra cost of £3,000.'

'Do you have a Visa Card that you can pay with?'

'I am sorry, but I do not.' Now, I had become a little wee irate with his constant badgering for money, especially after the initial cost of £10,000. And he had previously stated that he would come to me for the signature, before any mention of new costing.

'Oh. Ok, Emily. Are you alright?'

'Ye… I just need this nightmare to end. I need to get out of here and to get home,' I answered sharper than I would have liked to.

'Well, I will see you tomorrow, Emily. It will soon be here.'

Sarcastically I replied, 'Maybe sooner for some than others.'

'Yes. That is true. Well, goodbye, Emily.'

'Goodbye, and I will see you tomorrow.'

'Insha'Allah.'

'Yes, Insha'Allah. Goodbye, Omar.'

I returned to the cell where things had now become quieter, or possibly I had.

I explained to Anna when she asked what the lawyer had said that he would get a signature tomorrow and then I would be home possibly within three days. Oh, and they wanted another three thousand pounds from me.

'What three? You mean three hundred English pounds?'

'No, I mean three thousand, yes thousand.'

'What to get a signature for you leave?'

'Don't fucking ask. And before you start with fucking bastards, robbers and whatever else you want to say about them - well, yes, I agree, but they are going to get me out. And I need it so bad, Anna. I know this experience has changed me, but the longer I stay here, the more fucked up I know I am becoming. I want to go home as similar as I can to the Emily who came out here. I am scared I am going to change so much that I won't be the same. I am scared, Anna, because I am so angry.'

She grabbed my left hand with hers and said, 'Emily. You are good person. You see that? You will go home different, Emily. You have to. This is impossible… forget. We all suffer. But you will go home .. to your family and you will forget.'

'Anna, that's the problem. I don't think I will ever or could ever forget about this.'

'And the money - not pay. It crazy, Emily. Three thousand for signature. Should be done before.'

'I know. God, this bloody country.' We both smiled.

I know the others were listening, but I just didn't have the energy to converse. Of course, if they had asked me a question, I would have answered. If there were conversations, I would join in, but I had been put through so much emotionally that the impact on my physical and mental health were evident to me as I pulled away internally.

I did have the opportunity that evening when someone new came on duty to phone home and explain to my mother whose disbelief in Dubai increased every time I called her.

She ended our conversation by saying, 'Well, let's hope we have some good news tomorrow. God willing.'

To which I answered, 'Don't bloody start with God willing. That is what Insha'Allah means and they seem to say that here all the time. It doesn't bloody do anything,' to which she replied with a stern, 'Emily!'

I knew that was my cue to shut up and the time had funnily enough come to an end, but I ended with, 'I can't wait to come home, Mammy.'

And she concurred, 'I know, Em. I know.' With a 'Love you.'

After a restless night of tossing and turning, we awoke to the roll call for breakfast. I nibbled and sat chewing and contemplating, *I wonder what is happening now in the case of Emily?* I pondered whether Omar would come to see me today. I questioned whether another £3,000 was warranted for a signature - hadn't enough been spent? I could see Sah faintly in the distance and I smiled for a short time daydreaming of holding her with laughter and kisses.

The morning was long as usual and meandered into the afternoon as expected. Any noise all morning from the bitches of Bur Dubai would make me jump up like a meerkat investigating noise. Then, I could hear a male voice. You got to notice a male's voice in a female-dominated society, believe you me. I sat up and had a warm feeling start and grow in my tummy, building with strength and warmth, and I started to smile. I got up and walked towards the entrance of the cell, and in front of me was the man who had informed me the previous evening that he would indeed speak with me today. He had been true to his word, even though he now demanded £3,000 more. I stopped in my tracks to take him in as he had papers in front of officers and the Egyptian. It was a conversation where I could see they listened. He then turned to see me as one of them had clocked me and he turned fully with,

'Please, let her out.' He used his right hand to reference 'open.' I smiled, I think, the biggest smile I had made here and approached the cell as one of them got up to open it. Once through, he told me to sit down on one of the chairs that surrounded the desk, as did he. We faced each other, my legal team and the enemy opposite, the bitches of Bur Dubai. However, I had no interest in them and just looked at Omar anticipating the news I had been waiting for. At this moment in time, he was my sun and he shone brightly in this darkness which had become home and now embodied me mentally.

His deep voice was soothing too, not in a Barry White way, but it relaxed me. I looked up to him when he started,

'Hello Emily. How are you?'

'Hi. Ye, I am ok, but I really need to know what is happening?'

'We have the signature here.' He pointed to a document. 'I need you to come with me to a department in this building for another signature on this document and I will also need your signature. Now we go with a police officer, and we finish.'

I could see that the female officer who was going to accompany us had no emotion and was robotic in her motion. She went to get handcuffs to put on me when I saw a different side to my Omar. He started waving his hands and speaking loudly, it wasn't a shout, but you knew something had riled him. I just looked at all the faces around me, not knowing what on earth was going on, when Egyptian said something, and the handcuffs were returned to where they had come from.

I asked what was going on and he immediately looked at me and said,

'She was going to put handcuffs on you. I told her that there was no need as you have been found not guilty and you will be deported. We are in this building and not leaving it, so there is no need.'

We followed the officer up the stairs and I turned around to speak to Omar to continue the conversation. 'Thank you for sticking up for me back there with the handcuffs. The ones they use here are extremely uncomfortable, you know what I mean? I always get embarrassed when I wear them; I feel people stare at me and question what I have done.'

He responded quickly. 'I have never worn them, Emily.'

That was the abrupt end to that conversation, and I laughed to myself saying, 'Jesus Emily. Not much play-acting in his house.'

We went through corridors, doors, stairs until we got to an office. I sat down on chairs outside the office as instructed by Omar, with the officer standing not too far away from me, whilst he knocked and then opened the door before entering. I looked around me, then he reappeared and sat in the chair next to me. His black suit did not flatter his rather large body, and I immediately thought a dish dash would be more flattering to his size and height. He leaned close to me. He did not invade my privacy, but I didn't like the fact that I could smell his coffee breath. He quietly spoke, 'Now, once this is done, I will get your signature and then leave you to go to another department. Then, you will be processed. It will not be long now, Emily.'

I became emotional immediately and hunched myself forward, head lowered and wiped my tears.

'I just want to go home to my daughter.'

'I know you do. Now listen, once you get back to the UK, you never, ever return here. Do you hear me?'

I nodded.

'I will contact you for the £3,000 payment, but you try to forget what happened here. And you never come back.'

'Oh, believe me, I have no intention of ever returning here. I have now lost my job, apartment, daughter's education in Qatar and I am done. I want to go home to the safety of the UK and my family.'

'In life, Emily, you can lose everything, but you are lucky as you have a family and daughter that love you. Go home and forget everything.'

I looked up at him, 'But that's the problem. The things I have experienced and witnessed, well, I am not sure if I can. I know I have been lucky because I am British when I compare myself to some of the others and the mess they are in. And they are going to continue to be in this situation because they have no money, no embassy and no lawyer.'

'Emily, you have been lucky as this was not a normal case.'

'Normal, no. Are there normal cases out here? Hell, I was arrested for nothing, made to sign documents… the list could go on.'

'Well, you don't have long left here now.' He smiled and then his attention was drawn to the office door that opened with an elderly Emirati who passed the document back to him. They spoke and were looking at me when the old man smiled at me before returning to his office. Again, I had no understanding until I was told, 'Now sign this, Emily, and those are all the signatures that were needed.' I signed the document where I was told, and we stood.

'Now, you will go back to the cell Emily. It won't be for too long, and I would like to wish you a safe journey home.'

He placed his hand out to shake it. I obliged and I thanked him once more for all his help.

'I can never thank you enough. Thank you.' I placed my left arm around his shoulder and closed my eyes as I held on for a second or two.

We parted smiling. He turned to leave in the opposite direction as I watched his hasty departure. You could tell he was a busy man, so I questioned how many drugs cases go on in Dubai. Whilst I knew this was the last time I would physically meet with him in person, during this lifetime, I honestly didn't look forward to the discussion of the three thousand quid. That would be something to think about once I was home.

I returned to the cell and ached as it felt like it was the furthest I had walked in months, but it felt good to walk from one place to the other, through corridors where faces were passed. Faces that moved in different directions with purpose. The girls quizzed me as to my little adventure and I retorted the account without embellishing the story. It was a minute or two of difference to their lives and I was glad of it in a way.

That evening Lebanese and Moroccan were called for phone duty as one of the lazy ones was on. They had only been out a couple of minutes when Lebanese called me. They always hogged the phone and then would start on the rest of us who always phoned. But, for the first time ever, my name was called. I had my phone card ready but Moroccan said,

'Emily, look at the notice board, your name is up. It was not there yesterday.'

'Jesus, what does it say?'

'Public Prosecution document 2010/9/1 two days' time. The Government of Dubai say that you will leave in two days from this letter. You be deported in two days.'

I closed my eyes and held my left hand over my left eye and my right hand on my right eye. My head was tilted, and I breathed in big deep breaths through my nose. I pulled my hands down slowly over my face and looked at her. Hell, she was standing so close to me we were nearly touching, and I said, 'This is it, isn't it? This is my freedom, right?'

She gently laughed and put her arms on my shoulders. 'Yes, Emily, this is your freedom.'

I stood back, breathing deeper breaths and then turned and stepped back to the girls near my cell, and I loudly told them,

'It has bloody come through. I am to be deported within two bloody days.'

Anna came straight to give me hug whilst others smiled and came to tap my shoulder. The Filipinos were joyous and told me that they had been praying day and night, which was a lovely thing to say. I hugged them all as whenever I did pass their cell to go to the toilet, they were always praying.

Moroccan then questioned, 'You no want to use phone Emily?'

'Yes, bloody hell yes. I need to tell my mother.'

'Then quickly, ok?'

I quickly got my phone card, and bubbling with excitement and adrenaline, I phoned.

As soon as the phone picked up, I speedily blurted out, 'Mammy, my deportation letter has come through. I should be leaving within two days, Mammy. Can you believe it? Can you?'

My eyes were filling up and droplets poured out which then streamed down my face. I didn't care as my head pressed gently against the wall.

'Emily, oh God, this is wonderful. But are you sure now?'

'Mammy, Omar came today, well this morning and he got the signatures. He told me he was going to sort it out and then this evening the girls have told me my name is on the notice board, so ye, as far as I am concerned, I am coming home.'

'Oh Em, I bloody hope so. Jesus.'

'I know, Mammy.'

'Is Sah there? I really want to speak to her?'

'Ye, she is here. What are you going to tell her?'

'That the doctor has said I can leave within two days and that I am well enough to travel and fly.'

'Ok. She is here now?'

I waited for the phone to be passed to her tiny little hands and to hear her sweet inhales and exhales as she thought of what to say on the telephone.

Then, I heard my mother tell her, 'Go on. Who do you think it is?'

With a little giggle she answered, 'Mammy?'

Then I started, 'Sah, Sah, Sah! How are you, Cariad?'

'Mammy!'

Oh, my heart melted. 'Yes, it is me and I have the best news ever.'

'Mmmm.'

'The doctors have said I can leave hospital so I will be home in a couple of days. Isn't that good news?'

'Ye,' she answered.

'Well, Mammy will be home in a couple of days, I hope, and I am going to kiss you so much that you won't need a bath.'

'Nooooooooooooo!'

'I love you, Sah and I have missed you so much.'

'I love you, Mammy.'

'I know. Listen, I am going to have to go soon.'

'Ok, Mammy.'

And with that she was gone. I said my goodbyes to Mammy and that, 'I will try to call you to let you know what's happening.'

'Ok, Em. Good luck. I love you.'

'Love you too. Kiss Sah from me.'

'I will.'

I came from that telephone call feeling lighter. My breathing was more relaxed and effortless. I walked back into the cell and was deep in emotion. Whilst others spoke amongst and around me, I dreamed of what she was doing now with my mother. It was getting late here but with the time difference I couldn't work out if it was a 1- or 2-hour difference between the UK and here. Maybe she was getting ready for bed as I was? Or maybe they were watching something on TV, cwtched up on the sofa together. I just knew that I had to keep it together and not let my temperate emotions get too excitable. I also wanted to be sympathetic to the girls as I would be leaving the home, this home, I had shared with them from the very beginning. I had not only shared the cells with them but their stories, life, trials, and tribulations with men internationally. After many of our conversations, I did, in fact, conclude that the majority of us were here because of men, so I came to the conclusion that men have got an awful lot to fucking answer for.

When Lebanese and Moroccan came back to the cell from their telephone duties, we discussed deportation in more depth. I learnt that an individual is deported when the court issues an order of deportation against you, and this rule becomes final and enforceable. I was now classified as an unwanted visitor who legally could not ever return to Dubai for life. The good news was that I could still transit through the UAE airports if I stayed in the international zone.

I was also told by one of the ladies that there is a petition procedure to remove the permanent ban, but it is exceptionally granted and costs in the region of £100,000. I would never ever be paying that money to return to a country that I now detested everything it stood for and made it clear to the girls, 'Well, I know one thing, I will never be coming back here. Never! Ever! Fuck them, fuck Dubai!' And that is all I had to say on the matter.

But one thing is for sure, I slept so well that night. Anna and I shared the top bunk, it was a rolling rota of favouritism if you got lucky to share a bed, as otherwise it would be an evening on the concrete floor. Also, Anna and my body frame allowed us to share a single mattress comfortably, well, as comfortably as what was possible under the current situation. We both tossed and turned, don't get me wrong, but I woke with hope, excitement, and I suppose adrenaline. I needed to know what time I would be deported and the procedure of the process, and to question when the notice for my release came through and why didn't any, and I repeat, any of the police officers notify me? If it wasn't for the Arab girls in the clink with me, then I wouldn't have bloody known.

After breakfast and the start of the morning shift for the officers I waited to see if Egyptian was on duty. I peeped back and forth, and whilst some of the bitches were there, Egyptian wasn't. Maybe it was just my luck. The cell door was still open and so I walked through and faced them. It took me three times to get their attention and I was standing in front of them. Possibly, they had hearing problems too, but the evidence so far suggested that they were indeed fuckwits in a job that they should never ever have been allowed to interview for, let alone be appointed. My God!

So, I said, 'Excuse me?' I waited. Nothing. 'Excuse me?' louder. There was not a flicker of attention given to me. Now, I had been polite, to no avail, so the next one would bloody get their attention. I shouted, 'Excuse me?' Bingo! I had their attention and if looks could kill from big eyes with bright lipstick, well, I would have been a very cold stiff.

One of them said, 'What?' whilst rolling her eyes before saying something to the others and then they all looked at me and giggled. This made me mad as hell.

'Your rudeness is excused; however, I have three questions. Firstly, where is...' *(not Egyptian - fuck what is her name?* 'the Egyptian lady who is in charge - the captain?'

They looked amongst themselves and then thinner one said, 'Not here.'

'Well, evidently otherwise, why would I ask you. Secondly,

why was I not informed,' *(oh better break this down)* 'told that this had come through for me yesterday?' They looked to the document I pointed to on the notice board and said nothing. I continued, 'This states that I am to be deported. Agreed?'

One walked over to it, said something to the others, moved her hands around and sat her rather large bottom down. I focused on its size and questioned how her bottom balanced on a toilet and what size of turd stool passed her sewage system before I came back to my last question.

'Thirdly, when am I leaving Bur Dubai? I would like to know when I will be returning to the UK as I have been found innocent.'

There was no response from any of them, then the thinner one told me, 'Go back.'

'Excuse me?' I said for the fourth time. 'I don't care who you call, but I am waiting here until I know what is going on. I know you understood that.' I proceeded to sit down on a free chair opposite where the bitches sat. I was not moving my pretty little bottom until I had satisfaction and understanding as to what and when things would move.

To say they didn't have a clue what was going on was an understatement. They looked at one another as if to question, 'What?' This was not covered in their training.

Thinner one then piped up after speaking with the others and was firmer, 'Go back cell.' She lifted her head upwards and towards the cell door.

'Nah, that is not going to happen until someone can find out exactly when I am leaving. Do you understand me?'

A conversation erupted then one of the three big mamas called Lebanese from the cell. Something was said then Lebanese told me,

'Emily. They do not know. Come back to cell now.'

I shook my head back and forth and said, 'No. I am not leaving this spot until they pick up the phone or toddle off upstairs to ask someone exactly what is going on.'

Then Moroccan came and put her hand on my right shoulder. 'Emily. This not good. Come now. Come with us to cell.'

'Girls, I know you mean well, but the only thing I am asking them to do is to call someone and find out exactly when I am leaving. Now, surely in their capacity as police officers they can ask questions/give answers, so I really suggest they get on as I am not moving from this seat.'

Lebanese and Moroccan spoke amongst themselves and then spoke with the officers. They seemed to be talking, then looking at me and then talking again.

'Emily, please? This no good.'

'I am sorry, but all I am asking is for them to make a telephone call or to go upstairs and find out when I am leaving. I was found innocent weeks ago, and as far as I am concerned, I am still being held here illegally and I have human rights, you know. I, like you, am entitled to these international rights and freedoms set forth in their declaration.

So, what is the bloody problem in finding out what is happening?'

The thin one said something and then one of the larger ones got on the phone. The conversation she had with whoever she called wasn't long, and then the phone was passed to me.

'Hello. Who am I speaking to?'

'You wanted to speak with me about when you will leave?'

I recognised the voice immediately. It was Egyptian. Now she wasn't here, she was yesterday, but would she know? I doubted it very much.

'Yes, I know that the paperwork has come through for my deportation. I was told last night by the two Arabic girls in the cell with me.'

'Yes.'

'I would like to know when I will be leaving for deportation.'

There was hesitation. 'I will be in tomorrow, and I will find out.'

'I am sorry that isn't good enough. I would like to know when I will be leaving as my lawyer stated within two days. Does that mean I will be leaving tomorrow?'

''I do not know.'

'Then, can the officers here do their work and contact someone within the police station to find out please?'

'Finish now, Emily. Go back to the cell,' she pleaded.

'I am sorry, I can't do that until I have confirmation as to when I am leaving. I would like one of your officers on duty to contact whoever they need to find out. I know it is not difficult, and surely, they are contracted to do the best job possible as police officers. I hope you will inform them, tell them, to find out otherwise I will be contacting the British Embassy and my lawyer again. I have been found innocent and continue to be locked up. It is your responsibility now to do your job. Please?'

'Pass phone back. Ok?'

I was a wee bit frustrated with the incompetence of the whole organisation. 'I will pass the phone back.'

I returned it to the officer in front of me. I looked around me whilst the conversation continued on the phone. Everyone was watching and listening. Hell, my stance and refusal to move had attracted the whole cell's attention and eyes peered at me from all directions.

The phone was put down, and then she said something to the others. Then, she redialled and phoned someone else. The conversation was noticeably short and then the phone was put down again. They spoke amongst themselves, and I sat there waiting. Then, Lebanese and Moroccan returned to the cell. The confusion on their faces was clear, but I maintained my seating position. I sat there oblivious to what the officers were doing and sat comfortably in the chair. It was so nice to sit in a simple chair. For a few minutes, the officers just sat looking at me and I sat looking back at them. To say the atmosphere was icy was an understatement. Then, footsteps were heard coming down to the basement. A man in a dish dash stood in front of the cell door and one of them got the keys and let him in. He looked at me with no emotion displayed and spoke with them before turning to address me.

'The problem?'

Now, he was obviously senior, and I knew I really didn't need any more shit to be thrown my way, so I politely replied,

'Hello! My name is Emily. Nice to meet you. Could you possibly help me as I was found innocent and am to be deported? See there is a notice here?' I pointed to the document on the notice board. He had a quick look and then returned to me. 'Now I was found not guilty weeks ago and it has taken weeks to get the paperwork in order. So, my lawyer intervened and now the documentation is complete, and I would like confirmation of when exactly I will be leaving here, as I have been informed within two days. Now, my experience so far has taught me not to rely on what I am told, as communication is extremely poor here. Could you please speak to the department to find out what is happening please?'

He looked me up and down, so in turn I looked him up and down in his dress. He then instructed me, 'Go back to the cell. I will investigate and come back and tell you.'

'You promise that today you will come back and tell me?'

'I give my word.'

I stood up, thanked him, and shook his hand. Throughout our conversation, the ladies had sat like model students. I returned to the cell, and I assume, well, hoped, that when he left, he would indeed investigate.

The girls were bemused, and Anna questioned, 'What happened Emily?'

'He promised to look into it and let me know later.'

'Good for you, Emily.'

Lebanese had condemnation with, 'You are silly, Emily. You go home. You could get into trouble. Silly!'

'I have every right to ask such questions. I have waited weeks to be deported and because of Dubai's disorganised justice system, we are all suffering. Yes, I spoke to those bitches with contempt, but you must remember you get treated differently than us. I have never met such a group of women who should not be in this profession. It's fucking disgusting what goes on here and I am not sorry if you don't like the way I am speaking, but it is the way I am feeling and if I don't deal with this, I am going to lose it and then believe me you will see a different side to me. We all have the capacity to fight, and we have done it daily to survive here, mentally and physically, but what happens here is disgusting. People need to know what goes on in this hidden world beneath the bright lights of the city, and to be held accountable. Hell, we have.'

She had nothing to say on the matter and I had said my piece.

The Africans applauded me, 'Well done, Emily. You say how you feel. And yes, it is wrong what happens here.'

The excitement had ended, and everything returned to the same mundane routine. Lunch had come and gone, and then my name was called. I walked slowly, not knowing if this chap from upstairs had returned or if something else had occurred. But he was a man of his word, and he had returned. We were separated by metal, but I heard him clearly.

'You will go to get money from the cash machine upstairs, then you will be taken to buy a ticket. Please have your passport on you.'

'When?'

'Soon. Someone will come down.'

'Thank you so much for your help. It is a shame you don't work down here.'

He laughed, said, 'No,' and then left.

My steps back to the cell were like mini jumps of excitement. I didn't even look at the bitches. So, the wait continued and true to his word, a man did come down. There was a man in a dish dash awaiting at the cell door.

'Emily?' he said in a quiet manner. His pronunciation far improved from others working within the system.

I pelted from the cell and looked up to meet his gaze through the metal bars on the door and replied solemnly, 'Yes.'

He instructed to the point, 'I am here to take you to the bank to get money for your return ticket to your home country. Do you have your bank card and passport?'

I nodded. He said something in Arabic to the bitches, they let me out and proceeded to open the safe and give me my envelope with my personal possessions. The safe was opened and I collected my bank card and passport. We walked to the cash point machine I had previously used to get money for phone cards and shopping. However, the walk to the travel agent was lovely as it was outside of the building. There was no conversation between us just a few 'come's. The lady who processed my flight ticket treated me like any customer, and I was thankful that the handcuffs were off otherwise I am sure the experience would not have been as pleasant.

The flight was booked for two days' time, but it was booked and that was the main thing. The elation I felt walking back was pure bliss. I smiled and skipped with excitement.

I didn't have the tickets and would have to rely on an ex-inmate, my Mary, to help me pick them up. She was in communication with my mother, and I called her. She had said that if there was anything she could do to help me then I was to just ask, and I did so in a telephone call upon my return. I asked the officers politely and explained that the ticket would be processed in another agent's shop. I did not know the procedure for deportation, so I asked Lebanese.

'You taken to deportation and then fly home.'

This didn't mean much to me, so I waited and waited… and nothing happened. It was such a rollercoaster of ups and downs, misunderstanding and ignorance. The frustration of not knowing was cruel. I slept that night next to Anna and waited for the sun to rise, to eat breakfast and start my questions again.

So, after breakfast had finished, I went up to the cell door to speak with Egyptian. I asked politely, 'Excuse me, do you know when I will be leaving for deportation?'

I could see in her eyes that she was tired of having someone like me in her custody and possibly she found me somewhat annoying. I remembered when as a child whilst driving with my family I would ask so many questions that in the end, my father would answer, 'Emily, I don't know all the answers. Can we try and enjoy this spin?' My mother would reply, 'But that's how she will learn.' It made me giggle and wonder whether Sah would question me like I used to my father.

She returned my gaze and replied with a little, or the littlest, smile. 'Yes, today.'

'What today?'

She nodded to confirm. I started to jump up and down and then said a loud, 'Yes! I am leaving today.'

I returned to the cell and Anna gave me the biggest hug, which made me cry a little, and as I went to the bathroom the other ladies and nationalities shared my joy. When I finally got back to the cell and sat down, my name was called again. I went like a good inmate without hesitation and Egyptian was there.

She said, 'You go in twenty minutes.'

'Twenty minutes?' My forehead was crunched and eyes like saucers.

'Yes, Emily.'

That was the first time she had called me by my name and made me feel a little more human with rights.

I looked at her with watery eyes and said, 'Thank you.'

Within twenty minutes, I would be out and leaving the misery of this institution behind me. I walked slowly back to my cell and told the girls, 'I have 20 minutes before leaving.'

Anna was the first to hug me and get emotional, saying, 'I will miss you, Emily.' I held on to her tight as I knew inside, deep inside, and call it a sixth sense if you like that we would not meet again in this lifetime. I felt that with everyone here, the time I spent with these ladies was time that would not be returned elsewhere or at any time in this future. Did I unconsciously hope this to help me forget? No, it was something I could not answer, as it was just what I sensed.

The others gathered around except for Lebanese and Emirati, and we huddled together, hugging. It was bittersweet and the number of ladies that came to say goodbye was shocking. Some would slip me pieces of paper with their names, telephone numbers and email addresses to contact someone, hell anyone, on the outside world, whether it be family or their embassy for help and understanding. I assured them that I would do what I could for them and try to help in any capacity I could.

I had some of the girls' info and gave my home number to those who asked. I was pumped with running as I gathered all my crap under the bunk bed, and then I went back to the cell door to ask for my bag. I walked towards the holding area where all our bags were kept and found it after pulling out 15 bags. Mine was at the back and bottom and it had been moved since the last time I had opened it.

As I opened it to place objects back in, I noticed that some makeup I had purchased, as well as my wallet, were missing.

The contents of my wallet were kept with my passport in another safe, and I had purchased new makeup at Heathrow Airport and knew things had gone missing, namely, mascara, lipstick, and a few other things. I immediately told the officer who stood at the door.

She was a known bitch and I simply said, 'Things have been taken from my bag?'

'So, you want to stay or go?'

I shook my head at her in disgust. It was the tone she spoke in. So I said it louder to the others and no notice was taken. I questioned what the hell was going on here. The officers are thieves. What a fucked up system.

My bag was out and packed. My passport was ready, but I still didn't have my tickets. I had spoken with South African Mary who was going to collect my tickets as her work's office was near and she would drop them to me in between appointments. The conversation was short and sweet, and after asking Egyptian where I was being taken to, she confirmed, and Mary knew where the location was. She said she would be there sometime in the afternoon to drop the tickets off to me. I wasn't going to panic and just hoped that nothing negative would happen now in the final stage of this whole bloody saga.

I asked to go back into the cell to say a final farewell to the girls. I had one last hug with Anna and shouted to ensure that all could hear me.

'Girls, good luck. I hope you will all be home soon. Keep strong.' I had smiles back and as I walked back through the cell door for the last time, I turned for one last picture. Usually, when I leave home, any home I have lived in, I always thanked every room and said goodbye for housing me and for taking/looking after me, but I had no thanks for the shitty toilet, shower or cells.

Handcuffs were placed on my hands by the bitch who wanted to know if I wanted to go or stay, who smirked at me with her big fat red lips. I sat down waiting with my bag, then the same bitch said,

'Come. We go.'

I could see that she really liked her position, and the swagger she had with the contempt she had for me was visible. But, before leaving I wanted, no, needed to make a statement for all to hear. I turned to Egyptian and simply said, 'I would like to thank you for your assistance and help. You were on leave when I arrived, but since your return, things have been better here. The female officers have been actually working and not missing court dates. Visitors have had access. They have treated all nationalities better, and some of the ladies have not been hit and pushed by the officers. Thank you. I have nothing to say to the rest of you.' I made a facial expression as though I had smelt something that was about to make me vomit before standing tall with my bloody handcuffs again, and walking up those stairs for the last time. This part of the journey had ended, and I was ecstatic to leave, but seriously did it have to be with one of the worst bitches of all?

We left Bur Dubai in a police van. I sat at the back as far away from the driver and bitch. I didn't know exactly where we were going, but I embraced the start of my freedom by letting the sunlight energise me after the initial shock of the rays. The journey wasn't long, but it was enjoyable. And I couldn't bloody believe it when we got to our final destination. I was back at square one, the cell that had been my home initially at the start of this bloody story. A story that was true and that I had lived. I couldn't fucking believe it.

The attitude of the bitch did not improve and got worse. She had obviously been here before as she knew the directions.

She told me, 'Hurry now!' which was followed by, 'You quick!' and, 'Hurry, hurry!'. It was her tone and facial expressions towards me that made me mad.

We passed the same corridors and offices, but I made a conscious decision not to look around me and to switch off, as I couldn't cope with seeing and hearing the new echoes of the men who were detained here.

We arrived at the female cell and paperwork was handed over. There were no pleasantries between the female officers, and what struck me was the clear blue eyes of this new officer who I had previously not met. She was elderly with skin that was darkened with lines that had grown on her face over her long years of life. But those clear blue eyes were mesmerising and so unexpected. She was not an Emirati due to her colouring, but I questioned whether she would be like the others?

She placed the documents down on the table and then the bitch took my handcuffs off and she hurt me as she took them off awkwardly. I shouted 'Ow!' in pain to which she smiled.

Blue eyes calmly said, 'Gently,' to which bitch gave a look of disgust. I, in turn, gave her a look of disgust and said, 'Is there really any need for this kind of behaviour from you? Seriously? Good Muslim ay?' Well, if I did. Her eyes narrowed and if looks could have killed. I was not an angry, violent person but God, when pushed I knew I could have evil thoughts and I wished that one day I would bump into her in the UK. Now that would be fun. Then I had to remind myself of, 'Good Emily.'

She left with the handcuffs and a cow swagger of confidence that was really not warranted. I had pity for whoever her partner or husband was, and simply thought *what a poor bastard*. Then, I was left looking at blue eyes, who simply looked up at me and smiled, a smile of kindness. What a contradiction, or was this a test? She encouraged me to sit opposite her and not in this cell.

Then, our first conversation started, and it would be one of many.

'Are you ok?'

'Yes, I am now, thank you.'

'Officer not very nice. Sorry. We had one from Bur Dubai come work here and she was rude and bad to prisoners that she had warning. No need.'

'I can believe it. In Bur Dubai, the police officers, most of them, are very rude. I saw them hit some Filipinos and treat them the worst. We missed court appointments and to be honest they should be sacked.'

'Sacked?'

'Oh sorry. Not work as police officers and find other jobs as they are not suited. Maybe clean toilets and learn some respect!"

'Ah I see. Where are you from?'

And the conversation continued. I told her my story and she told me hers. Her daughter lived in London, and she visited yearly. After an hour or two, she informed me that I should go in the cell, and I did as she had shown me kindness that I hadn't experienced from any of the other female officers. A male officer came to speak with her, and I recognised the voice before turning to see him. They spoke and then I interrupted, 'Hello.'

He looked at me and then replied. 'Hello. I remember you.'

'Yes, and I remember you. You told me not to worry when I was arrested and that I would go home after I had the good cop and bad cop in your office. You were nice and helped me. Thank you.'

'Yes, and you are here ready to go home?'

'Yes.'

'You, ok?'

'I will be once I am on the aeroplane on my way home.'

He smiled and then he asked if I smoked. My eyes lit up literally and I answered, 'Yes, I do smoke cigarettes, but under my current situation, sadly, I haven't been able to.'

'You want one?'

'Seriously? Yes please? Is that ok? I won't get in trouble?'

'No trouble. Come?'

Blue eyes opened the cell and I followed him in the opposite direction to which I had entered the building, and he opened a door that was more like an escape exit with steps leading down from it. He allowed me to take a cigarette and then lit it for me. *What a gentleman,* I thought, and I gratefully said. 'Thank you.'

I sat down, looked up at the crystal blue sky, and inhaled. The heat penetrated through my skin and even though I was still incarcerated, I felt closer to my freedom and coming home to the safety of the UK, and Wales. More importantly, and to what I knew was true, my family. When I returned to the cell door, blue eyes did not lock it but left it open. Food was delivered, the usual shit of rice and bones. However, I could not face eating it and left it outside the cell door. It was odd as I had been conditioned to prison life and I felt safe in the cell and nervous when outside of it. Blue eyes did close the door when she had to leave her desk, which wasn't often. However, luckily for her she did as I had a visit, a visit from the big boss of the police station, to my residence. He looked down at my food which had remained untouched.

'You not eat? You not hungry?'

I laughed and said a firm, 'No!'

'Why?'

'Have you tried the food here? Please try it.'

He laughed and answered, 'No, thank you.'

Ye right. He knew it was shit.

'Who are you?'

'I am in charge here. Where have you come from?'

'Bur Dubai?'

'Were you treated well?'

'I think you know the reputation Bur Dubai Women's Jail has, and still nothing changes. It is disgusting.'

'Well, you go home soon and forget.'

'Do you honestly think that I can forget? Really? I wish that were true, but when you see the worst that humanity can do from people who personify religion... well, it is laughable when the reality of what has happened is ingrained into your very being. I hope I can live to learn with what has happened and that I will not become prejudiced against a people and country.' He looked at me longingly looking for an answer. He had none. He smiled at me and was gone.

Later, blue eyes and I had a visitor, and it was Mary. She walked in with my plane ticket in her hand and held my hands through the bars and gave me the biggest kiss on my right cheek. Blue eyes asked who she was, and she said that she was a lawyer, but she didn't give the name which I had known her by.

I was puzzled and thought, *what are you doing woman? You have been in and out of Bur Dubai for bloody debt and I was sure, in any country, it was illegal or there would be consequences for lying to authorities when impersonating someone and gaining access in this manner.*

She handed me a ticket and said, 'I don't have long, Emily, as I have to go to an appointment. I have prayed and my church has prayed for you, Emily, and God bless you. You are going home.' Her heart was so pure and innocent, and I know she had been in contact with my mother, as she had informed me sometimes when I could call. Whilst she was speaking, the nice police officer came to see if I wanted another cigarette.

I smiled and nodded and stated, 'It will be nice to stand outside with you, Mary, whilst I smoke. We have never been outside together in the fresh air.'

She smiled and we followed him to the steps outside. He was on his phone speaking to someone when I said to Mary, 'Why did you say you were my lawyer and give a false name?'

'I panicked, Emily, and thought that they would not let me in. So, I wrote a false address and give them a wrong name as I just don't want to get into trouble with the police again.'

I honestly didn't know what to say, so I stated, 'Well, I want to thank you, Mary, for being there for my mother and myself. I will never forget what you have done for me.' We hugged after I had finished my cigarette and kissed each other on the cheek. She departed as I returned to my open cell. As she walked away, I knew that I would miss Mary, and I sincerely hoped that her situation changed for the better for her and her son. She was a kind, gentle, and very religious soul, and I truly loved her for being her.

Blue eyes continued to chat to me and she was extremely interested in Wales as she had heard of it but had never visited. I described it passionately as it is a beautiful, cultured, historic country with passionate people. I couldn't believe it when she asked, 'Can I have your address, so when I come to visit my daughter next, I would like to visit Wales and you?'

I was gobsmacked and, like Mary, out of fear, gave my correct name, as she knew it with a false address. There was no fucking way she was visiting me at my home even though she had been nice to me. At the end of the day, how could I physically warrant one of them visiting me knowing the system they work for and under?

It wasn't long until an officer entered and asked for me. 'We go now?'

I jumped up with such enthusiasm that I nearly tripped over my own feet. I looked at blue eyes and knew she would possibly know that I had lied to her one day, but I felt the need to thank her for her humanity. 'Thank you so much for being so kind to me. It is a tragic shame that not all female police officers are more like you. But then again, the majority of them are Emirati, aren't they? Thank you.' The male officer had handcuffs for me to wear, and I automatically placed my hands out for him to constrain me. I hoped that I had made my point to her, and it is a funny fact that in 2009, the UAE nationals, Emirian, made up less than a fifth of the population. Around 80% of the population were expatriates, with the Emirian only accounting for 19%. Expatriates made up most of the population and were drawn from South Asia 50%, Westerners and East Asians 8%, with other Arab and Iranian nationals accounting for 23%. I hoped that in the future more expatriates would be employed in the Dubai police force to help it develop and grow to the best that it could be because by employing the local Emirati females it was failing miserably, nationally, and internationally. I shook her hand and she smiled at me. Why she was still working I did not know, as her age must have been near retirement.

It was strange that those who were not pure Emirati were nice, compassionate, and accommodating. But then, on the flip side, would she have treated me differently if I hadn't been found innocent? I would never have that answer, nor did I really care at this point.

I followed the officer to a car and a driver drove us a short distance to a holding area, near the airport, where a small bus awaited outside. The planes were in the distance, and I felt so close to my freedom. Once we parked up and got out of the car with my bag, I could see as we approached the building that there were people congregated in a room through the glass door. Standing inside were mostly men with different sized bags in front of them, surrounded by a few male officers. We stood in a line in an industrial area, an open holding cell, in some part of the airport that whilst being part of a police station felt more like we should have been putting overalls on to start our daily job before sitting down on old battered wooden chairs.

We were a mixed bag of nationalities and ages with different cultural fashion senses. It was hard to interpret what their characters or stories were from looking at this fine bunch of misfits. I imagined that they had a diverse array of careers from gardeners to cleaners and possibly middle management/office workers. They called out our names to confirm that we were present and asked to see our passports and plane tickets. Then, we were told to take our bags 'There!' When I turned to look, I saw an x-ray machine to the right, which I had missed in my nosiness to look at the other inmates with me. They went through, thankfully for all of us with no issue. I was so grateful as I couldn't have coped with a situation arising and then a delay or even missing my flight due to having to give a witness statement or something. We were handed our bags back and then they were taken away with our passports and plane tickets. I assumed we would get them back later.

Even though our freedom was so near, the handcuffs which held our aching wrists together were a harsh reminder that we were still prisoners in this country, even when innocent. The American who sat near me looked American, if you know what I mean, with the baseball cap, baggy sports t-shirt and pants, and with the accent that confirmed his presence that kind of gave it away. I analysed him, looking him up and down, questioning, *what on earth could you have done to end up here like me?* I would never know the answer to this question, as this was not the time or place to start friendly conversations. Further, the men and women who found themselves in the same situation as I found myself in now, looked as though their energy and hope had been sucked out. I assumed that they were former shells of themselves with little emotion, just as I was.

To the right of the American was a Filipino gentleman, who had a weathered face, his shoulders slouched, and his eyes seemed vacant and emotionless. I dreaded to think what he had endured due to his nationality and guessed his treatment and that of the American had been worlds apart. If it was indeed like what I had witnessed and experienced. Perhaps, he was a female version of someone I had encountered, a hungry worker who had been caught eating out of his employer's bin for food, or a man whose visa had expired. Whatever his reasons, I will not forget, ever, the lost hope I saw in that man's eyes. I sincerely hoped that he would return home to his loved ones, be at peace and have safety.

A younger East European lady dressed in fashionable clothes, clothes that I would not wear, reminded me of a young girl I had met in my incarceration who worked in the sex industry. An industry that is apparent throughout the wealthier Middle East countries as there is a need on behalf of these sex-starved and depraved Arab men. But it is these women that are persecuted and reprimanded, whilst their clients, those that use them, get away with it literally, both native and ex-pats. Her facial expression was hard, and I summarised that her life, like many others in this industry, must have been desperate. For her to return home with the stigma of not being able to return to this country to where she had lived, worked, and supported her family back home could possibly be devastating. I feared for her and the others who were in a similar situation, as legally, they were the bottom of the barrel in most societies. I hoped her life would work out and that she would find health and happiness in whatever career she continued to do, new or old.

One by one, our names were called. We were instructed to leave the room we had sat in patiently. The door was fixed ajar and as I walked out into the hot autumn day the sunlight blinded me and hurt my eyes. It took me seconds to release my eyes from their squint and to be able to focus, as the sun had moved position from earlier.

We were led onto a bus, a 30-seater medium-sized bus, with our bags. We were all seated separately by two or three seats. A Pakistani man sat in the driver's seat and smiled at each of us as we stepped onto his bus and made our way to our seats. He was the second jovial person I had met since my ordeal had begun, and whilst it was refreshing it was to no avail because each one of us had experienced horrendous, life-defining changes to our personalities, emotions, and mental health. We were lost to him and caged in those experiences even if we hadn't realised it yet.

As we commenced our journey to who knows where in the airport the driver asked, 'Are you all ok?'

It was the first time I had been asked sincerely by a convict bus driver. He was paid to drive us, but the passengers on the bus had logged out and sat with their heads lowered.

I lifted my head and responded even though the police were ever-present observing us on this bus. I ensured my voice would be heard over the rumblings of the engine and with a serious voice of contempt I stated, 'I am just happy to be leaving this God-forsaken country, to get home to normality and a justice system that is fair and just. It is bloody disgusting what is going on here. Seriously!'

He retorted, 'I have been here 15 years and it has changed. Not good anymore. Bad. Very bad. Crazy.'

'Bad? Very bad? You have no idea. People are being locked up for such stupid, stupid reasons. And they are guilty until proven innocent. How can someone defend themselves if they have no money, do not speak the language, and have no help whatsoever? And they keep Emiratis in jobs they are not qualified or fit to do. It's a bloody disgrace and shambles.' I then stopped at the fear that I could be re-arrested as sometimes inmates are, in fact, officers undercover and knowing my luck, I could end up fucked again. I sighed. It was time to shut up as I was nearly free, nearly. I remembered Daddy's wise words, 'Think before you speak.' So, I bowed my head and shrugged my shoulders to mimic my compatriots. The driver had not finished and responded, and as I heard his voice, I looked up to his mirror to see his face.

'Go home. Get out of here and forget what you have seen.'

I gave a wrinkled smile but how could I? How bloody could I?

The journey didn't take long to get to our destination, but it did make me feel like a dirty convict held in caged metal bars. When we came to a standstill and our designated area of arrival, the door opened and a plain-clothed obese man, what I believe to be a policeman, approached the bus and simply stated, 'Out!'

One by one, we departed, and the atmosphere changed again. I turned to the driver and said, 'Thank you.' Whilst we made eye contact, nothing else was said, not even a flicker of a smile, and I left for the next process/stage of my deportation. We were lined up and not gracefully like troops on parade. We were hunched and stood in all directions trying to cope with the situation we all found ourselves. One by one, we followed our instructions of holding our arms in front of us, and individually our handcuffs were removed. The relief was immense, and I twisted and turned them. Freedom was nearer yet again.

We were led into a large metallic door that opened, opened into the airport and bloody duty-free. I couldn't believe it! We had obviously missed check-in and our bags awaited us, in a line, on the right side of the wall, having been processed. We individually collected them from the row they were organised in. With that, we were handed our boarding cards and passports and told to go. One by one, we left and entered a doorway where a wealth of sound; music, speech and space awaited us. The smell of different perfumes and foods were abundant, and I could taste them. It was wonderful.

We all went our separate ways, and I stood in the centre of where I could only describe as being one of the many duty-free shopping and eatery areas. I could feel myself start to quiver, then shake with my eyes watering. If I could have curled up in a corner and cried, I would have, but I couldn't. I was in shock and didn't know what direction to go.

I watched around me: families, children, couples smiling and happy, businessmen on their phones and smartly dressed. Everything gleamed and looked so clean with brightness. I once had been one of those smartly dressed individuals, enjoying duty-free with the impending flight for work or a well-deserved pleasurable holiday. But now, I didn't know what to do or where to go. I was lost with not being told what to do.

I started to walk, endlessly taking everything in - the smells, sights, and sounds. The once confident Emily was not the same. She had been lost on this journey, and I don't remember the exact breaking point, as there seemed to be so many.

I had my flight ticket and passport in my right hand still clenched and saw the screen with the flight details. I had just over two hours of more waiting. I saw the Irish Bar in the distance, and I slowly made my way to it with each step that my legs instinctively walked.

I sat at the bar on a stool and an Irish man asked, 'Can I help you?'

I looked and answered, 'A Foster's lager shandy please.' I watched the process from when he left me to the end result. My card payment went through successfully. I opened my right arm and clenched the long-chilled glass. I smelt it and a flash of emotions, tastes and memories overflowed. My breath was shallow and deep. I looked around me and then motioned to take my first long- awaited sip. It tasted so nice, as the liquid made its way down my throat from its first touch on my tongue and inside my mouth. But I was uneasy and questioned all around me. It was such a big space, and I was scared. Was I being watched? Could I be arrested for having a pint? Was I safe here? Were these feelings logical after being institutionalised within a legal system?

Then, there were those that I left behind, those innocent and guilty souls, who had faces, names and real-life stories who were not a government statistic on a piece of paper. They were a daughter, mother, aunt, granddaughter, grandmother, friend, colleague, or acquaintance of someone. What about them? I had shared my daily life with those ladies, and they were still incarcerated in such bloody awful conditions with those bitches from Bur Dubai in charge of them.

I held my head in my left arm, feeling the build-up of tears fill my eyes until they poured relentlessly down my cheeks. I wiped them away and placed my focus on the menu. I hadn't eaten a proper meal that tickled my taste buds in so long, a meal that had made me feel complete and fulfilled from when I left that apartment. I cannot put it into words eloquently, but I felt as though I was peering out distantly, as though part of me had left and was continuing on autopilot.

I quickly tried to compose myself and got my mobile phone out of my bag. I was wired and I needed to calm down before even contemplating phoning home. I couldn't afford to lose it emotionally now that I was here. Could you imagine if I had been arrested at the airport for breaking down emotionally after an Emirati had reported me for something so innocent? My God! Once I had composed myself, and I had relaxed slightly after exercising my neck and shoulders with deep breathing, I turned it on and waited for it to load. Once ready, I input the numbers and waited for it to be answered. A voice answered, one that I loved unconditionally and had missed daily beyond words. My heart missed beats as my eyes watered.

'Emily, is that you?'

I hesitated quietly before answering, 'Yes, Mammy. It is me. I am finally out and in the airport. I am coming home.' Her cries of joy were audible as were my cries of happiness.

I got to speak with Sah too and she just kept repeating, 'Mammy's comin home.'

I was wished a safe journey home and when asked what time I would be home, I couldn't answer a definite time, as I would have to book a National Express from Heathrow to Swansea and then catch a bus from Swansea to home. 'I know I am coming home, but I don't know what time I will arrive, Mammy. I will come back as soon as I can, I promise.'

'Is there anything I can buy that you want to eat when you come home?'

I laughed and said, 'No, Mammy. I am sure what you have in the fridge and freezer will be fine. We can go shopping when I am home.'

Everything seemed so surreal around me, and life had continued uninterrupted for the majority of people who surrounded me in this airport, I theorised, whilst I had been locked up. I ordered a Great British Fry Up and waited eagerly to have it.

Upon its arrival, I could smell the sizzling sausages, bacon, baked beans, and mushrooms. My first mouthful consisted of a slice of bacon, sausage, baked beans and egg with some salt and a slight basting of brown sauce I had squirted on my white plate. The burst of flavours was enormous, and my juices flowed to liquidise my food as it went down my gullet. I couldn't finish the plate as it was just too much for my now shrunken stomach. To say I was full was an understatement, and with the last drops of my cool shandy I felt very bloated and gassy.

I had promised Sah a present, so I paid my bill, thanked the server, and took a deep breath before setting off in the direction of the duty-free shops. I walked slowly, concentrating on the displays around me. There was so much to take in with shoppers moving swiftly around me. Music and conversation surrounded everything and the smell of the perfume fragranced different areas. I found the toy area and scanned the different toys. It had to be pretty special, as she had suffered in her own way of missing her mammy. Then I saw it, and my initial reaction was 'Bloody hell!' It was a pink electric guitar that had buttons to play music and keys that created sound or noise. I knew she would love it, and she would have hours of playing it whilst jumping around dancing. It wasn't too bad in price and its size meant I could carry it under my arm. Whilst standing by the till, I then saw a sweet container full of chocolates. It was really cool, as when you lifted the big dude's arm up a funnel let some sweets out to eat. I knew she would love playing with this and eating the chocolates. She also knew that she was the only one that liked this brand of chocolate, so there would be even more for her tummy.

I purchased them with a smile, knowing that they would bring the biggest soppy smiles and kisses from my favourite person in my world as a thank you. I wanted to arrive early at my departure gate, as there was no way I was missing this plane. I was early. However, there was a scattering of people sitting around. I sat facing the runway so I could see planes landing and taking off. I looked out and got lost in the vastness of blue outside, then it hit me, this would be the last time I would ever be here in this life. I was not coming back. I was being deported and even though I had been found innocent, Dubai would not allow me back in again. I would be re-arrested and re-deported again. And I was sad. I had had so many fun times here over the years, but they were of times past in an old country that I once knew. The new Dubai was somewhere I did not want to be even as a visitor, as my eyes had been opened, and they would and could not close to what I had seen and witnessed. I watched planes land and I wondered how many innocent individuals on those planes knew the true Dubai? Were they hypnotised like I had been into seeing the beauty of wealth that had built Dubai, the richness of its weather, coast, and services? I know my eyes had been opened to the truth.

Time flew by and soon the flight was called. I nervously lined up in the queue with my passport and ticket ready. I was not used to having so many people around me, and whilst I had longed to be in this position for weeks and months, daily, I was left feeling scared in this big place. The South Korean air stewardess had once visited Bur Dubai on a three-day visit. She had been arrested for being drunk on a layover, but luckily her company helped her, and she got out quite quickly. She had been lovely, and I asked her if the airline knew who on the plane had been deported from a country. She stated they were aware of each person who had been deported but not to the circumstances. I gather that had something to do with human rights, I imagined. She informed me that it was due to the security of the plane, but she had stated that she would no longer question people's deportation, as after being arrested herself and hearing the stories of other offences, she had concluded that it was also 'Crazy!'

So, as I stood in line, I knew that they knew that I was being deported. This was just so embarrassing and degrading. I was processed through and as I waited to board, I realised that this would be the last time ever in my life that I would be here, and that I was never to return. It was another sad aspect. My last step on Dubai soil was consciously remembered and felt as I made my way onto the plane. I showed my ticket and was pointed in the direction of the left from the beautiful-looking and fresh-faced air hostesses. I was lucky as I was mid-way up the plane next to an exit, which gave me a little extra legroom and I sat in the window seat with two seats beside me. I placed my items in the overhead carriage and sat down. A man sat two seats away from me on the aisle seat. I looked up and smiled before trying to buckle my seat belt on correctly. I fiddled around and couldn't work the bloody thing out. Now, I knew it was a simple thing to attach, but could I do it? Hell no! I started to panic, and I could feel perspiration on my forehead and my facial heat rise in temperature. Then, the man leant over from his aisle seat, over the middle seat and helped me buckle it up.

I looked up at him and quietly said, 'Thank you.'

I rested my head back and looked out of the window. I just wanted this plane full and to take off immediately, but I would have to wait a little more as everyone settled in their seats. I had plenty of time to sit and let my mind wander whilst the air stewards did their thing of ensuring bags were stored and that people were sitting. The doors had been locked and no one was going to sit in the middle chair. However, I couldn't get the fact of them knowing that I was being deported out of my mind, and the Korean air hostess saying about security. Then my paranoia started whirlwinding, and was this guy sitting to my right, next to the aisle, security and sitting by me because I was a security risk on this airplane? All I could say was, *fuck me! Is that why he helped buckle me in when he saw that I was getting stressed?* Oh God. Then I questioned, and this was the important point, could I get an alcoholic drink on this aeroplane? Was I even allowed? My God! I looked at him as closely as I could without raising suspicion by reading the onboard magazine. I couldn't see a gun or anything in his pockets which resembled a gun, but it could have been under his jacket like they have on TV. What I could see from his colouring is that he was a Muslim of Arab descent, but not Emirati. He was in plain clothes, and I thought it could be plausible because I knew the Americans had such on the domestic and international flights, or so I thought. So, I made a conscious decision to get my head down and keep myself to myself.

The information started on the tannoy and the hostesses positioned themselves ready for their safety instructions/emergency exits presentation. I always watched as I thought it rather rude and dangerous not to. The plane started to move gently and then with more pace. My breathing quickened and I held on to my chair as I peered out of the window. It was getting late and whilst the sun was still warm, the night sky was preparing to make an entrance. The lift of the plane was gentle after the increase of speed, and my visit and time in Dubai were over. I knew that this aspect of the flight, the take-off, was the most dangerous as when flying out of Tel Aviv once, I was lucky enough or unlucky to be seated by someone who worked within the industry. When he informed me, I really shat myself, and it made me paranoid on that flight, especially upon take-off.

I was unsure when we would be leaving Dubai aerospace and hoped it would be soon after a successful take-off. Headphones were handed out, and I placed them straight on my ears and flicked through the radio channels. The seatbelt lights went off, and movement ensued, whilst the hostesses delivered drinks. My turn came and I looked up anxiously. My heart beat quickly, and she asked me what I would like to drink. I replied, 'Would it be possible to have a white wine please? Is it allowed?'

'Yes, certainly.' She poured out the contents of the small bottle, and security did nothing. I patiently waited to taste it before firstly thinking that it tasted of vinegar, and secondly, finding the Black Eyed Peas and Meet Me Halfway. Oh, how it made me feel now listening to it on my return journey. With the beat playing I visualised Mammy and Sah. I wanted them, no, I needed them so much, now.

The journey back home was peaceful, dark, and quiet. After eating the airline food that was edible, and 100 times better than any of the shit that was served in Bur Dubai, the atmosphere changed to people switching off, reading, watching a movie, or sleeping. A calm flooded me as I sat here amongst these strangers in comfort with air conditioning, TVs, and alcoholic drinks when I was reminded of the ladies from Bur Dubai. They too would be relaxing in their cells. It was such a contrast of contradictions, and whilst I did think of them in their specific seating/lying areas I was thankful to be going home. I pulled off my headphones, positioned the blue blanket over me and closed my eyes. It was time to rest my eyes because in a few hours, and tomorrow, I would be home.

Walking through and leaving customs in the UK was quick and easy. Thankfully, I had no issues and no stares from the customs officers throughout the process of leaving the aeroplane to customs as I wasn't sure if they too would take me in for questioning as to why I had been deported. And my journey to the National Express Office was a quick walk to ensure I could get on the next bus home. To say that the whole process was stressful was an understatement. I honestly didn't feel comfortable with so many people moving and speaking. It was just too much noise, and it literally made my head pulsate. I made the payment, and I had a ticket for the next bus back to Swansea. I then proceeded to find a seat outside, purchasing a pack of fags to smoke whilst I waited patiently with a fizzy drink.

I then got my UK phone out to call Mammy and let her know I was back home in the bloody great United Kingdom. It was then and there that I had the thunderbolt that I was home in the UK. I was here, and I had made it home after weeks/months of living a nightmare.

I started to break down and my breathing became rapid and emotional. I physically felt sick as my stomach turned. The concentration that I had used since landing and departing the plane with the anxiety I felt inside and all around me had clouded me, and it was only when I sat down and relaxed that I could access my personal feelings and feel my emotions. I tried to compose myself as quickly as possible as I didn't want people around me thinking I was an emotional weirdo or something.

I got up, moved to the smoking area, and lit one up. With each inhale I felt the negativity and emotion leave with my exhale and I relaxed. The cigarette was sucked dry with a couple of puffs. I was re-composed. Even though people stood and sat around me I didn't see them. Yes, I knew they were there, but they were shadows in the background. I was in my own little world of confusion and misunderstanding with the need to phone home.

And, after a little time I was ready, and I made the phone call.

'Hi, Mammy. I am home.'

'Oh, Em. Finally! You, ok?'

With a huge sigh I replied, 'Yes, I am. I am so bloody happy to be here, back on British soil, even if the weather is miserable and shitty. Jesus!'

'Oh, Em. Thank God it is over, and you will be home soon.'

'Is Sah there?'

'Yes. Hold on.'

I heard her breathing and clumsy hold on the phone when I yelled, 'Sah. Sah! Mammy's coming home, and I will see you soon.'

She replied with a long, 'Mammy,' and with a 'When?'

We spoke and laughed at all the same things of how I was going to tickle and kiss her so much that she would wee herself and get in trouble with Mam to which she replied, 'No!'

I explained to her that I would be catching the next National Express back to Swansea, as we usually did, but that I would be catching the bus from Swansea to home. She wanted to know whether she had any presents and I jokingly played with her on the phone, teasing that I was her present. I could picture her and her smiles as she spoke with the facial expressions she made with certain words and feelings. My heart lifted after that conversation, and it carried me home to Swansea.

The traffic on the roads from Heathrow was relatively busy and my eyes were drawn to the green and lush countryside we passed. The cows and sheep that grazed lazily, trees that moved in the wind, cars that veered off going to who knows where and the housing estates and industrial areas that were always present near the big towns and cities.

Life was all around me, and like a good bubble bath, I soaked it all in. What a contrast this was to the Middle East.

The journey didn't seem long, but I was tired from the overthinking and concentration of taking everything in. It was beautiful and a stark contrast to the isolation and boredom of prison life. We made the journey in good time, and I had only a few minutes to wait for my connection home. I listened to the chatter of two elderly friends who were chatting about the prices going up in the shops and the weather - such innocent and normal chatter - whilst a mother tended to her child's chocolate face with a wet wipe.

I paid the driver and made my way to the back of the bus before placing my bags on the seat next to me. I loved the feel of the bus as it revved up, its vibrations and the smell of the fuel. It was something as a child I had enjoyed and it brought back many memories, happy memories.

The route hadn't changed in my lifetime, and it was a very predictable journey home with all the major stops. Once we left Pontardulais, and made our way up to Llanedi, the countryside to my right took my breath away. As we came down the hill into Tycroes and down to Penybanc, I knew I was nearly home. We passed the pubs of the town and then came to the main bus stop. It had not changed one iota except possibly for the increase of rubbish and graffiti on the adorning walls that I noticed.

I thanked the bus driver then proceeded to get off the bus to get my connecting bus and then I continued to walk home. I had walked these steps so many times, and as I pulled my bag and carried the gifts, it was the first time I noticed that I walked home with sheer joy and excitement. I could not wait as each step brought me closer to the home I had always known and loved, with the people that were the beat of my ever-pounding heart.

I didn't pass anyone that I knew walking or driving as I walked, which was a bonus. I wasn't ready and didn't know how I would react. I just wanted to open our gate, walk through the open door and then to sit myself firmly in the safety of my kitchen with a nice cup of tea. I wanted to sit opposite my mother, see her in front of my eyes while I held my baby and felt her breath against my cheek. My heartbeat rose as I neared the door, and as I entered there was Mammy putting the kettle on with beautiful, honest eyes, that showed me just how much she had missed me with a smile of love. I walked in, dumped everything on the floor and walked up to her kissing her on the cheek.

She held onto my arms and quietly told me, 'It is good to have you back here, safe and sound, Emily.' She shook me gently as if to confirm her meaning. Then I looked around, puzzled, that I could not hear Sah, or any of the programmes she enjoyed watching in the living room. 'Where is she?'

'Her father phoned and has picked her up. They won't be long now, see. She has missed you. It has broken my heart, Emily.' She became emotional whilst she poured the boiling water into the mugs.

I looked on knowing how much I had missed her, and my eyes filled. She gave me the cuppa, which was in a cup I had used many times, and there I sat in the wooden armchair sipping one of the nicest cups of tea I could ever remember having. I was offered food, anything I wanted, but there was only one thing I wanted and waited for. I didn't really want to talk about what had happened, but I needed to say how sorry I was. Yes, I needed to do this. We had many conversations, and in one of them when I mentioned trying to phone my school in Qatar, Mammy stated, 'I didn't want to tell you, Emily, but one of your colleagues out there called me on the phone and said you had lost your job. They said an announcement had been made in a morning meeting. They were shocked that I didn't know.'

'I tried to call them, Mammy.'

'Emily, I tried to call them and left messages. They never replied. I am sorry.'

It was only when I opened my emails that I read the email I was sent from my place of work and home. It was sent on the 16/09/2010 from the headmaster whom I had served loyally.

Dear Emily,
Having not received any news whatsoever regarding your continued absence from school, I regret to inform you that your contract has now been terminated. If you do return, please do not enter the school as you will not be permitted to stay.
Regards,
Headmaster

There were no words to describe how I felt. Even if I could have returned there, I couldn't. I had lost my possessions - all my possessions, my daughter's possessions from birth and all our photographs from Sah's birth, a career that I loved with students who were a pleasure to teach, and our home.

My mother kept apologising with, 'I'm sorry, Em.' But she didn't have to be sorry. She had left messages asking the school to contact her regarding me. I had instructed Mammy not to leave a message with my sordid story, as I theorised at least by speaking, no misunderstanding and exaggerating could occur prior to any discussions. I had observed enough of school politics whilst working there to understand the bitchy and two-faced personification of their professionalism. It was for a little self-preservation, I suppose, but they never called her back. And so, that was the end of my job as a teacher in Qatar. I was now also blacklisted from Qatar for breaking my Employment Contract. So, I was now excluded from two countries on this planet where I had lived and worked in places I had once called home, never to return. I would never have believed it if someone had told me when I was younger that this could have ever happened. But it had, and there was no getting away from this fact.

Another conversation had ended, catching up on how my uncle and auntie were, and it affected me deeply. I became angry inside when Mammy had told me she had had to tell them what had happened and what was continuing to happen, as when Rob went back to Africa, she had no one to talk to. One morning, well, every morning they spoke to each other, and my aunty had told my uncle to go and see Mammy as she knew something was wrong as she heard it in her voice, and it was then that my mother had told my uncle. I felt ashamed, embarrassed, stupid… and all these emotions made me anxious beyond belief, as I felt as though I was being taken back there to that place that nearly broke me. I felt panic with the more people knowing that it would make it more real to me here, in the safety of my home, as I did not want to think about it as I just couldn't. I just felt sheer panic, scared with no control. I needed this under control, and I had lost a part of that, but I understood and was sympathetic to my mother's needs with another, 'Sorry!'

I continued to sip my tea and then the loud slam of a car door could be heard. It was a noise I had become accustomed to when it did happen, as it was outside the house I had been brought up in, all my life, and it meant that it was probably Sah coming back from spending time with her father.

The front door opened and closed, and then the gentle steps she took became heavier into a jumping run as soon as she saw me in the living room. The surprise on her face, even though she knew I was coming home, was immense as it spread from cheek to cheek and she shouted, 'Mammy,' as she ran to my arms. I held her and kissed her forehead, cheeks and give her a big smacker on her beautiful rosy lips. I pulled her up, held her on my lap where she snuggled in, and I tickled her until she squirmed into my neck, laughing so much that it was intoxicating. Then, she placed her hands on my cheeks and said, 'Better now, Mammy?'

I smiled at her and held my forehead to hers and said, 'Yes, Mammy is better now because I am home with you. I missed you! I don't think you will ever know just how much.' I lifted my head and then pulled her close before she replied with one word, 'Presents?'

'Oh, that didn't take long, did it?' I lifted her up and flew her to the bags. As she stood there quietly, I told her, 'Close your eyes,' and she did so. I then got the guitar out of the bag and told her to place her hands out and with some help she did. Then, I placed it in her hands and told her to open her eyes.

When she opened them, she jumped up and down repeating, 'Guitar! Guitar! Guitar!'

We pulled it from the cardboard box and then she went to sit in the living room having mastered the on/off button. The music, or more apt noise, was played and initially, it was a nice kind of different, but after a while, well, it ached the eardrums. Luckily, I had the chocolates to take her attention and once she worked out that she had to lift an arm to release the chocs, well, let us say there were frequent giggles. It was as though I had never been away and that evening, we sat down for a family meal and enjoyed it together. It had been a long road and journey to get back and that night, when the house was asleep, I had my first glass of Lambrini. Mammy had thought that I may need a drink, and she was right in a way.

I was outside having a cigarette looking up at the sky, the stars that twinkled in between the clouds and the fresh cold air made the hairs on my arms leap up as though someone was walking on my grave. I could see the girls in Bur Dubai sleeping in the cells in their places as I turned to go back into the kitchen and drank some more Lambrini. I flicked the cigarette in the ashtray before entering the house and turning to close the door. As the keys locked the door, I smiled. I was home. I went to bed, and whilst my sleep was interrupted by intervals of confusion and checking my surroundings, I did manage to close my eyes. But I was still scared, and I didn't know what or how to cope with everything. Sah was at my side when I woke, and I had my arm touching her firmly to make sure that she was real and that this was not a nasty game of the imagination played by the Bur Dubai Police. But no, I was here, the place I should have always been. Home.

Part 5

I was bloody right - now I'm fucked up = mentally!!

I can honestly say that my head was a turbulent storm, whose epicentre was a mess, and I had changed both physically and mentally. I was a shell of my former self; I would not leave the house unless I absolutely had to and I drank. Boy, did I drink Lambrini and at £5.00 for two one point five litres, it was a bargain, and it allowed me to go to sleep, numb.

Whilst my little girl and mother remained the same and life continued as my daughter started her new school in Wales, I was a different case. Within a few days of being home, I found the phone number for the Philippines Embassy in London. I had told the girls back in Bur Dubai that I would help them when I got home, so I phoned after days of contemplating and working up the confidence to be able to do so, and I rang. I finally got through after being transferred to someone and when I explained who I was, where I had come from with the names of Filipino women who were being held there, I was told I had to put it in writing. I explained how difficult it had been for me to contemplate phoning and having the confidence to do so, but she reiterated their policy and would only accept a written document. I was emotional on the phone and pleaded to no avail. I came from that phone call crying, and when questioned by my mother, I told her that I didn't think I could write it down, that I simply couldn't do it before retreating to my bedroom and breaking down yet again.

During the day, well, every day, I would go out for numerous walks over to the river with my beautiful dogs, spend hours by the river watching and listening to the river flow continuously with a soft sound which was accompanied by the fresh open fields that surrounded me. The wind would blow sometimes, and rain would pour, but it didn't matter. As I stood there, I felt my freedom physically. I always looked up to the sky and heavens and thanked God. I also thanked Daddy, as in my darkest moments, and there were many, I felt him and his love surround me; giving me the strength to continue this journey in Bur Dubai. I felt free in this place, and it became my haven for hours before I then returned to the safety of my home and family. But I could not forget the souls I left behind, and whilst I lived in my present here, I could be transported back there at any moment. Sleeping was the same. I would sometimes wake up not knowing where I was and would have to touch my surroundings and put the light on immediately to ensure where I was. The sweat would wet me literally, and it also affected my breathing as my heart rate increased with the palpitations.

There was no way I could work, let alone stand up and teach, in my ability, even my spoken language as I was not as eloquent, and in immediate moments I had to escape and walk away from anything that I found challenging, upsetting, or made me concentrate. I just didn't have the confidence to leave my surroundings, mentally or physically, and I jumped at the slightest sound. I could manage taking Sah to and from school, but that was it.

I had cut ties with the individuals I had shared friendships with after my father's death. I learned the hard way that those who you think are the closest to you are not always. They were not there for me when I had needed them the most, and they were not there for my mother when I returned to the Middle East. My father's death showed me my truth, and it was a sad truth that hurt. The realisation that I was alone and that I could never rely on them made me retaliate with the conscious decision to unfriend them. It was for self-protection as I couldn't hurt anymore. To this day I sincerely wish them health and happiness. Am I sorry? Yes, but whilst one can be sorry, one can also accept that it was meant to happen when it did, because it happened. It was my fate as if it hadn't happened when it did, I know I would not have been able to control my story of what happened in Dubai and where it would have spread to. They would not have helped my healing process and were not meant to be a part of and continue with me on my path and journey through life. I know the true meaning and definition of what friendship is now and am grateful for it.

One of the informative documents given to me by the British Embassy was of Prisoners Abroad. I phoned them for advice sometime after coming home, and they informed me that I needed to claim benefits. They instructed me that they would write a letter of support and that I was to hand this over to the Benefits Department. The lady suggested it would make things easier for me, and so a letter arrived a few days later after our discussion.

This letter assisted me to claim benefits with ease and do you know, I even had a phone call from a Jobcentre Plus worker stating that they had received the letter from Prisoners Abroad, that my paperwork was being processed and to question if I needed a loan to help me. I did not have the mental capacity to understand documents and letters. I was so foggy and forgetful. I was nervous continually as I raced from existing in two worlds, two divergent worlds that kept colliding in one body. I know I thanked the Resettlement Worker on the phone call and the Jobcentre Plus worker, but words are simple. They will never know how they made a difficult case easier for someone, and I will forever be grateful to them.

I obviously went to see my family doctor at the local surgery. I informed him of what had happened to me, my experience, symptoms, and emotions. He immediately stated that he thought I was suffering from post-traumatic stress disorder (PTSD). I had heard of this whilst servicemen were being discussed on the news previously, but I had no formal understanding. I stated that I did not want it written down on my medical notes, as I did not want my future career to be affected by having such a condition. I asked for help, and he instructed me that he knew of a good counsellor within the local area, and that he would contact her with my details. He also offered me antidepressants which was something I had never had previously. He told me that they would take about three weeks to take effect. So, I waited for the antidepressants to work and for contact from the counsellor until a letter finally arrived.

It was hand posted and arrived on the 5th of November 2010. It read as follows:

Dear Emily,
I have been asked to get in touch with you to offer you counselling. I have been unable to get through on your landline so please call me on (a local number) or (mobile number) so we can arrange to meet.
Name MBACP
Counsellor

Contact and appointment were made. Obviously, I was nervous as I knew I would have to address my ordeal in Dubai. I questioned her credentials, which if I am honest were questionable from lots of different certificates and courses, but not a definite degree. But I needed hope and so we moved forward together. I spoke, she listened, and after four sessions her advice was, 'Whenever you think of your experience you need to stop it and think of something else.' I affirmed that I had always believed that when such things occurred it was good to address it and to not ignore. She specified, reiterating to 'think of something else.'

So, for the foreseeable future, this is what I did. My mother and brother both stated that they thought this was the wrong advice too, but my doctor had recommended her, and she was qualified, right? I mean she had her qualification, certificates, and photo of her on a Welsh show.

With time, patience and being kind to myself, I turned my life around. It took me months to get in contact with a Supply Teaching Agency I had previously worked for, and they signed me up immediately. I started to work in an old secondary school in Swansea that I had previously worked at. The school had a high proportion of Arabic Muslim children, and I was thankful that I had no reaction to them whatsoever. However, watching Muslims on television was another story, and as soon as I heard the accent and a view of women especially, well, my breathing changed becoming more deeper and I had a need to run. I enjoyed teaching there, and eventually, they employed me. At the same time, I worked two evenings a week at a college lecturing students in another county. I was offered more lecturing hours there, so I left the school to work at the college. I felt as though I was slowly growing with confidence and in control again of my life, and more importantly, building a secure future for Sah and I.

We remained living with my mother and in time I also got involved with local politics. Now, that is another bloody epic story and laughable. Put it like this, growing up, my mother always said she never wanted to read my name, or that of my brother's, in the local paper, and sadly my name did appear in that paper sometimes due to my honest contributions at meetings.

I even started a relationship with someone my brother knew and who strongly stated, 'He is a good one.' Well, I think you know what my luck is like by now, and he was not a good one. He was another one who used and abused my goodwill. We were together for nearly two years, and I supported him emotionally and economically whilst we were together, but the relationship had been more one-sided from the beginning, and sadly, I didn't know this.

That was many years ago now, and I have not met anyone, kissed anyone, nor had any sexual interaction since that relationship ended. The sad thing is that through all of the relationship, I had a love for him and his family, and so had Sah.

However, what I didn't realise during this time, was that by taking the counsellor's advice, I was a ticking time bomb. I found by keeping busy, and I mean I was a workaholic as I worked full-time and I volunteered politically on a weekly basis in meetings where I observed adults behaving like children. I sat amongst some proper ignorant and rude people, who lacked the common sense to work together and put political parties' ideologies away when bettering the area, we lived in.

I then had my daughter, mother, my demanding boyfriend and his child, and I was pushing myself to extremes not to have to think about Bur Dubai. It had been achievable, but what I didn't realize was that any stress would be a trigger point, and when my relationship with User became stressful, my eating habits changed, and I just couldn't cope with the stress and any negativity. I mean, I ate, but the upset in my stomach wanted to make me heave and often the contents re-emerged. The constant arguing made me want to turn to Lambrini more and things were said in hurt. It came to an end, thankfully, after months of mental abuse and pure frustration. The only positive was my loss of weight, but the negative developed quickly. My head would start to pulsate, hurt and it got to a stage where I wanted to smash my head against the wall. I would hyperventilate and be short and angry, not at work, but always at home. They say that you hurt the ones you love the most, and sadly my mother was the one to have my attitude. I was out of character and had become so straight and conservative with my viewpoints that I had become offensive. Luckily, I had resigned from my volunteering months previously, as the constant meetings and votes made no changes to the empowerment, improvement and development of my much-loved town and home.

I made the conscious decision to seek help and searched and contacted online post-traumatic stress disorder doctors in Wales, who would work privately with me. I wrote emails and letters outlining my traumatic experience, symptoms, need for help and finally, after weeks of waiting and many meltdowns, hiding away, freaking out and crying, oh, so much crying, I had a letter from a local hospital. Someone there had discussed my case, and a colleague had been interested. We finally made contact and an initial first appointment was made. I was so desperate to understand how to deal and heal myself.

I had arranged for my mother to have Sah so that we would have peace. I couldn't remember his name as I had become forgetful, so I aptly named him Dr Help on my mobile. He had such a nice, welcoming smile and soothing voice that made me feel instantly safe. He informed me that he only took private cases on that interested him and after a long discussion during that first meeting at my house, he stated that he wanted and would help me, which was to my immense relief. For the first time in ever so long, I believed, passionately believed, that this man could help me live with my demons, or whatever was going on in my head mentally, because now it was also affecting me physically. We forget, you know, that just because someone looks fine it doesn't mean that they are inside, and I certainly was breaking with violent episodes that made me feel so alone and helpless. I was simply falling apart and didn't know what to do, but I now knew where to go, and it was to the man before me who worked within the psychotherapy department, as a trained cognitive therapist. He left me 10 A4 sheets that consisted of a questionnaire, and others that necessitated my personal information and details. It was all very professional, and I was to answer truthfully, as a comparison would be made from the beginning of the treatment to the conclusion. I was to post them to him at the hospital before our next meeting in a week.

I duly returned to my mother's and informed her of my hope, trust, and belief in my Dr Help. Sah was playing a game on the rug in the living room, amusing herself happily and contentedly. We returned home, and after putting Sah to bed comfortably, I endeavoured to work through the documents to post them in the morning, as I needed my doctor to have the information before we started our treatment. I subsequently posted three copies in three different envelopes to ensure that he received one of them. And he did receive those copies to his amusement. And so, we started my therapy.

Dr Help explained and in layman terms I translated that at the back and base of my head, just above my neck, is where our memories are stored in a thing he drew like a bubble. Now these memories are all the experiences, both negative and positive, throughout our life. Then, the top bubble that was located midway between my eyes and the back of my head transferred my new memories to the lower bubble, where all memories are stored long-term. I could follow this explanation and when he confirmed that my terribly negative experiences in Dubai had caused PTSD and that there was, in essence, a blockage in my transference from new memories to long-term memories, so, therefore, I was reliving moments at a flash. Dr Help stated that there was an American therapy that consisted of tapping my head, then with his finger or pencil moving it in front of my eye line to ensure that I followed his movement to and fro continuously and that the questions he asked would allow the right and left side of my brain to be open and hopefully, in theory, let these new and recurring memories pass to my long-term memory.

After questioning, I would always feel exhausted and emotional but also hopeful, as with each week, my answers were always sincerely honest and through his clever questioning, my answers developed to reveal the continuous ache that I carried with me, which encouraged the broken link between my short- and long-term memory. And it was my guilt: guilt for what I had put my family through, and the guilt of not being able to help those women, those poor women back in Bur Fucking Dubai. We discussed how I had phoned the Embassy of the Philippines to inform them of their nationals who were experiencing awful conditions lost in a legal system, but they would not accept the information unless it was in written form. I could not put pen to paper and broke down. I couldn't do it. Dr Help also questioned me, 'How could you have helped them, Emily?' This question was re-asked in different sessions until I stated, 'I couldn't have. What could I do? I didn't have the money to help them all. I couldn't help them. They must go through the legal system. There was nothing, nothing I could do.'

The fact remains that to this day, if I hadn't met my Dr Help when I did, I don't think, no, I know, that I would not have been able to cope daily and would have had a mental breakdown. He will never know the gratitude I have for the help, support and kindness he showed to me. I just wish cognitive therapy was more widely available to help all that need it.

Over time, I was able to speak with a few of the ladies from Bur Dubai as I had given them my home phone number. It was bittersweet as I wanted to hear their voices, but I got taken back there, and it wasn't fair for Sah and Mammy. They could and would never see the darkness that I had, but it didn't mean they couldn't feel it.

Sheila called and had been phoning over the weeks as she had heard from a Scottish colleague who had remained in Qatar working that I had not returned and lost my job. Mammy just said that I wasn't here. When we did speak, and I initially heard her voice, I just started to cry and say, 'Oh, Sheila.' I told her that I couldn't tell her what had happened but that I would one day. And do you know what she said, 'Emily, I am just glad to hear your voice. I have been worried, really worried, and your mother wouldn't say anything. I don't know what has gone on, but know I am here for you and when you want to talk, I am here. Ok? No pressure, but I am here.'

It took me eight years to finally tell her what had really happened. Her response was one of sympathy and anger with Abe and of the school, but she had no judgement. She ended that conversation with a simple, 'Oh well, Ems, I knew you would tell me when you were ready, and that is alright. God, I wished we lived closer!'

I think this story has shown the goodness of our Sheila and how our friendship continues to prevail.

Scottish colleague was also helpful to me in giving me the all-clear to call my ex-head of department with his permission. I had respected my head and his wife, who also worked in the same department, as they too had lost a parent a few weeks previously to me. One had had to return home whilst my head of department had stayed with their children. I helped with the kids if he was working late, with alcohol upon her return and took their son to a sporting event in the capital, as they weren't going, and he really wanted to go. I thought a lot of them and wanted to apologise, but when I called with such nervousness, and she answered to my, 'Hi, it is Emily. Thanks for speaking with me. Is it possible to speak to….'

I was firmly cut off and told, 'Emily, I am sorry but after speaking with the headmaster today, we cannot speak to you. I am sorry.'

I retorted emotionally, 'But I just want to….' only to hear a repeat in such a cold hard tone of what she had initially told me.

'I see,' I replied, crying, whilst managing to put together my final conversation that I would ever have with the people I had previously viewed as colleagues firstly, but also as friends. 'Well, I just want to say that I am deeply sorry that Sah and I did not return, and I wanted to thank you for... um…' I didn't have the chance to finish because she harshly stated, 'Goodbye.' The phone went dead, and I sat down on the stairs, clutching the phone before I broke down and sobbed, just shaking my head. My mother came to get me after some time and shook her head, before boiling the kettle to make a cup of tea. 'And I thought you said they were religious Christians?' she questioned.

I nodded, confirming with a, 'Yes, they are.' She concluded that there was nothing worse and that they were usually hypocrites.

I informed Scottish colleague of what had happened, and she was full of apologies stating that she would never have told me to call if she had known what they would have done, but he, my ex-head of department, had stated it was ok. I understand that we, all of us, have and use self-protection, but do I honestly believe that my apologising would affect his job, no I didn't, and I still don't. In the same conversation with Scottish colleague, she had stated that whilst I was away from the beginning of the new academic year, in the staffroom, my department had laughed, joking, wondering if I had joined Abe's harem because I hadn't returned and started the new academic year, may I add, with Sah. There was no thought for my care or for that of Sah's. I concurred that possibly they were not the best personification of Christians in this situation.

I have learnt with time, patience, and kindness to myself to live with who I am now and try to be the best that I can be as a mother and daughter. I have learnt that I can love unconditionally, but I am not the same person I was after what happened. I am the best I can be. I was found innocent of all charges in a foreign and alien legal system; justice was and had been served. That must be and must be the truth of it right? That, I smoked marijuana in my mother's garden and not in Dubai?

I thank you for reading the words that have helped to heal me. It has been a long process for myself to live with the new me and for that of my family too. My journey has been a difficult one, and I still, to this day, get taken back to that place. I can be doing something as simple as watching television, cooking in the kitchen, or driving the car when I can be taken back with immediate effect. It takes my breath away each time as my heart rate increases and heat rises from my neck upwards. I wish that I could say it has been easy, but it most definitely hasn't. In fact, it took me eight years before I started to even write these words, even after encouragement from Dr Help, as after meeting me initially, he started to research what you can be arrested for in Dubai and he was horrified. He told me to write my story for others to read, as he was shocked with what he found. I bumped into him a few years back and he immediately asked me how my book was coming on, and I was pleased to inform him that I had started it. He informed me that he looked forward to reading it, as do others that I have shared my story with, those whom I trust implicitly.

I honestly wish I could tell you that I returned home and lived happily ever after. I live day-to-day and try to be the best person that I can be. I try not to judge and to be kind and kind to myself. That's all one can do. My family are the best, and through everything, we are there for one another. My journey since has taken us to many places, and Sah has been with me continuously to share these memories. I am glad that no police force in any country we have visited has caused us issues, as we too went to live in Africa for a short time. Now that was an adventure with many tales to speak of. I guess the point I am trying to make is that no matter what life throws at you, you will survive, and you will be surprised as to what you can physically and mentally go through before breaking point. We all have our limits, that is true, but if anything positive comes from the words I have written, even if it helps one person to not make the same mistakes as I did, then I can smile and say, 'I am happy.'

Printed in Dunstable, United Kingdom